SHAPING JAZZ

SHAPING JAZZ

Cities, Labels, and the Global Emergence of an Art Form

Damon J. Phillips

PRINCETON UNIVERSITY PRESS

Princeton and Oxford

Library of Congress Cataloging-in-Publication Data

Phillips, Damon J., 1968–
Shaping jazz : cities, labels, and the global emergence of an art form / Damon J. Phillips.
pages cm
Includes bibliographical references and index.
ISBN 978-0-691-15088-8 (hardcover)
1. Jazz—Social aspects.   2. Jazz—History and criticism.   I. Title.
ML3918.J39P48 2013
781.6509—dc23   2013003222

British Library Cataloging-in-Publication Data is available

This book has been composed in Adobe Garamond Pro

Printed on acid-free paper. ∞

Printed in the United States of America

10 9 8 7 6 5 4 3 2 1

To Arthur and Grace Glass, Rev. P. T. and Ase Lue Phillips,
and all those who shaped me before I was born

Contents

Acknowledgments

Given the number of years of research that this book represents, I'm quite certain that there have been people who have helped me in critical ways whom I'm forgetting at this moment of writing or whose important feedback I have blended with the advice and feedback from others. That said, I am indebted to a particular set of institutional communities. I would like to first thank my colleagues at the Stanford Graduate School of Business. More than any other group, the organizational scholars in Stanford's business school and sociology departments have seen this project from its uncertain beginnings before pen was put to paper about ten years ago to its current status. Many of you have seen so much of this book's material that you probably could have written the book yourselves. And among this group no one affected this trajectory more than Glenn Carroll. As you will see, the influence of your writings and feedback over the years is represented here, and I thank you for that.

Over half of this book was written in the fertile intellectual soil of the University of Chicago in the latter half of my eleven years there. It was an extraordinary privilege to bring such a book into fruition in that intellectual culture, and I benefited not only from some of the best faculty and graduate students in the world but also from a culture that would allow someone to develop a multiyear sociological project on the emergence of jazz in the 1920s as a respected member of the business school faculty well before I was tenured. Chicago provided me not only with the space but also the resources, encouragement, and contacts to further my work. It also fostered key conversations with Matt Bothner, Ronald Burt, Stanislav Dobrev, Steve Kahl, Elizabeth Pontikes, and Sean Safford. It was truly special. Thank you so very much—I certainly do not take it for granted.

The last institution that was critical for me and this book was the Center for Advanced Study in the Behavioral Sciences at Stanford—the place where the remainder of the book, except for the conclusion, was essentially completed. I could not have benefited more from the culture of the center and my colleagues. In pursuing a topic that required such broad intellectual connections, the fact that I was able to think through my ideas with an amazing cadre of historians (Robert Beachy, Allan Issacman, Ted Porter, Robert Proctor, Anupama Rao), media scholars (Arvind Rajagopal and Jonathan Sterne), and sociologists (Amy Binder, Gary Alan Fine, Rhacel Parrenas, and Nancy Whittier) was a transformational experience during which I grew as a scholar. I especially want to thank Marianne Nikolov. Our conversations by the library magazine stand when I was struggling with the introduction, as well as your amazing talent for suggesting how I might communicate complex ideas, to this day represent the most unexpected but impactful influence on the overall framing of the book.

I also can't forget that as a first-time book author more accustomed to writing journal articles, it took several people to encourage me to write this book. Chief among these were Howard Aldrich, Ronald Burt, Frank Dobbin, Tim Dowd, Michael Hannan, and John Padgett. Howie and Frank, the independent conversations we had about my project and jazz in general were uniquely energizing and, more than that, gave me the sense that my topic might have a much wider audience than I had expected. Your passion was a real boost of confidence. Ron, not only do I want to thank you for your encouragement but the empirical focus and conversational style in this book are due to your influence and advice. Tim, thank you for helping me understand who would be most excited by my work, introducing me to many of them, and suggesting that a book would be an effective way of conveying the historical context and natural richness of the topic. Mike, your confidence in me and patience throughout this process, as well as your ability to see the connections in my work well before I did, has had an immeasurable effect. John, you were the first person to tell me to write this book on jazz, a thought I had been considering but before then never confidently voiced. That short conversation—along with the copy of Hebdige's *Subculture* you handed me—still resonates for me as a pivotal moment.

This type of work does not happen without learning from great archivists, those who live with the source material so intimately that they themselves become living reservoirs of knowledge. I met many jazz curators in person, by phone, or online, but I want to especially thank Debbie Gillaspie of the Chicago Jazz Archive at the University of Chicago Regenstein Library, who first opened my eyes to early jazz with such intelligence and kindness that she was my lead compass in the messy sea of data. I also want to thank Wolfram Knauer at the Jazzinstitut Darmstadt, who, in a ten-minute conversation, saved me at least nine months of research and opened my eyes to how a scholar's biases can affect the interpretation of historical data.

This book contains several images and historical references that required time-consuming detective work from many people around the world: from Julia Seiber Boyd of the Cambridge Szeged Society and Mátyás Seiber Trust in the United Kingdom, to jazz historian Hans Pehl and Caroline Prassel of Dr. Hoch's Konservatorium in Germany, to Aurora Perez at the Stanford Archive of Recorded Sound in the United States. My interactions with these experts had the additional benefit of teaching me rare and detailed insights on the history of jazz. Thank you so much for taking time to hunt down what I feared could never be found, as well as everything you taught me along the way.

Just as critical as the curators and archivists—but largely unknown to me—is the vast community of jazz aficionados and collectors who have passionately, diligently, and meticulously documented jazz music and made the work the rest of us do possible. Not only is a book like this built upon your collective efforts, but you often know more and educate academics like me. For those of you who allowed me to see your private collections, to those who let me "listen in" on your online discussions, to the friends and relatives of many of the musicians I will never have the opportunity to meet in person, thank you. I understand why a new discovery can bring you to the point of tears, and I'm very glad you share those discoveries with the world.

I am unusually blessed to share my world with Kathy W. Phillips: my wife, life partner, and my intellectual, emotional, and spiritual anchor. You did more than give me space to write the book; you provided the intellectual nourishment to maintain my focus throughout. I only stop at "thank you" because I can't find stronger words . . . but I'm still looking. Kinara and Amali, though I'm not surprised by your love throughout, I never realized that children of ten and five years old would make suggestions that would be implemented in the book—you are insightful beyond your years. Thank you. I love you all.

Much of *Shaping Jazz* has been collaborative, and I want to thank those who directly contributed as collaborators on the studies and projects that preceded it: Sujatha Fernandes, Steven Kahl, Young-Kyu Kim, Greg Liegel, and David Owens. Thank you all for your gifts of insight and friendship. I have tried to note the insights that I owe directly to you, but I undoubtedly forgotten the many ways that good collaborators like you have positively influenced this book.

Thank you as well to Noah Askin and Kim de Laat, two stellar graduate students who read and provided feedback on the entire manuscript. I feel fortunate to know such talented young scholars, especially those who are kind enough to juggle reading the manuscript alongside their other demands. Thank you for helping improve the book.

To the Princeton University Press team, I could not appreciate your help more. From the initial encouragement from Tim Sullivan, to the stewardship of the manuscript by Eric Schwartz, Janie Chan, and Ryan Mulligan, to the editorial prowess of Karen Carter and Jennifer Backer, you have all ushered *Shaping Jazz* to publication with more professionalism, patience, and clarity than I thought was possible.

SHAPING JAZZ

INTRODUCTION

Sociological Congruence and the Shaping of Recorded Jazz

Since jazz is an improvisational music, recordings offer
perhaps the only valid way of its preservation.

—MARTIN WILLIAMSON, INTRODUCTION TO THE
Smithsonian Collection of Classic Jazz

Records not only disseminated jazz, but inseminated it . . .
in some ways they created what we now call jazz.

—EVAN EISENBERG

I have an unusual confession to make. When I go to high-end grocery stores I like to read the food and beverage narratives printed on the products. Beyond what you see on wine bottles in these stores, you can even find narratives on a bottle of water. For example, "[xyz] begins its journey high up in the remote native forests of New Zealand's Kaimanawa Ranges. Its voyage takes it through layers of volcanic rock and sandstone to a vast aquifer where it has collected for millennia." Another bottle states, "Our water is bottled at the source only weeks after falling as rain on Mauna Loa." Many scholars who study the sociology of markets will tell you that more than making the company's water memorable, the narrative may lead us to evaluate the water as more appealing, distinctive, and maybe even tastier than if there were no narrative at all.

Now I don't like just any narrative. I am particularly drawn to narratives that mention the "where" and "who." I find most interesting the narratives that tell me that a bottle of water is from some "distant" land like New Zealand or Mauna Loa (Hawaii) or that provide information on the firm or its founders. And even though I have not independently tasted water from New Zealand or Mauna Loa (or maybe it is actually *because* I have not directly tasted it, but more on that later), the appeal might be different than if the same water were associated instead with upstate New York, Colorado, or Atlanta. I may be even more accepting of unusual-tasting water if I believe it came from an unfamiliar place.

So, yes, I have a strange habit of reading product narratives for fun. But my fascination with product narratives has little to do with water per se or even high-end grocery stores. Instead, it has a lot to do with this book.

One of my memories from my adolescent years is thumbing through my parents' LP record collection and occasionally placing selections on the turntable. A few records will always be with me. Marvin Gaye's *Let's Get It On* is one of the first that comes to mind, although as a child I was more interested in the cover photography than in the music. There was also Prokofiev's "Peter and the Wolf," the first child's drama I ever heard told through music. After a few listens I didn't even need the narrator; the orchestration vividly told the story. Then there were albums by Aretha Franklin, Stevie Wonder, and Mahalia Jackson. But the one I listened to the most, often as secretly as I now read bottled water narratives, was the 1973 *Smithsonian Collection of Classic Jazz* set of recordings. Listening to that collection and reading the forty-six-page text that accompanied the recordings planted a seed that, decades later, has resulted in this book.

Despite disclaimers by the collection's author and compiler, Martin Williams, I had no doubt at the time that the Smithsonian collection was a first-rate compilation of the best and most important jazz recordings, organized chronologically so that one could follow the historical trajectory of jazz. That said, I initially disliked many of the tunes. It was only after I read the text (liner notes) associated with the music that a great many of them became appealing. After reading those liner notes, the confusing songs became clearer, annoying songs became art, and everything seemed to naturally belong in the jazz canon. I began to understand not only that there were styles associated with different geographical locations (New Orleans, Chicago, Kansas City, etc.) but that there was an auditory and stylistic inventory that gave jazz its logic. The Williams narratives gave me that inventory.

To be sure, not every selection in the jazz collection benefited from a narrative. Some of them were great without the accompanying text. For example, I was blown away by Sarah Vaughan and Harry "Sweets" Edison on "Ain't No Use" and didn't need a narrative to judge its appeal. The same was true of the Modern Jazz Quartet's "Django." But for many of the selections, I initially had either no reaction or a negative reaction to the music. It wasn't until I acquired greater knowledge of who performed it, the location of the performance, or other circumstances behind the recording that I could categorize and evaluate it.

Another invaluable aspect of the Smithsonian collection was that it provided different recordings of the same tune—either by the same artist at different times or by different artists. For example, the collection begins by comparing two separate recordings of Scott Joplin playing "Maple Leaf Rag" and later compares back-to-back performances of "Body and Soul" (the first by the Benny Goodman Trio and the second by Coleman Hawkins). In fact, Williams's text repeatedly refers to multiple versions of the same tune (e.g., urging the reader to compare the Modern Jazz Quartet's and Ornette Coleman's versions of "Lonely Woman"). The implication was that to understand jazz, one can use key songs and tunes that many artists recorded as reference points. In this way, the tunes that have been recorded multiple times serve a particularly important role in orienting and understanding jazz across its different contexts and styles. Sometimes the only thing that two different types of jazz have in common is that they perform or reference the same tunes. For instance, it is difficult to simultaneously label both Paul Whiteman's "symphonic" music and pianist Aki Takase's "modern" music as works of jazz. While Whiteman's 1920s music was a highly orchestrated and arranged syncopated style where improvisation was common but not central, Takase's music is experimental, minimalist in terms of arrangements (often just a duet), and improvisationally willing to abandon standard harmonic structures familiar to Western ears. Listening to both of them side by side would stretch one's ability to place them within the same genre, as there is very little stylistically to link the two. But what the artists do have in common is that they have each recorded similar pieces like "St. Louis Blues," and it is this commonality that allows one to place each artist in the universe of jazz—with jazz standards as one of the key forces that holds wide-ranging styles together.

The Smithsonian collection's music and text have simmered in my mind for decades now. It led me to discover volumes of jazz tunes and performances. I eventually took up the alto saxophone as a teenager, learning a bit here and there, and ultimately became a serious fan and consumer of jazz. Yet as my love of jazz grew, I became more and more perplexed as to why some tunes were noted as jazz standards while others were not. There have been over a million recordings of jazz songs and tunes,[1] but only a few hundred have been recorded over and over again. Many in this often-recorded subset are very good compositions, but there are also a lot of great compositions that failed to have the same influence and appeal as the select few that today are considered jazz standards. What sort of factors led a small minority of songs, a subset of a population of great compositions and performances, to get a disproportionate amount of attention and appeal such that they have become the "standards" that help define the genre? Why are some songs re-recorded by many musicians over time while others receive no such following?

This is the fundamental puzzle that I seek to make some headway on in this book. It is a question that I believe can be better understood by looking at the context of the initial production of a song or tune, in particular the narrative associated with the music's production. Specifically, my focus in *Shaping Jazz* is on the "where" and the "who."

Better understanding the "where" is manifested in particular ways. Just as I suspect that people evaluate water differently depending on its source (New Zealand, Canada, Hawaii, or New York), a tune's appeal as legitimate jazz depends on where it was produced as well as the record company associated with that song. Much evidence from scholars who study the perception of art indicates that if I play a new tune and tell you it is from Calcutta versus New York, you will hear the song differently.[2] In *Shaping Jazz*, I explore why places like New York were less often sources of appealing songs than we now understand them to be and served bigger roles as engines of diffusion rather than as sources of diffusion. I explain why and when geographical references in tune or group titles were particularly privileged in terms of their appeal. I also explain why a place like Berlin, which produced substantially more jazz than Paris in the 1920s to mid-1930s, is now on the historical sidelines of jazz's history.

With respect to the "who," I focus on firms instead of individuals. This is not only because I believe that we have much more to learn by studying the organizations that produced recorded jazz but because I have been trained as an organizational and economic sociologist to study the role of social structure and identity in markets. I find that firms in the recording industry had an immense role in shaping jazz, just as the geographic context of production did. I explain why and how the identity of record companies affected not only what music they chose to record but also the music that they sought to be publicly associated with and how they deployed their marketing resources. In the end, I show that a tune or song's appeal as jazz is related to the narrative around its creation. The identity of the geographical and organizational context really mattered to the evolution of jazz.

This book uses empirical puzzles to better understand the early years of the market for jazz and to try to understand why some tunes had long-term appeal while others did not, and how the market boundaries of jazz evolved as a part of this process. My strategy has been to follow recordings that were re-recorded by different musicians over time and eventually gave rise to a canon of commercialized jazz. Thus "St. Louis Blues" or "Take the 'A'-Train" are part of the canon of recorded jazz, or more specifically the *discographical canon*, to the extent that many jazz recordings are made of these titles over time. I take songs and tunes that were recorded before 1933 (a pivotal year in global societal turbulence) and try to understand what distinguishes the titles that are re-recorded repeatedly over time. In this way, I treat recordings as cultural products that are, at least in part, geographical and organizational in origin.

I hope it is clear by now that this is not a typical book on jazz, in part because I am not the typical scholar to write about jazz. I am not a musicologist or a historian, and I'm too amateur a musician to speak with any legitimate authority from that perspective. Rather, I am a quantitatively oriented sociologist attempting to employ the great deal that I have learned from the works of my peers in sociology, ethnomusicology, and history. At the same time, though social histories of jazz abound, I hope this book convinces you that there is real value in integrating the conceptual and analytical tools of organizational and economic sociology. *Shaping Jazz* reframes current knowledge to yield new insights as a case study of market emergence, boundary dynamics, and evolution. As a consequence, this book speaks to how cultural markets emerge and evolve. But even here cultural markets are an instance of markets for experiential, consumption, and symbolic goods where the quest for underlying quality is elusive, deceptive, and sometimes downright misguided.

I often think of *Shaping Jazz* as my second dissertation, and it is indeed a work that took longer than my formal dissertation. Beginning in 1999, but not intently until 2003, I have been uncovering and collecting data, reading first- and second-hand sources, listening to oral histories, interviewing musicians and audiences who experienced the music of the 1920s and 1930s, using my musical abilities to play compositions or alongside recordings of early jazz, camping out in archives in the United States and Europe, and conducting quantitative analyses on discographical data covering tens of thousands of recordings. My motivation at each step was a particular puzzle rather than an overarching research agenda. And in that way this project did not begin as a major undertaking. At the outset I just wanted to know why the largest record companies seemed to have such a difficult time producing and marketing jazz music that sounded more like that of Louis Armstrong, Jelly Roll Morton, and the Original Dixieland Jazz Band but an easier time doing so with more symphonic music closer to Paul Whiteman's performance of *Rhapsody in Blue*. Ten years later, here I am.

(SOCIOLOGICAL) CONGRUENCE

As I focused on this project, it became clear that each topic that comprises *Shaping Jazz* has a particular type of congruence as an underlying mechanism. A sociological use of congruence helps explain the role of geographic and organizational origins specifically and more broadly contributes to our understanding of how cultural markets emerge and evolve. Conceptually, my model of sociological congruence draws upon a longstanding idea across the social sciences that we evaluate certain objects, like products (e.g., a musical work), according to the cues and characteristics that exist as the context of that object's production. To the extent that there are characteristics of a cultural product that are consistent with a receiver's understanding of the context, the more the cultural product will flourish. Just like most bottled water narratives mention that their water comes from one mountain or another, we as audience members tend to think of certain types of cultural products as affiliated with particular locales or types of organizations, with some sources having more authenticity than others.

Thus the more sociologically congruent a cultural object is, the more the product and context of production match for that audience, the greater its authenticity for that audience. This is an insight I first learned from reading or talking to Howard Becker, Pierre Bourdieu, Gary Alan Fine, Wendy Griswold, Michelle Lamont, Paul Lopes, Richard Peterson, and Harrison White, in part because it mapped so well onto the work of organizational sociologists such as Glenn Carroll, Neil Fligstein, John Freeman, Michael Hannan, John Padgett, Walter Powell, and Huggy Rao. It is an insight that undergirds the thinking of many of my more immediate contemporaries such as Shyon Baumann, Amy Binder, Tim Dowd, David Grazian, Greta Hsu, Jennifer Lena, Martin Ruef, Olav Sorenson, and Ezra Zuckerman.

Hence my use of sociological congruence is not to introduce a new concept but to recognize that there is a concept that both ties together needlessly disparate strands of sociology and provides clear guidance to understanding how markets such as that for recorded jazz can organize. I believe that sociological congruence can affect the salience of cultural products, as well as instill them with meaning and value, and thereby influence the boundary dynamics of a market. In this light, jazz tunes are "symbolic resources" that affect the creation, maintenance, contestation, and dissolution of cultural market boundaries.[3]

It is not enough, then, that bottled water comes from mountains but that water that tastes "normal" comes from "typical" mountains while water that tastes unique comes from unique or unusual sources. I don't know what water from New Zealand actually tastes like, but as an American when I taste bottled water that claims to be from the mountains of New Zealand I'm not expecting it to taste like water from a U.S. source. I expect as well that the more distinct the taste, the more authentic I would imagine the New Zealand water to be.

This match between a product's characteristic and the context of production is what I would consider one form of sociological congruence (which I will explore in some detail) where "sociological" refers to components of identity that relate to the context of production. I believe it also applies to which jazz songs and tunes received disproportionally greater appeal such that—all else equal—some jazz music has creation origin narratives that are more legitimate to the receiver than others.[4] The nature of the origin is also affected by characteristics of the song. Thus a tune or song known to have been recorded in New York is more appealing if it "sounds" like it was made in New York to the receiver, just as the descriptive "New York rapper" has a distinctive set of aesthetic characteristics associated with it. A recording by an artist introduced as a New York rapper is more appealing to the extent that the characteristics of the recording are congruent with the identity associated with New York–based rap music. A hip-hop recording that features a rap artist playing a pan flute will suffer in appeal (with an American audience) if it is associated with being from New York, but it will have relatively more appeal if it is associated with Peru (as "authentic Andean rap") or even the mountains of New Zealand if the U.S. audience for the artist sees the pan flute as an instrument associated with being "foreign." In fact, it is this very point that provides one of the pillars of Peterson's (1997) analysis of authenticity in country music.

Similarly, there are many examples that contrast the market identity of a large incumbent producer with a smaller, newer, and more "authentic" firm. Within music this often takes the form of the smaller independent label that produces music that is both unique and appealing, almost by definition. To be sure, I will provide evidence in *Shaping Jazz* that some of the differences between the larger incumbent record companies and the newer firms founding during the Jazz Age led to variance in the music produced. Even with that taken into account, my contention is that the perceptual differences were even greater. Whether (according to my data) smaller record producers recorded more small African American jazz groups in the 1920s is secondary to whether records with such origins are now seen as more authentic and thus appealing, and both could be true.

In short, in *Shaping Jazz* I emphasize that the value and meaning of cultural products are in part socially constructed through the use of the congruence of a product's characteristics and the context of production, where I privilege the geography and record-producing organization.

This notion of congruence is a common observation in classic sociology and cultural sociology but also in other fields like social psychology, marketing, and even critical economic geography.[5] I am not a student of the humanities, but I have no doubt that some form of this idea is present there as well. The power of sociological congruence for *Shaping Jazz* is in the implications for both creativity- and innovation-based settings, allowing a parsimonious and intuitive explanation—*that jazz was shaped by a drive toward congruity between songs and their sources.* The congruence between a producer (such as a record company) and its output (such as a song or tune) influences everything from (1) the producer's strategy on what to produce; to (2) how the output is interpreted immediately and over time; to (3) the subsequent evolution and social order of markets.

SOCIOLOGICAL CONGRUENCE AND THE MARKET FOR JAZZ

My focus here is not to define jazz per se. I've seen too many people more qualified than I struggle, flounder, and ultimately embarrass themselves in their attempt to define jazz. In fact, many of the people we imagine as great jazz musicians don't bother themselves with defining jazz in any detailed manner. As an art form it is too dynamic for anything close to a universally satisfactory definition to emerge. Rather my goal is to better understand what tunes and songs, as components of the market for jazz, come to be privileged in representing jazz in its recorded, commercialized form. It is through these recordings that *Shaping Jazz* shows how jazz has been influenced by the social structure of the geography and producing organizations. Moreover, this influence is dynamic in that it affects how our understanding of jazz varies over time. What was agreed upon as jazz in 1925 is not the same as our understanding of jazz in 1970, and neither completely captures our understanding of jazz today. As we will see, even if we look at jazz in the 1920s alone, a wide variety of music was labeled as jazz.

At the same time, it is possible to define the *market* for jazz. That is, it is possible to capture and trace what sells for jazz and what has been marketed as jazz, and there is enough in the historical record to come to grips with it from a market perspective. Jazz recordings are critical in part because they can help bound a market and give a sense of a dynamic market center, indicated by what music is recorded and re-recorded as jazz. Take the blues-structured jazz standard "All Blues" from Miles Davis's *Kind of Blue*. A jazz musician typically has a multitude of blues-structured tunes to choose from and can choose to perform them in different ways stylistically (e.g., modal, bebop, etc.). The musician may also choose to play an extemporaneous melody over the blues chords. However, while there are thousands of possibilities, the subset of blues-structured tunes that are actually recorded by multiple musicians over time—like "All Blues"—is small and serves the critical purpose of facilitating the coordination and evaluation of all market participants that encompass an art world. An artist records "All Blues" instead of another similarly structured tune because she is making an identity claim that in part positions that artist in the landscape of a cultural market in a way that a lesser-known but otherwise equivalent tune cannot.

In fact, I posit that a market for jazz could not have formed, flourished, and maintained legitimacy without a smaller set of tunes to serve as a common point of reference by musicians, record companies, consumers, and critics. So while defining the entirety of jazz may be depressingly elusive, capturing recorded and commercialized jazz is a more tractable exercise, as long as one comes to terms with four observations that make up the foundation of my analysis. First, the market for recorded jazz is oriented around recordings that maximize long-run appeal within a community of musicians. The market center from the perspective of recordings is anchored in the tunes and songs that were recorded more often than others. Second, jazz as a category, while porous, is also path dependent in that we reference the past categories of jazz when assessing new categorizations of jazz. Third, jazz markets can be defined around exemplars rather than the typical. In 1945, few jazz musicians sounded like Charlie Parker or Dizzy Gillespie, although many consumers remember them as representing jazz in 1945. It is more appropriate, however, to see them as exemplars that redefined the typical.[6] Fourth, the boundaries and meanings of jazz are dynamic. Much of the music in 1925 that was thought of as legitimate jazz now lies at the periphery of the genre. We now recognize Duke Ellington as much more central to the development of 1920s to early 1930s jazz than was Paul Whiteman, but with respect to the market for jazz during this period, Whiteman was the key exemplar and point of reference. Ellington wasn't even close. While today we may use Ellington to assess the authenticity of Whiteman's more symphonic music as jazz, in the 1920s it was Ellington who was advertised as the "Paul Whiteman of Colored Orchestras"[7] among the (white) audiences who drove the sales and commercial direction of jazz.

The point of *Shaping Jazz* is that the context of the production of the recording is an important factor in understanding a recording's appeal. Sociological congruence is the mechanism that explains how the context of production affects the appeal of recordings. From the perspective of the receiver, the more congruence the context of production has with other characteristics of the song (who is performing it, the instruments used, how the song is titled, etc.), the more appealing the song. I am leaving for another book the dynamic understandings of jazz history, as well as how the national identity around culture and aesthetic taste affects what we see as congruent. In *Shaping Jazz* I will focus most of my analysis on the period 1917–33, with an emphasis on how congruence rooted in that period influenced the long-run appeal of individual recordings.

UNCOVERING CONGRUENCE, ONE PUZZLE AT A TIME

I demonstrate the import of the context of production and the mechanism of sociological convergence through the examination of six puzzles. While each puzzle is distinct, they present aspects of my thesis and evidence, which ultimately lead to a fuller understanding of how jazz was shaped. The first three puzzles relate to the role of geography.

In chapter 1, I begin by asking why it matters that jazz was produced in sixty-seven cities worldwide. That is, jazz up to 1933 was primarily recorded in a small set of cities, including Chicago, London, and New York. Does it even matter that in understanding the evolving market for jazz, and the music that formed the market center, that we also pay attention to jazz recordings from more disconnected cities such as Minneapolis (Minnesota), Hilversum (Holland), Sydney (Australia), Buenos Aires (Argentina), and Calcutta (India)? The answer, through understanding the mobility network of musicians across these cities, is a resounding "yes," but that is just the beginning. The real puzzle is why there seems to be a disproportionate advantage for recordings that emerged from these more disconnected cities than when compared to the more central cities like New York.

As is often the case, solving this puzzle gave birth to additional questions. Although I could identify how a city's structural position in the network of musician mobility mattered, the mechanism that firmly linked the city's structural position to long-run appeal was less clear. My model requires that musicians years after the original recording would have access to the information about where and when the original recording took place. This naturally leads to such questions as, "How could a musician in 1950 know that 'Milenburg Joys' was originally recorded on the Gennett label in Richmond, Indiana, in 1923?" In other words, the results of chapter 1 lead one to ask whether more can be understood about the process of diffusion that led to long-run appeal for jazz from a highly disconnected source. Tackling these questions is the main task of chapter 2.

An additional puzzle arose because my chapter 1 model explains the results of nearly every city with one exception: Berlin. Thus chapter 3 explores why Berlin is such a singular exception. A close examination of this question led me to jazz archives in Germany, which yielded fascinating and unexpected results that enrich our understanding of the relationship between the context of production, sociological congruence, and cultural product appeal. Not only is German jazz better understood, but this research adds insight into how the legitimacy of certain styles of jazz has varied over time.

The remaining three chapters focus on record companies and labels as the context of production. Chapter 4 examines why the firms that introduced a type of recorded jazz that was successful switch to champion another type of jazz that was less successful. Incumbent firms were first movers in recording illegitimate (but profitable) jazz. However, they distanced themselves from this type of jazz and responded to elite anti-jazz pressure by inserting symphonic elements into the original form. In chapter 4, I focus on the role of the cultural elite and their attack on jazz and its producers. The firms that had incongruence with respect to their social structural position and jazz feared being penalized (incurring a loss of status and legitimacy). Using both qualitative historical and quantitative analyses, I show that firms founded in the years when classical music dominated the market for recordings (Victorian-era firms) were less improvisational and minimized their association with jazz's low-status racial and stylistic elements.

Chapter 5 examines what was perhaps the most perplexing of the puzzles that I encountered in trying to understand the market for early jazz recordings. In the course of examining the discographies, I found that many recordings were re-released by the same record company under a pseudonym. For example, a recording under the name the Wisconsin Roof Orchestra was re-released by the same firm as Miami Society Orchestra. King Oliver and his Dixie Syncopators was re-released as the Aurora Aristocrats. In fact, pseudonyms were used in 13% of all recordings in my discographical sample. And while one common explanation is that competitors wishing to profit from the original recordings of the focal firm created pseudonyms, 85% of pseudonyms in my sample were created by the same firm. Only 8% of pseudonyms were created by competitors. Herein lies the puzzle: Why these pseudonyms? The solution reveals particularly important information about the operation and organization of the early market and requires a deeper understanding of firm identity than was uncovered in chapter 4. This deeper understanding ends in an interesting answer that involves evidence of deception by incumbent jazz record companies, which actively sought congruence between their identity and the characteristics of their products and deceived observers into believing that their production of cultural products was consistent with their Victorian-era identity.

The final empirical chapter, chapter 6, focuses most intently on the narratives of cultural products, in particular on the identities of the individual recordings and groups in concert with the identities of record companies and labels. This chapter is not so much a puzzle but an opportunity to link the role of product descriptions mentioned at the outset of this book with the findings of the subsequent chapters. In this way, chapter 6 serves as a transition to the conclusion, where I outline the implications of my research for a conceptual model of product appeal in emerging markets in which meaning and value are dynamically constructed. Specifically, chapter 6 examines the significance of whether a recording's originators and early adopters are of the same or different race. This is done by determining whether a tune or song with black originators and white early adopters had different long-run appeal than one in which the originators were white and the early adopters black. What about the long-run appeal of songs whose originators and early adopters are of the same race? The answer and the rationale behind it cannot be understood without also examining the record companies associated with originators; this finding in turn helps propose a new means for capturing the building blocks of genres.

In chapter 7, the concluding chapter, I use smooth jazz as a way to capture some of the implications of *Shaping Jazz* for our current market for commercialized jazz. I then use this discussion to synthesize each of the chapters to provide general statements and propositions for the organization of recorded jazz and other markets, as well as to consider some limitations. I close the book with a discussion on how these insights apply not only to other theories on market categories, positions, and identities but also to other markets where boundaries and notions of quality are dynamic and where novelty is rewarded. I pay particular attention to the markets for nanotechnology and green technology. Finally, I reengage the market for bottled water.

A METHODOLOGICAL NOTE

Uncovering the role of sociological congruence required drawing upon my examination of multiple discographies, as well as archival material from the Chicago Jazz Archive, Jazzinstitut Darmstadt (the largest public jazz archive in Europe), and the Stanford Archive of Recorded Sound. I was able to access oral histories, sheet music, record label data, advertising and marketing information, and so forth. In addition to purchasing recordings from collectors and vintage record stores, I also benefited from online sources (www.redhotjazz.org and www.centerforjazzarts.org). I read musician autobiographies, articles on jazz from dozens of local and national newspapers, and related material in other popular and trade press publications (e.g., *Ladies Home Journal, Etude*),[8] which further helped me understand the characteristics of jazz during the 1920s and 1930s. Finally, I was able have enriching conversations with musicians and consumers who were teenagers during that period.

At the most aggregated level, these data were employed to analyze jazz from sixty-seven cities across five continents. However, I also examined recorded jazz from specific regions, such as jazz from the U.S. Midwest and Germany to obtain deeper explanatory power. I listened to and analyzed thousands of individual recordings. This quantitative analysis was largely made possible by directories on record companies and discography data contained in the Brian Rust (1969) and Tom Lord discographies (2005, 2010). The Lord discography (2010) is an electronic database (building on Rust's 1969 work) that provides information on the record labels of over 38,000 band leaders, 195,000 recording sessions, 1,111,000 musician entries, and 1,190,000 tune entries. Much of my analysis, however, is from 1917 to 1933. An online version of the discography is available from http://www.lordisco.com/tjdonline.html.

One substantial advantage of these discographies is their near completeness. These data are quite amazing, as they include not only recordings released but also those recorded and rejected. Rare errors are typically found by expert online communities of aficionados and collectors, and these communities helped me check and modify my sample. In general, the discography captures critical data for my analysis: titles of each recording, recording dates, record company/label, group leader, and musician names, as well as the instruments played. The discography also keeps track of critical details such as artist and group pseudonyms. All of these data exist in a database for much of the quantitative analysis.

I employ these data in various ways, but when doing quantitative analyses for this project (where the nature of the data makes the direction of effects more reliable than the point estimates) I employed the inferential power of interaction effects instead of relying simply on main effects. The main effects, such as the statistical relationship between a network position of a city and the appeal of the music from that city, are subject to more alternative explanations than I can probably imagine (and I have imagined many). Rather, I draw on the inferential power of specifying under what conditions the established effect (e.g., the city's network position) matters to better establish *why* it matters. Determining what interaction terms to include is driven by the historical context and institutional detail that my colleagues and I have uncovered. Except for chapter 5 (on the role of pseudonyms), the theoretical statements are based first on a close reading of the historical context, then followed by quantitative analyses that attempt to demonstrate the more historical qualitative investigation.

Finally, to enhance the coherence of *Shaping Jazz*, I employ an appendix to minimize the cumbersome tables of quantitative analyses in the main text of the book. Where the analysis was previously done in a journal article (chapters 5 and 6) I refer instead to the analyses in the respective article. Tables for the quantitative analyses for chapters 1, 2, 3, and 4 are in the appendix.

In the end, I hope that *Shaping Jazz* evokes a fraction of the excitement involved in writing it.

Chapter 1

THE PUZZLE OF GEOGRAPHICAL DISCONNECTEDNESS

I managed to play a couple of compositions together with Bud Shank
at one of the festivals. He invited me because I was one of the best
players, and an exotic stranger from remote Russia. . . . At the end,
the people applauded to the strange Russian on foot.

—OLEG KIREYEV, PROFESSIONAL SAXOPHONE
PLAYER AND COMPOSER, 2010

As they chant esoteric Arabic words, the lute, a sitar like
instrument, begins slowly and deliberately into the next song. . . .
This is the nature of Arabic music. Intoxicating, spiritually savage
and untamed. A far Eastern form of jazz that requires not only a
lot of talent to play but a strong unquenchable love.

—ROSIE FAULKNER, REVIEW OF "HOUSE OF TARAB," *Seattle
University Spectator*, OCTOBER 9, 2011

As these epigraphs illustrate, we tend to reserve a special type of appeal for music that is from locations that are far away or disconnected from us. Of course, one of the questions is whether that appeal is based on the inherent uniqueness or qualities of the music or whether our interpretation of the music alters its appeal given that we know the music's source is foreign to us. Our biases and understandings about the source of a cultural object often inform our evaluations. For me, the implications of this are powerful as they point to the fact that to study how jazz was shaped one needs to integrate thinking about both the production and the reception of music. And as I learned over the course of writing this book, the integration of production and reception matters a great deal when trying to understand the emergence of the market for recorded jazz.

My investigation into jazz begins with a focus on jazz recordings before 1934, with the closest attention paid to recordings in the 1920s when the market for commercialized recorded jazz became robustly competitive for the first time. There were several features of these data that I found quite interesting, especially when looking at the social structural aspects of how musicians traveled, how firms were positioned economically as well as socially, and how these factors seemed to affect the production and reception of music in ways that depended on the geographical origins of jazz recordings.

TABLE 1.1. Cities Where Jazz Was Recorded before 1934

Amsterdam	Copenhagen	Long Island (NY)	Plattsburgh (NY)
Ashville (NC)	Culver City (CA)	Los Angeles	Prague
Atlanta	Dallas	Louisville (KY)	Richmond (IN)
Barcelona	Detroit	Melbourne (AUS)	Richmond (VA)
Berlin	Framingham (MA)	Memphis	San Antonio
Birmingham (AL)	Ghent (BEL)	Milan	San Francisco
Bristol (TN)	Grafton (WI)	Minneapolis	Savannah
Brussels	Havana	Montreal	Spokane
Budapest	Hayes Mid (UK)	Moscow	St. Louis
Buenos Aires	Helsinki	Newark (NJ)	Stockholm
Buffalo	Hilversum (HOL)	New Orleans	St. Paul
Butte (MT)	Hollywood	New York City	Sydney (AUS)
Calcutta	Houston	Oakland (CA)	The Hague
Camden (NJ)	Indianapolis	Orange (NJ)	Vienna
Chicago	Kansas City	Oslo	Winston Salem (NC)
Cincinnati	Knoxville (TN)	Paris	Zurich (SWI)
Cleveland (OH)	London	Philadelphia	

Source: Lord 2005.

For example, I was fascinated by the fact that before 1934 jazz was recorded in sixty-seven cities according to the discographical data (see Table 1.1). Over 40% of these cities were outside the United States, spanning five continents and often disconnected from major markets such as Chicago, London, or New York. That was interesting, but for me there were more interesting follow-up questions, such as, "Does it matter that jazz was recorded in so many cities, and if so, how can this be understood?" "Is it necessary to consider jazz recordings from Minneapolis, Hilversum, Sydney, Buenos Aires, and Calcutta when understanding the emerging market for recorded jazz?" and "Do we learn all we need to know about the emergence of the discographical canon by just considering cities like New York and Chicago that were at the nexus of musician mobility and recording activity?"[1]

Two additional facts made these questions even more compelling. First, as I began to rank jazz titles by the number of times they have been re-recorded over the years—a measure I call long-run appeal—it appeared that there were a disproportionately high number of songs and tunes that emerged from these more disconnected cities than when compared to those that came from Chicago and New York.[2] Many of the top recorded tunes and songs that constitute the discographical jazz canon were originally recorded in Chicago and New York, but much of this music was also originally recorded outside these cities.

The second fact emerged when I examined the mobility of musicians across these cities up to 1934; I tracked them through the discography according to where they made recordings. Figure 1.1 is a network diagram of the flows of jazz music bandleaders across cities. For example, the top of the diagram shows that

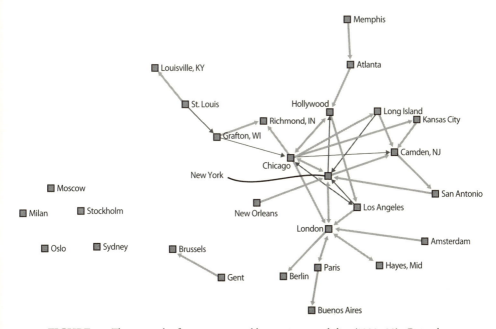

FIGURE 1.1. The network of cities connected by musician mobility (1930–32). Cities that are not listed here did not produce jazz from 1930 to 1932.

during the window of 1930–32, musical groups first recorded in Memphis, Tennessee, then traveled to Atlanta, Georgia. Not surprisingly, cities like Chicago and New York are highly central in the network.

I will explore many features of this network throughout this book, but what initially drew my attention was that there were cities that were actively participating in the production of recorded jazz but lacked the mobility ties to the core of activity in Chicago and New York. The most obvious examples were Milan, Moscow, Oslo, Stockholm, and Sydney (see Figure 1.1), but Gent and Brussels can also be included, as well as cities on the periphery of the main set of connected cities such as Amsterdam and Atlanta. Do these cities matter in understanding the emergence of the discographical canon of jazz? If so, what role do they play?[3]

DEVELOPING A THEORY OF DISCONNECTEDNESS AND SHAPING JAZZ

It turns out that answering what I thought were simple questions involved a process that was richer and more nuanced than I had initially imagined. Answering these questions has sparked several qualitative and quantitative analyses, readings of hundreds of books and articles, and traveling to several archives in the United

States and Europe. One reason that these were not easily answered questions is that although there are many scholars who have contributed monumentally to the understanding of cultural markets in general and jazz in particular, there were two critical but underaddressed issues.

First, within the study of innovation-based markets, socially distant or disconnected sources of innovation (whether they be people, organizations, or locations) are often recognized as relevant, but there is not much theory to support this recognition. That is, scholars have developed theory on how accumulated advantages from highly connected sources can occur independently of the intentions of those highly connected sources.[4] Disconnected sources, however, lack a comparable level of theoretical development, especially where meaning and value are driven by the interpretation of actions, rather than the intention of those actions.

Second, the present state of mainstream network analysis falls short in studying social systems such as those represented in Figure 1.1. That is, if there is a social system that has (cultural) producers who are active but disconnected to varying degrees, there are very few methodological tools that can be employed for the purpose of analysis. In fact, most studies of networks disregard isolated actors, and this neglect too often lacks theoretical justification. Looking at Figure 1.1, attempting to understand the emergence for the market for jazz and the rise of a discographical canon without Brussels, Gent, Milan, Moscow, Oslo, Stockholm, and Sydney would represent not only poor empiricism but also a poor understanding of history. Thus to answer my questions I needed to develop a way to consider cities as they vary in the degree that they are disconnected from others.

In this chapter I focus on how disconnectedness—a term I will define more cleanly in the next section—can have a unique role in social systems, particularly in innovation-based social systems familiar to scholars of organizations and markets (e.g., cultural markets, technological systems). Despite the explicit role that structural perspectives have played in organizational and economic sociology, too little of this work has engaged the role of disconnected sources. At the same time, there is much evidence to suggest that disconnectedness plays a critical role when such sources are seen as socially distant or dissimilar, such as members of subcultures, those considered exotic and foreign, or artists who are economically and psychologically disadvantaged.[5]

What is missing, however, is a structural account that brings the role of the exotic, foreign, and "authentic outsider"[6] under a single concept—what I refer to as disconnectedness. To develop this concept I expand a structuralist approach on social network positions using scholarship on the reception of cultural objects (products) to show that objects from disconnected sources can be more appealing, particularly when the outputs in question are difficult to categorize. This congruent match between (disconnected) sources and (difficult-to-categorize) outputs is the key mechanism that underlies my theoretical framework.

Disconnectedness: Setting the Stage

Georg Simmel's theory on the "tertius" and Ronald Burt's studies on structural autonomy present atypical structural positions that act independently of structural and normative constraints.[7] Subsequent work has often emphasized the strategic intentions of focal actors; however, both Simmel and Burt point out that often it is the interpretation of actions and not necessarily intentions that drive differences in influence and attainment. Indeed, more recently sociologists have found that when considering everything from the social position of Florentine leaders to that of government agencies, there is ample evidence that the influence of central actors is partially due to the imputed meaning of their actions.[8]

As a complement to these insights, I call attention to the fact that the value of a source's output is also imputed when that source is socially dissimilar (or disconnected). I believe that this argument, bolstered with well-rooted scholarship by Wendy Griswold and others within cultural sociology, allows us to consider the value of disconnected sources' outputs.[9] This literature draws attention to actors who are defined by the structure of relationships that they lack rather than the relationships they have. In settings that reward novelty, dissimilar, distant, and distinct sources are more likely to have outputs successfully labeled as exotic and more highly valued precisely because they are removed and "free" from connections to others. For example, Gary Alan Fine (2003) draws out the implications for being disconnected when understanding authenticity within the world of self-taught ("outsider") art.[10] In his rich ethnographic study, he finds that self-taught artists represent a social position and identity defined by the lack of connections: "Within the art market, they [self-taught artists] lack *social capital*, ties to elite communities, and are not fully integrated professionals in this mainstream art world. It is their *lack* of, rather than their attributes, that defines them . . . their reputation to be established by others" (2003, 156; emphasis original). The combination of a structural view of an artistic source outside a social system with research on how value and meaning of such an actor can be constructed independent of that source's intentions forms the foundation of my answer to the questions of this chapter. That is, I suggest that disconnectedness, as a social network characteristic, positively affects others' interpretation of a source's cultural outputs independent of that source's intentions.[11]

A Motivating Example: Jazz and the Disconnected

Figure 1.2 is a simplification of the problem I highlighted in Figure 1.1 and is presented as a motivation for us to consider disconnectedness as a distinct sociological construct. The figure displays two network structures, A and B. They share in common an isolate (the larger unconnected circle with the gray center). In Figure 1.1 this might be a city like Oslo or Sydney. It turns out that most theoretical and

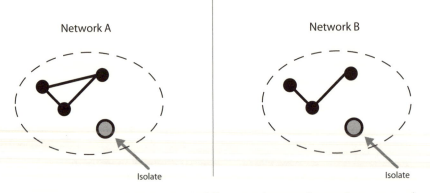

FIGURE 1.2. Two isolated actors, two different implications for social structure and action.

empirical approaches treat the two isolates similarly, where each is a network isolate to the larger component of three connected actors. As I noted, many scholars, when seeking to understand the network structure of a social system, disregard isolates altogether.

However, the two isolates are not similarly situated, and this difference is important when we are interested in evaluating a source's actions and outputs. We should not assume the same association between social structure, action, and evaluation for the two isolates in Networks A and B. The isolate in Network A is on the outside of an interconnected group and is likely viewed as having an identity distinct from members of that group in at least one of two ways. First, its social position and role identity may be due to conflict between the isolate and the group, as Simmel might note, where the isolate is defined explicitly in opposition to the interconnected group. In this case music from the isolate would be seen as explicitly opposing music from the interconnected groups. Second, the disconnected actor may have a distinct and independent identity orthogonal to the members of the clique.[12] In this case, the identity of the isolate is interpreted by other members of the social system as a distinct "other"—not oppositional to the clique but also not similar to any of the connected members of the social system. I focus on this second case; not only does it more closely capture the epigraphs at the beginning of this chapter (where the Russian and "Arab" musicians are seen as a foreign "other" rather than oppositional), but it also more closely corresponds to the context of early jazz where global social organization was still emergent and few fixed identities had evolved sufficiently for oppositional identities to form.

Returning to Network B on the right side of Figure 1.2, we observe a network with an isolate as in Network A. However, here the other three nodes are not the interconnected triad observed in Network A. Indeed, Simmel would suggest that Network B features two types of actors: *tertius gaudens* and the "isolated individual."[13] The *tertius gaudens* reflects the position of the node that serves as an intermediary between two disparate nodes. Both Simmel and Burt suggest that this intermediary is unencumbered by constraints associated with network closure and has the capability of innovating through the unique integration of knowledge.[14] In my study, some cities (New York, Chicago, and London) serve as central intermediaries between other cities, and I will examine their influence on the evolution of jazz.

The isolate in B (referred to as Isolate B), as in Network A (referred to Isolate A), is unencumbered as well from Simmel's standpoint. But we cannot expect that the resulting social action and evaluation in Network B would be equivalent to that in Network A. Isolate B is less disconnected than Isolate A. Its isolation is less striking, and with it there is a reduced likelihood that its identity is equally distinct from the other nodes in Network B. In other words, *Isolate B is less structurally disconnected than Isolate A.* Consider once again the intercity network in Figure 1.1. How music from a city like Oslo or Sydney is understood and evaluated by those in other cities depends in part on how interconnected all of the other cities are. That is, whether the music an isolated city produces is distinct is not my primary concern here. I instead place greater emphasis on the variance in reception of (cultural) outputs from sources rather than their production. The more interconnected the core of the intercity network is, the more places like Oslo and Sydney will be viewed as distinct "others" by that core. The implication for shaping jazz is that music that came from disconnected sources had a particular appeal to those in the core of the social system because of the distinctiveness of those disconnected sources.

With this in mind, I articulate my answer to the central puzzle of the role of disconnectedness in three parts. First, conditional on the production of a new output, its appeal to a particular audience (peers, critics, or consumers) is driven by how they impute value and meaning from the source's level of disconnectedness. In markets where uniqueness is given salience, disconnected sources have a novelty, foreignness, or exoticism advantage.[15] To the extent that outputs with appeal influence the emergence of a genre's canon,[16] disconnected producers also have a disproportionate influence on that emergence. Second, I argue that disconnectedness is associated with one's membership within a social system but outside interconnected alters. High disconnectedness means being clearly outside a set of interconnected alters, even if locally central. Third, I claim that the appeal for the outputs of disconnected producers is greater when the outputs are also difficult to categorize since they are more congruent with disconnectedness.[17] We expect someone who is unique to produce something that is unusual (e.g., "Arab" jazz music), and this congruence increases the salience and appeal of difficult-to-categorize outputs.

My goal, then, is to incorporate this into the context of early jazz by drawing attention to the role of cities as sources of music and thereby gain insight on their role in the market for recorded jazz. Here, cities differ to the extent that they are disconnected. I expect to find evidence not only that, all else equal, recordings from cities with high disconnectedness are appealing to musicians over time but that the appeal is best captured when the musical recording is difficult to categorize.

JAZZ'S EMERGENCE AND THE INFLUENCE OF DISCONNECTED CITIES

I am exploring the impact of structurally disconnected cities and the rise of jazz standards through the discographical canon, where jazz standards are a key component of jazz that ethnomusicologists and other jazz scholars use to organize jazz.[18] Songs or tunes that are re-recorded by many jazz musicians over time represent the music most identified as the "jazz standards" that members of the genre's community would recognize. Jazz standards not only are a means of conveying identity but also provide members of the jazz art world with a basis of comparison and evaluation.[19] For example, a performance of Strayhorn and Ellington's "Take the 'A' Train" is typically considered a "jazz performance" independent of how well it is performed or what instruments it is performed on. Moreover, without any other information, whoever performs this song is likely to be considered a jazz musician by audience members.[20] It would not even have to "swing." Granted, many would conclude that it was "bad" jazz or even "impure" jazz, but it would likely be classified as jazz nonetheless. The importance of jazz standards persists in the academy among music theorists and musicologists.[21] For instance, composer and music theorist Steven Block uses a jazz standard recording ("Bemsha Swing") to define free jazz (a subgenre of jazz thought to be lacking form and defying definition).[22] Without the jazz standard, there would little reference point with which to evaluate free jazz.

Thus, just as the consumption of types of music reflects a consumer's identity, re-recording a song or tune can provide a musician with greater legitimacy by demonstrating her membership in the category of jazz.[23] A song or tune may also be re-recorded because it is unusual or exotic, leading some musicians to draw upon the music as a means to differentiate themselves from other musicians. In my model music associated with the first rationale (to garner legitimacy) was associated with established, central cities in the jazz community. The second rationale (differentiation) was associated with cities high in disconnectedness.

From this standpoint I conducted two quantitative studies to better understand the role of a musical source's network position in the construction of the discographical canon of jazz. My main interest was a city's level of disconnectedness and whether that disconnectedness mattered for understanding the market for recorded jazz and the discographical jazz canon. In a market like jazz where novelty is rewarded, I expected that outputs from disconnected cities would be more likely to receive broader appeal. If this appeal occurred early in the rise of the genre, as was the case with early jazz, this appeal might also have influenced the canon of recorded jazz. Similar to the way that marginalized artists can be seen as authentic sources of iconoclastic art,[24] the congruence between the role identity associated with a disconnected city and a non-normative recording that emerged from that city increased its appeal. For example, a difficult-to-categorize song in 1929 from New York would seem like a mismatch and thus unappealing, but that same song from Sydney would have greater appeal.

As I proceed, it is important to note that network centrality and disconnectedness do not operate in opposition. That is, while disconnectedness is most easily illustrated when examining isolates (as in Figures 1.1 and 1.2), *all* actors and entities within a network structure have some value of disconnectedness. For example, a city can have a high value of centrality from local ties and a high value of disconnectedness due to a position outside a large cohesive network. There may be social structures in which a city's centrality strictly covaries with its disconnectedness but others in which there is little relationship. Conceptually however, centrality and disconnectedness are distinct and analytically orthogonal—a point I elaborate in a companion article to this chapter (Phillips 2011) and display later in Figure 1.3.

AN EMPIRICAL APPROACH TO THE RISE OF JAZZ (1897–1933)

Jazz scholars generally acknowledge that recorded jazz began in 1917, although jazz's roots in ragtime and blues extend back to the turn of the century.[25] This is important as some of the music recorded before 1917 entered the repertoire of jazz musicians. I used jazz discographies for the period 1897–1933 to capture the *discographical* jazz canon and created two data sets: (1) city-level data that capture a city's output of recorded jazz as well as its position in an evolving network based on musician mobility; (2) recording-level data from the U.S. Midwest that looks at the long-run appeal of individual recordings. Each data set was designed to run statistical analyses that employ dozens of predictor and control variables.[26]

The end of the observation period for the city-level data (1933) corresponds to a cultural transition in Europe that culminated in World War II—an exogenous shock that radically altered the evolution of jazz.[27] The observation period for the Midwest recording-level data ends in 1929 owing to the U.S. stock market crash. This and the subsequent depression led to the failure of many record companies and a sharp decrease in recordings.[28] The year 1933 is a historical nadir—a low point in the production of jazz. After 1933, the swing era of jazz and its spread during World War II would fuel a second peak by the early to mid-1940s.

My main quantitative thrust in this chapter involves estimating the long-run appeal of a city's music, where long-run appeal is represented by music that is recorded multiple times from its first recording until 2004, which increases a song's likelihood of being in the discographical canon and, as a consequence, of being a jazz standard. Table 1.2 provides a sense of which songs or tunes had the

TABLE 1.2. Examples of Jazz Standards (Using the Discographical Data): Top Ten Most Recorded Jazz Songs up to 2004

Song Title	# Times Recorded
St. Louis Blues	1,569
Body and Soul	1,530
Sweet Georgia Brown	1,212
Summertime	1,161
Take the "A" Train	1,125
Stardust	1,046
'Round Midnight	1,028
Caravan	1,024
Honeysuckle Rose	986
All the Things You Are	986

Source: Lord 2005.

highest appeal according to this metric; it lists the top ten most frequently re-corded jazz songs up to 2004. As an indicator that recordings before 1934 were critical to the discographical jazz canon, each of the songs or tunes in Table 1.2, with the exception of " 'Round Midnight," was originally recorded before 1934. Thus the recordings from this early period are the foundation of the discographi-cal jazz canon.[29] Moreover, the appeal of these songs was driven by key people who decided what music would be recorded: musicians or, more specifically, bandleaders. This does not mean that record companies and labels did not influ-ence what was re-recorded (see chapters 4–6 for the role of firms in the construc-tion of the discographical canon); my point is that bandleaders were critical to the music selection process.[30]

My first goal with the discographical data, organized as Study 1, was to statisti-cally establish a link between the disconnectedness of a city and the long-run ap-peal of music from that city. I will also use Study 1 to establish that disconnected-ness cannot be explained away by network centrality or isolation—two of the most common variables in network analyses. Study 2 moves from establishing whether disconnectedness matters to why it matters. Here I tested whether the strength of disconnectedness was driven by the reception of difficult-to-categorize music using detailed recording-level analyses. Identifying difficult-to-categorize music is necessarily contextual. Thus to conduct this second study I focused on the data from Midwest jazz recordings and qualitative evidence on three indicators of a whether a jazz recording in the Midwest (or in the United States more gener-ally) would be considered either difficult to categorize or easy to categorize. Using these indicators, I tested my prediction that disconnectedness was only advanta-geous when the recordings in question were difficult to categorize.

Many supplementary analyses and robustness checks were also conducted. Moreover, there are a rich set of control variables to address a number of alternative hypotheses and factors. For example, I included fixed effects for city, record label and company, and year.[31] I also controlled for whether the city is an isolate (as something that is independent of its level of disconnectedness); how much production of jazz is occurring in the city; the propensity of a city to produce original music; whether the city is new to the jazz scene; whether recording musicians from the city stay in the focal city or travel to other cities; group characteristics; the arrangement of instruments; the collaboration network of musicians based on past recordings; how many takes it took to get the song; how commercially successful the song was up to 1943 (short-term commercial success); and how many re-recordings the song had up to 1943 (short-term appeal) (see Phillips 2011 as well as the appendix).

Study 1: City Centrality and Disconnectedness as a Main Effect

To keep track of the evidence for my arguments, I distilled them into a set of predictions. While I also examined the role of a city's network centrality, I expected that a city's disconnectedness was positively associated with music that had long-run appeal since cities high in disconnectedness were associated with nonnormative (or difficult-to-categorize) music. Highly disconnected sources were distinct sources of music, and this salience should have drawn more attention to songs and tunes that emerged from them. This leads to my initial prediction that independent of a city's network centrality, the more disconnected a city in the musician network, the more often recordings originating from that city were re-recorded by musicians over time.[32]

Study 2: Difficult-to-Categorize Recordings as the Key Mechanism

In order to empirically verify the mechanism of congruence between a recording's source and its characteristics, I used data on individual recordings to test for the whether a recording was difficult to categorize with respect to a particular region (the Midwest) and time (1920s). My claim is that difficult-to-categorize recordings received positive appeal (greater number of re-recordings) when the originating city had high disconnectedness. Disconnected cities had an identity consistent with recordings as difficult to categorize. Thus, all things equal, recordings with difficult-to-categorize elements should have been re-recorded more if they were originally produced in a city with high disconnectedness in the musician network.

These recording-level analyses took advantage of the richness of the data set of U.S. Midwest recordings from 1920 to 1929. In addition to the Tom Lord discography (2005, 2010) and Brian Rust's jazz discography (1969), I used data on individual labels and firms from the *Directory of American Disc Record Brands and Manufacturers, 1891–1943*.[33] I included original recordings in the Midwest, the region where recorded jazz, especially improvisationally oriented jazz, emerged.

The data set also includes recordings by record companies with headquarters outside the Midwest, as it was common for larger record companies to own recording studios in multiple cities. The data from the Midwest encompassed Chicago, Minneapolis, St. Louis, Cincinnati, Milwaukee, Richmond (Indiana), Peoria (Illinois), Kansas City, and Cleveland. After losing some cases due to missing data, the final data set for analysis constituted 1,752 original recordings by 355 groups.

The key to Study 2 lies not just in the quantitative discographical data but in the opportunity to engage the rich archival and historical data made available in archives and by music historians. Using music history and my own archival work, I extracted three indicators of whether a song was difficult to categorize in the Midwest during the 1920s. That is, in addition to readings on jazz and popular culture during the 1920s,[34] I drew upon archival material from the Chicago Jazz Archive and the Stanford Archive of Recorded Sound. This provided me access to oral histories, sheet music, record label data, and advertising and marketing information. I also read musician autobiographies,[35] jazz in the public discourse from dozens of local and national newspapers (from the *New York Times* to the *Logan Republican* in Logan, Utah), and other popular and trade press publications such as *Etude* and *Ladies Home Journal*.[36] Finally, in developing the indicators I used Rutgers' Institute of Jazz Studies, www.redhotjazz.com, and www.centerforjazzarts.org, which enabled me to view images and listen to hundreds of audio files.

The first indicator explicitly captures whether the recording would have been difficult to categorize while the second and third capture the ease of categorization: (1) recordings using rare instruments were more difficult to categorize; whereas (2) recordings by groups that purposely labeled themselves to clearly signal their musical style were easy to categorize; as were (3) songs that explicitly signaled sexual context. The first indicator should have made a re-recording *more* appealing when it originated from a city high in disconnectedness. A recording with the second or third indicators should have been *less* appealing when the song came from a city high in disconnectedness. In other words, songs that fit categorical rules were a mismatch with disconnectedness.

None of these indicators was "perfect" and each can fall prey to alternative explanations. However, my logic was to demonstrate an overall pattern of results using different indicators that describe a recording in diverse ways (the instrumentation, the name of the group, and sexual content of the song). To the extent that these indicators show a consistent pattern, there is greater confidence that I understand the relationship between the social position of cities and the early market for jazz.

The first indicator I employed was *the use of rare, non-normative instruments* within the context of U.S. jazz. For example, a pipe organ was considered an unusual and generally improper instrument for jazz.[37] I was less concerned with whether disconnected cities in my Midwest sample were more likely to use pipe organs in jazz; I wanted to know whether jazz music using pipe organs was more appealing if it emerged from a city high in disconnectedness. Hypothetically speaking, a jazz recording with a pipe organ would experience greater appeal if it had emerged from Minneapolis compared to Chicago. The use of a rare instrument may also be a proxy for other unique features of the recording that are unobservable to me as a researcher (such as the song's use of timbre, color, harmonies, accents, sound effects, etc.) but nonetheless experienced by past consumers and the community of musicians.[38] Thus I expected that the higher a city's disconnectedness, the more appealing was music that featured rare (difficult-to-categorize) instrumentation.

For the second indicator, I examined the name of the recording group to see if that *group's musical style* was clearly signaled in the group's name. For example, the terms "orchestra" and "hot" both denoted clear styles of jazz recorded during the time period under study. Consider two groups led by Louis Armstrong from 1928 to 1929. The first, Louis Armstrong and His Hot Five, featured the term "hot," which referred to a more improvisationally oriented sound, closer to the more original type of jazz rooted in ragtime that emerged from New Orleans. By contrast, the second group, Louis Armstrong and His Orchestra, used the term "orchestra" to signal a more symphonic form of jazz with larger groups and more highly arranged music (see chapter 4 for a discussion of the use of "orchestra" in jazz group names). U.S. audience members knew the distinction between "hot" jazz and orchestral "sweet" jazz well,[39] and many jazz groups used this public knowledge to signal their music's style to consumers, fellow musicians, and other constituents.[40]

My goal here is not to offer an ethnomusicological analysis of the differences between these types of musical groups; that is far from my expertise. Rather, I wish to draw attention to the fact that terms such as "orchestra" and "hot," as well as other terms such as "jazz," "hotel," and so forth were used to signal the stylistic characteristics of a group. Groups with particular name identifiers gave a strong signal of their sound (48% of the groups in my sample on recordings provide a stylistic identifier in their name). Groups without clear identifiers were more difficult to categorize to those seeking to evaluate a group's music across time.

To the extent that a group's name facilitates categorization and classification, their association with cities high in disconnectedness should diminish the appeal of that group's recordings. A group that self-identified as a "hot" jazz group, "orchestra," "hotel," and so forth should have released less appealing recordings when the recordings originated from highly disconnected cities. Future musicians would have expected that good "hot" or "orchestral" jazz be originally recorded in a city like Chicago. At the same time, recordings by groups claiming to be "hot" or "orchestral" did poorly over time when the cities were more disconnected, as disconnectedness was associated with an unclear or orthogonal relationship with the emerging genre.

For the third indicator, I used *explicit sexual references*, capturing whether the tune or song's title used a popular (and at the time unambiguous) slang for sex: "jelly."[41] Examples of the titles in my sample of recordings include "You'll Never

Miss Your Jelly Till Your Jelly Roller's Gone," "Shake That Jelly Roll," and "Got Jelly on My Mind." This African American use of slang eventually reached academic and literary audiences with Zora Neale Hurston's "Story in Harlem Slang" (1942). The meaning of the term varied within the category of sex (e.g., male or female sexual organs, intercourse) but was never ambiguous as a signal of sexual content.[42]

For an empiricist, the nice thing here is that the use of sexual references was both unambiguous and a taboo. This allows me to test whether central and disconnected cities were affected by moral violations (taboos) versus those that were difficult to categorize. This is an important test, since one may expect that music from disconnected cities was appealing because it was counternormative (such as a taboo), whereas I am arguing that the appeal stemmed from the fact that the music was non-normative (difficult to categorize). That is, if the appeal of music from cities that were highly disconnected were influenced by violations of post-Victorian moral values, then music with clear sexual references would have had favorable appeal when coming from highly disconnected cities.[43] However, I am claiming that what matters is whether a song "fits" in the category of early jazz with respect to cognitive schema. "Jelly" reduced a recording's categorical ambiguity, increasing its appeal when produced in a location perceived as a legitimate and salient source of jazz, such as a city that was minimally disconnected (such as Chicago). At the same time, recordings with clear sexual references constituted incongruence when coming from a city with higher disconnectedness (Minneapolis, Richmond, etc.) since sexual references were easy to categorize in the emerging genre of jazz.

Note that this final indicator is a conservative underrepresentation of jazz's association with sexual activity. After all, I am looking at only the title of a recording and not any potentially more sexually charged information (e.g., lyrics) associated with the recording. Also, as Ivan Light among many has noted, jazz was often associated with "whorehouse music," and other recordings with sexual overtones would have also been clear to Americans in the 1920s.[44] Thus I am likely undercounting sexual references within jazz recordings. Keep in mind, however, that my logic here is twofold. First, the title of a recording is by far the clearest signal of a song's sexual content. Its content could have been derived without even listening to the song. Second, to the extent that I am missing music that can be categorized according to its sexual content, it should only make it more difficult to demonstrate its impact statistically.

QUANTITATIVE DATA AND EVIDENCE

An attractive feature of the intercity network data is that cities make valuable nodes for the dynamic form of network analysis that I need to employ. First, cities as nodes are temporally fixed. They do not, at least in my observation period, "fail," "die," or otherwise cease to exist. In many dynamic social networks, re-searchers have to grapple with the entry ("birth") and exit ("death") of nodes. That is not a concern in these analyses. Second, because the network between cities is based upon musician mobility, a city can be isolated (with no musicians traveling to and from that city) but still be a source of music if the musicians that reside in that city recorded music locally during that time period. Moreover, the actual flow of bandleaders between cities was critical to the diffusion of conventions, pre-ferred instruments, and so forth among musicians, making intercity mobility a critical mechanism.[45]

It is important to stress that following the movement of bandleaders is key because they largely controlled the musical selections and arrangements as jazz traversed the globe. In other words, the network of bandleader mobility captured those most consistently responsible for creating and re-creating jazz.[46] The ob-served network between cities reflects a jazz group's investment time in the city and the group leader's decision to assemble the group to record music.

At the same time, my data do not capture all forms of group leader mobility. For example, Sam Wooding and his Orchestra recorded in Berlin, Paris, and Bar-celona, but they also traveled extensively across Europe (this group was the most prolific touring group in Europe during my observation period), including a set of performances in Moscow in 1926 to rave reviews.[47] Actual recordings (which is what my data capture) typically occurred in places in which a group had an ex-tended stay on the order of months or years rather than days or weeks. For ex-ample, Wooding's group performances in Moscow spanned a seven-week period in which no recordings were made. In contrast, his group spent at least thirteen months in Berlin where they made eighteen recordings. Thus the observed net-work between cities reflects a jazz group's investment time in the city, the group leader's decision to assemble the touring group to record tunes from their evolving repertoire, and the existence of at least a recording studio in that city. Because re-corded jazz did not emerge from Moscow until 1932 it is coded as an isolate in the mobility network, but Muscovites would have heard jazz through recordings brought into the country and very limited touring engagements by musicians such as Wooding's group in 1926. Similarly, any of Moscow's fourteen recordings could have diffused to other cities through the distribution channels of record compa-nies and the friendship and communication network of musicians, as well as lim-ited radio airplay.

Thus a network tie means that bandleaders (as carriers of musical conventions) were moving across local markets that were oriented enough toward the produc-tion and reception of jazz for the group to have an extended stay and invest in making recordings. The tie also reflected an evolving repertoire by the jazz group. Not only did groups practice songs that they thought audiences at their next des-tination would positively respond to, but they also learned new songs during their extended stays and interaction with other musicians. Moreover, while bandleaders making single movements from one city to the next created many of the network ties, other ties were created by the same sets of bands, spinoffs of these bands, or others who were part of the same community of musicians.[48]

Operationalizing Disconnectedness (for Studies 1 and 2)

I measured centrality using effective size, a standard measure of (first-order) centrality in network analysis. Those familiar with the work of Ronald Burt will recognize effective size as form of the measure of centrality that emphasizes nonredundant network relationships. With this measure centrality not only increases when a city is connected to many cities but also increases to the extent that those connections are not themselves conntected. For example, if you recall Figure 1.1, London had high effective size centrality because it was connected to seven other cities and several of these cities—such as Los Angeles and Paris—were not themselves connected. The use of effective size centrality allows cities like London to be appropriately represented as legitimate sources of jazz, known as a nexus of musician mobility.

More novel is my measure of disconnectedness, which captures the social structure of which other cities the focal city is *not* connected to. Whereas centrality yields an identity associated with broad legitimacy, I am arguing that disconnectedness corresponds to a salient social distance or dissimilarity (e.g., foreignness, degree of exoticism) of a focal city's role identity. I measure disconnectedness as a time-varying continuous variable, based upon the complement of the annually updated asymmetric bandleader mobility matrix.[49] It is a property that all cities possess. This way of capturing disconnectedness allows one to construct theories in which a city can have high centrality *and* high disconnectedness, where even central cities can benefit from non-normative action.

I also created a dummy variable if a city produces jazz recordings but is an isolate in the musician mobility network. This is a control variable and a point of comparison with the measure of disconnectedness. In my operationalization, each network isolate in year t is given the same disconnectedness score, controlling for the fact that it is an isolate in the first place. Each of the network isolates has the same role identity in a given year, but with role identities that vary across time as the overall social structure evolves. Thus in my model music from Oslo and Sydney (as two isolated cities) is viewed similarly with respect to the cities' disconnectedness. Both would be seen as equally exotic or foreign to the worldwide community of jazz musicians, but they do not share a collective identity (i.e., musicians in Oslo and Sydney did not communicate with one another). If my operationalization of disconnectedness is merely a complicated method of measuring network isolates, this variable should sharply attenuate the estimated effects of disconnectedness. However, while network isolates are an example of disconnectedness in its strongest form, my measure of disconnectedness is distinct. Not only are the capabilities of network isolates uniform across social space and time but so is their role identity. An actor cannot be both highly central in the network

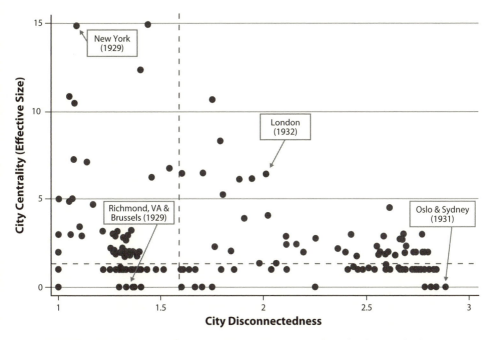

FIGURE 1.3. Scatter plot of city centrality and disconnectedness for the worldwide data set (1897–1933). Examples are selected to represent the four quadrants.

and an isolate, but an actor can be highly central and highly disconnected. Moreover, every actor in my model possesses some degree of disconnectedness, while this is not the case for the model of network isolation.

Figure 1.3 provides a scatter plot to further clarify the relationship between centrality and disconnectedness. The vertical dashed line represents the mean level of disconnectedness; the dashed horizontal line represents the mean level of centrality. Using these dashed lines we can simplify Figure 1.3 into four quadrants. The upper left quadrant represents city-years in which centrality was high and disconnectedness low. New York (in 1929) is in this quadrant. In the opposite corner quadrant are city-years in which centrality was low but disconnectedness high. Here I highlight one data point that is simultaneously occupied by two network isolates, Oslo and Sydney, in 1931. Cities that tend to have both greater-than-average centrality and disconnectedness are in the upper right quadrant. London is often in this quadrant, and its position in 1932 is identified in the figure. Recall from the intercity network diagram (Figure 1.1) that London's position in this quadrant is due to its centrality within Europe and relative disconnectedness from a relatively large network of U.S. cities. Finally, examples of actively producing cities low in both centrality and disconnectedness are Richmond (Virginia) and Brussels in 1929. These cities were isolated (centrality = 0) in years where the core of other interconnected cities was not particularly dense (lowering the disconnectedness score).

OPERATIONALIZING THE THREE INDICATORS OF
DIFFICULT-TO-CATEGORIZE RECORDINGS (STUDY 2)

To test my prediction about the relationship between difficult-to-categorize elements of a recording and the disconnectedness of a city, I first coded a dummy variable for whether the song featured a *rare jazz instrument*. I defined a rare instrument as one that is used in less than 5% of the Midwest recordings during the entire observation period. The list of rare instruments in this analysis are: bassoon (.1% of recordings), bass saxophone (2.1% of recordings), C-melody saxophone (2.0% of recordings), flute (1.0% of recordings), harmonica (.4% of recordings), piano-accordion (3.3% of recordings), pipe organ (.1% of recordings), steel guitar (.4% of recordings), ukulele (.1% of recordings), violin-cello (1.7% of recordings), vibraphone (1.0% of recordings), viola (.1% of recordings), and washboard (4.9% of recordings). Note that these instruments may be listed as rare for multiple reasons. For example, some never became popular within jazz (bassoon), some were losing popularity by the time of the observation period (washboard), and others were not yet popular (vibraphone). I captured instruments that were rare in the U.S. Midwest at the time of the respective song or tune's recording as a proxy of whether that recording was difficult to categorize.

As a point of calibration, I took advantage of Kraus and Harap's (1931) study, "The Musical Vocabulary of Newspapers and Magazines," in which they sought to determine how familiar a wide range of the U.S. reading public was with musical terms by counting the number of times musical terms (including instruments) were mentioned. Kraus and Harap listed each of the 214 musical terms that were mentioned more than five times in their sample of fourteen publications. Using this as a baseline of musical instruments and terms that the average literate American would be familiar with, I examined how frequently the instruments in my own sample were mentioned, using Kraus and Harap's study. The rare instruments from my Midwest sample have a median of only seven mentions in Kraus and Harap's study, whereas the remaining more common instruments in my sample have a median of seventy-three mentions, or more than ten times greater familiarity with the U.S. public. To put seven mentions in perspective, instruments not in my data but that also get seven mentions in Kraus and Harap's study included the musical saw and castanet. In other words, given that they only noted instruments that had more than five mentions, my selection of rare instruments would be equivalent to instruments that the 1931 U.S. public would have been unfamiliar with. As such, recordings with rare instrumentation should have greater appeal when they originated from a city high in disconnectedness.

Using the work of jazz historians and other scholars I constructed a dummy variable for whether the group's name in the discography explicitly signals the style of music it plays. The variable *clear music style* equals 1 if one of the following terms is in the name of the group: "hot," "orchestra," "jazz," "jass," "blues," "rhythm," or "syncopation"; each conveys a familiar style of music during the 1920s in the United States.[50] Finally, to capture whether recordings had an explicit sexual reference, I coded a dummy variable capturing whether a song's title contains the word "jelly." The descriptive statistics for these other variables I used in my analyses are in Table A.1.[51]

STUDY 1: CITY-LEVEL RESULTS (MAIN EFFECTS FOR CITY DISCONNECTEDNESS)

Before testing for the influence of a city's disconnectedness on a recording's long-run appeal, I first examined whether disconnectedness affected a city's propensity to produce original music. I needed to determine whether cities high in disconnectedness were more likely to be the sources of original music. If they were, a powerful counterargument to my theory is plausible: (1) cities high in disconnectedness typically produce original work; (2) original work is valued by the community of musicians over time; and, as a result, (3) music from cities high in disconnectedness had greater long-run appeal. This counterargument emphasizes the production side, whereas I am arguing that disconnected sources are not particularly unique or original but that their outputs are more likely to be seen as unique—giving them an exoticism advantage. To make this claim I have to determine what the propensity for producing original music was among cities high in disconnectedness.

My analysis revealed that disconnectedness was *negatively* associated with the production of original music (Phillips 2011, 472–74). That is, cities high in disconnectedness were more likely to copy and re-record the music of others rather than be the sources of original outputs. Indeed, close examination of the data revealed that cities high in disconnectedness were most often re-recording music that originated in highly central cities. A typical recording from a place like Sydney or Calcutta would be a re-recording of a tune that originated in New York or London rather than one that had never been recorded before.

This is important to consider as I test for the appeal of recordings, since disconnected sources were not more likely to be original and novel; there is little from their actual production to suggest that they would have been viewed as sources of original and unusual music. I believe that it is more accurate to say that while disconnectedness was negatively associated with the production of original music; the original music that did originate from disconnected cities had a disproportionately positive appeal. Even today, I would posit most Russian jazz artists do not sound unique in a way that is attached to their being in Russia. Your randomly selected Russian jazz artist sounds like your randomly selected jazz artist from the United States. This point complements work by scholars like David Grazian, who nicely explores the audience's role in constructing value independent of the actions of the artists in the context of blues.[52]

In the appendix I report statistical tests of whether a city's disconnectedness positively affected the long-run appeal of its recordings. My first analysis uses the data set of worldwide cities with control variables and different model specifications to take into account alternative explanations (Table A.2). These analyses show that not only is there a positive association between a city's disconnectedness and the long-run appeal of jazz from that city but that disconnectedness matters even after considering the city's centrality, the overall production of recordings (to capture market size), the city's production of original recordings (capturing the city's capability to produce), other city-level characteristics that might capture the commercial aspects of a music scene, and time period effects. The effect of disconnectedness even holds after taking into account time-invariant city differences with city fixed effects. I also verify that disconnectedness is more than mere network isolation and more generally a property based on the degree to which ego is distinctly disconnected from other actors in the social system.[53]

The more detailed recording-level analysis in the appendix verifies that on average a city's disconnectedness increased a recording's long-run appeal (Table A.3). Moreover, this effect exists controlling for the short-term appeal (number of re-recordings before World War II) and commercial success of a recording (number of reissues of the original recording before World War II). These controls adjust for any effect of the recording being a "hit" or other unobserved advantages such as the inherent "quality" of the recording. Thus the model is specifically capturing the appeal of the song or tune after World War II (the long-run appeal) independent of its success before World War II.

To take advantage of the recording-level data I collected, I coded and tested the influence of dozens of control variables. Table A.3 demonstrates the robustness of the disconnectedness effect. For example, the statistical effect of disconnectedness is independent of whether the record company was one of the largest in the market (as these firms had substantial advantages in the distribution and marketing of recordings), how much marketing the firm did in the *New York Times* (to capture its marketing presence with the newspaper's readership), and whether the firm was already in existence before the first "jazz" recording in 1917 (Victorian-era firms). The model also takes into account the possibility that appeal and disconnectedness were different when the recording was made in the same city as the company's headquarters, as there may have been differences when the record company's management was proximate to the recording studio.

One may question whether my measure of disconnectedness (and later my indicators of whether the recording was difficult to categorize) was correlated with demographic and structural characteristics of the recording group; to ensure that the effect of disconnectedness was net of these characteristics, I controlled for the size of the recording group, how unique the combination of instruments it used was, the race of the group and whether it had any female members, whether it had vocals, the group's recording experience (the number of recordings to date and whether all of the members of the group were recording for the first time), the studio productivity of the group (the average of recordings in their previous re-cording sessions and whether the recording was the first take), whether the group recorded in multiple cities (thus leading them to generate ties in the intercity network), and the average centrality of the musicians in the collaboration network based on previous recordings. I also used the discographies to control for whether the group had a designated and advertised leader, as this may have been correlated with appeal or the geographic network position of the recording. In a similar vein I controlled for whether the group had a designated "arranger," whether the group performed outside the recording studio, if the group was labeled as a "band" (my research revealed that these groups were more likely to have rare instruments), or if the group featured a geographic reference (see chapter 2 for a deeper discussion on geographical references). Finally, I netted out stable differences between record labels and cities and included variables to capture the particular year the recording was made.[54]

In short, my analyses include every factor I learned about and could collect data on across my decade of research. Many of these variables influenced a record-ing's long-term appeal and are interesting in and of themselves. But my main goal was to statistically verify that disconnectedness could not be explained away or dismissed. After including dozens of variables to address myriad alternatives and potential confounds, the relationship between disconnectedness and long-run ap-peal was robust.

In other words, to answer the first question of this chapter, city disconnected-ness mattered in that it was positively associated with long-run appeal. To further illustrate, Table 1.3 presents a summary of quantile regressions using the Midwest data that complement the regressions discussed in the appendix. While both the quantile (Table 1.3) and negative binomial (appendix) regressions demonstrate the relationship between city disconnectedness and long-run appeal, each has differ-ent advantages. The negative binominal models allowed me to more directly ad-dress concerns such as the interdependence of data. However, the quantile regres-sions gave me the opportunity to understand whether disconnectedness is influencing not only the most appealing music (the "big hits"), such as "St. Louis Blues" with 1,569 recordings, but also songs of more modest appeal, such as "Har-lem Flat Blues" with 11 total re-recordings.[55]

Table 1.3 shows that the effect of a city's disconnectedness is robust from the median level of long-run appeal to the 90th quantile, although the effect increases exponentially at higher quantities. A unit change in a city's disconnectedness (mean = 3.4, s.d. = 2.27) has a larger positive impact the higher the quantiles. At the 90th quantile of long-run re-recordings, a one-unit change in disconnected-ness results in an average of 62.4 additional times the song is re-recorded up until 2004. These results, displayed in Figure 1.4, suggest that to the extent that re-recordings capture the discographical canon, disconnectedness matters most for the songs in the upper quartile (the 75th quantile and above).

TABLE 1.3. Role of Disconnectedness across the Distribution Using Quantile Regressions

Variable	Quantile (median = 3)	Quantile (60th = 6)	Quantile (70th = 12)	Quantile (80th = 30)	Quantile (90th = 135)
Representative recording	*Get up off That Jazzo-phone*	*Blues of the Vagabond*	*Harlem Flat Blues*	*Don't Ever Leave Me*	*Mahogany Hall Stomp*
City centrality	−.01	.09	−.02	1.04*	.50
	(.08)	(.15)	(.23)	(.50)	(1.96)
City structural disconnected-ness	1.98**	6.39**	9.63**	16.84**	62.40**
	(.49)	(1.08)	(1.74)	(3.91)	(16.25)
City is network isolate	.67*	1.61**	2.10*	13.04**	46.76**
	(.28)	(.61)	(.97)	(2.12)	(8.49)
Log-pseudolikelihood	—	—	—	—	—
Pseudo R^2	.04	.07	.10	.14	.22
All remaining control variables?	Yes	Yes	Yes	Yes	Yes

*$p < .05$
**$p < .01$

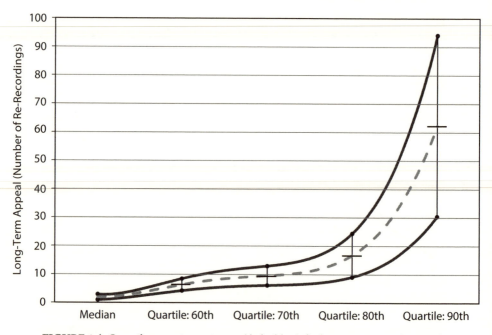

FIGURE 1.4. Quantile regression estimates (dashed line) for long-run re-recordings with 95% confidence intervals (solid lines); Midwest data ($N = 1,752$).

Study 2: Recording-Level Results

Figures 1.5a–c show the results of Study 2 (Table A.4), which used recording-level data to test whether the advantages of disconnectedness occur when some aspect of the recoding is difficult to categorize. Figure 1.5a shows that rare instrumentation in association with higher disconnectedness (the solid line) leads to greater long-run appeal. While the line for recordings with no rare instruments (the dashed line) is positive, the effect is not statistically significant. This is the first piece of evidence to support the thesis that disconnectedness improved the success of recordings that were more difficult to categorize.[56] The results shown in Figure 1.5b support the prediction that recording groups that clarified their music style were less appealing if emerging from a city high in disconnectedness (the solid line). Here, the upward-sloping dashed line indicates that higher disconnectedness improved long-run appeal when the musical style was unclear from the group's title. Not only is this effect statistically significant but so is the finding that recordings by groups with a clear style were negatively associated with long-run appeal when the city's disconnectedness is high (solid line). Figure 1.5c shows the results of testing the prediction that recordings with clear sexual references fared

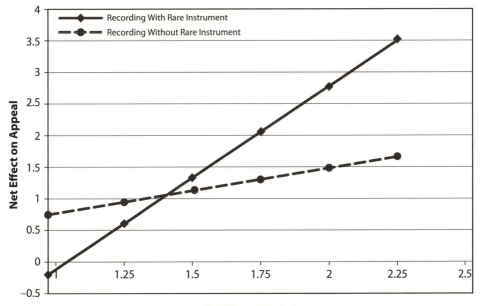

FIGURE 1.5. How city disconnectedness operates with three difficult-to-categorize indicators to affect the net appeal of recordings: (a) city disconnectedness and recordings with rare instruments; (b) city disconnectedness and recording groups with a clear music style; (c) city disconnectedness and explicit sexual reference ("jelly").

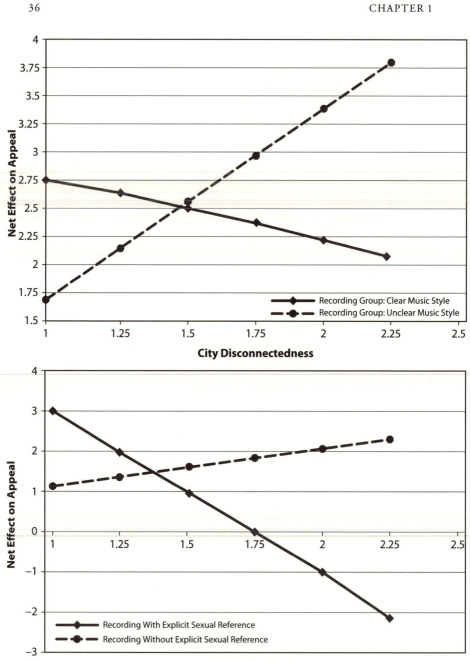

FIGURE 1.5. (cont.)

more poorly the more disconnected the city of the recording's origin. As predicted, the greater a city's disconnectedness, the less long-run appeal a song or tune had when the word "jelly" was in its title (solid line). Although the upward-sloping dashed line suggests that higher disconnectedness improves long-run appeal when the sexual reference is not made in the recording's title (dashed line), the effect is not statistically significant. Altogether, these figures paint a particularly compelling picture. Across all three indicators, difficult-to-categorize music fared better the greater the disconnectedness of the music's city.[57]

IMPLICATIONS FOR THE SHAPING OF JAZZ

I began this chapter with the observation that less prominent cities were active in producing jazz during the period of early jazz (before 1933), which led to the question of whether they influenced the emerging discographical canon through the long-run appeal of their recordings.

To answer this question I advanced the concept of structural disconnectedness by emphasizing that nonexistent relationships, when viewed structurally, is as valuable to members of a social system as the relationships that do exist. The greater the degree of disconnectedness, the more one is isolated from members who themselves are densely interconnected. While this concept is more general than the context of early jazz, I believe that it is quite helpful in understanding the emergence of the discographical canon. My focus is on the interpretation and imputed value associated with disconnectedness, which is distinct from other constructs, such as centrality or isolation. It also provides a link from a social structure of production to a social structure of reception and reorients attention to normative versus non-normative actions and characteristics.

Disconnectedness did indeed matter but not because disconnected cities are more original. On average cities high in disconnectedness were low in originality. However, when a disconnected city's music was difficult to categorize (even though this was a statistically unusual event), that music's long-run appeal was greater. I am treating appeal as something driven by the worldwide community of musicians. It was this community, in regular communication about the newest songs and trends, which drove the appeal of some songs over others. As Michael Danzi, an early jazz musician based in Berlin, noted, "We would play all the latest imported records, the latest hot music from the States."[58] This and other comments by practicing musicians of that period are supported by the fact that bandleaders were key determinants of what music a band would play and record.

This is not to say that the appeal to musicians (bandleaders) is the only factor that drives my results. Bandleaders were responding to their audiences, which included a generation of new consumers who were attracted to novelty and culture from socially distant and dissimilar sources.[59] Moreover, as I demonstrate in the latter half of this book, record companies were cognizant of evolving consumer tastes and played a key role in locating, evaluating, and disseminating music.[60] With my controls for record labels, as well as other research showing that record companies' attempts to champion particular songs in jazz often met with difficulties,[61] the influence of record companies is typically less than that of bandleaders in this chapter's analysis. Thus my focus on bandleaders is best understood as drawing attention to a principal set of actors in the diffusion of jazz music and an empirically tractable group. While they often influenced the appeal of some songs over others, it is likely that they were also representing a consensus across the different audiences for jazz.[62]

My chapter 1 findings are robust and consistent as a result of using both a broad worldwide database and a rich regional database that together allowed me to address multiple concerns. The role of a city's disconnectedness was in its association with elements that defied categorization. When deciding on which songs and tunes to re-record, bandleaders did not see disconnectedness as favoring *counter*normative characterizations so much as they saw it favoring *non*-normative characterizations. This is important in any social system, but in jazz it is critical as it identifies one way in which conventions and innovations were incorporated into the genre and formed the structure of the recorded jazz market. More broadly, my findings are important in that they allow us to better understand the emergent social organization of jazz.

PRODUCTION, RECEPTION, AND DISCONNECTEDNESS

This will sound comical to many jazz insiders, but there are those who would argue that recordings from disconnected cities were successful because they are somehow of higher "quality" or better in some way. And indeed, if I were focusing on the *production* of cultural objects this would be a much more compelling explanation, but because we are focusing on *reception*, a critic would need an account that does a better job of explaining the long-term appeal of difficult-to-categorize music from disconnected cities that is not already captured by the control variables I noted earlier in the chapter. In addition, my analyses revealed that difficult-to-categorize music had *lower* appeal on average, and disconnectedness is *negatively* related to the production of original music overall. It is only when original and difficult-to-categorize music is coupled with the disconnectedness of the source that the appeal is positive. Moreover, actually listening to early jazz from disconnected sources soon reveals that the assertion that music from disconnected sources is of somehow higher quality is difficult to defend.

IMPLICATIONS AND NEW QUESTIONS FOR THE SHAPING OF JAZZ

Cities high in disconnectedness shaped jazz when they happened to produce music that was difficult to categorize, since this was music that was deemed distinctly odd and thus congruent with the disconnectedness of the location. Jazz was shaped in part by congruence between the geographic source and the characteristics of the original recording. In short, we cannot understand how jazz was shaped without understanding the social structure of geographic origins.

At the same time, many questions remain, and some of them were inevitably generated by the very studies I conducted. What is it about the process of diffusion that links disconnectedness and congruence? How reasonable is it to expect that the geographic origins of a recording would have been salient to future musicians? How did musicians and other audiences of jazz from other cities receive that music? Can more be said about the characteristics of the record companies and the groups themselves?

The more I pondered the results presented in this chapter the more the remainder of the book project emerged as a set of puzzles relating to and extending this study. Chapters 2 and 3 further explore the role of geography, while chapters 4–6 focus on the characteristics of the firms and groups. What emerged was a consistent, but nuanced, narrative on the evolution of the discographical canon linked together by the role of sociological congruence. Jazz offerings that were congruent with schema and narratives flourished more often than offerings that were seen as incongruent. I soon realized that my task was to study the history of the early jazz market to extract some of the relevant dimensions along which congruence operated.

Chapter 2

FURTHER EXPLORING THE SALIENCE OF GEOGRAPHY

All night long, with that Dixieland strain,
Play it down, then do it again,
Ev'ry time I hear that tune,
Good luck says I'll be with you soon,
That's just why I've got the Milneburg joys.

—"MILENBURG JOYS" (WALTER MELROSE, 1925)

In chapter 1 I emphasized that the initial location of a recording matters for those receiving and evaluating music. In particular, disconnectedness in the network of geographic mobility has greater influence for how jazz is received than for how it is produced. The evidence suggested that disconnectedness operates though sociological congruence, where difficult-to-categorize aspects of a tune or song make the music more appealing if the (geographic) source is highly disconnected.

Part of my point is that sometimes we shortchange the fact that location effects how people categorize and evaluate a piece of music. Difficult-to-categorize music from a place that is perceived as unusual is often appealing to audiences (including fellow and future musicians). A musician evaluating a tune years after its first recording should attach meaning to that recording as a function where it was initially recorded.

My goal in chapter 2 is to further elaborate and use cases from the data to unpack two unanswered questions from chapter 1. First, chapter 1 focuses on the long-run appeal of a piece of music, but it remains unclear how musicians removed in time could have been aware of the location of the initial recording. For example, how might a musician in 1950 or 1970 have known that "Milenburg Joys" was recorded in Richmond, Indiana? Second, can more be understood about the process of diffusion that led to long-run appeal if the source was high in disconnectedness? The first chapter made progress on establishing the fact that disconnectedness matters. The goal of this chapter is to better understand *how* it matters. Chapter 3 furthers these efforts by examining a case that did not fit my chapter 1 models: early jazz from Germany.

CAN MUSICIANS REMOVED IN TIME BE AWARE OF THE ORIGINAL LOCATION OF A RECORDING?

In chapter 1 I claimed that a community of musicians is aware of a piece of music's (geographic) origin and that this origin is one important factor in the music's appeal. This is more intuitive when the location is New York or Chicago, but what about places that were high in disconnectedness? Is it reasonable to expect that musicians over time would know, for example, that a musical piece came from Sydney and not London? The answer, I believe, is yes for three reasons.

First, many times an exchange of songs and tunes occurred as touring musicians on different routes were co-located for short periods in the same city. Musicians who had recently come from the United States or a major city like London were especially valuable to others as they were more likely to know about new trends or styles that those in peripheral cities might have been unaware of. Indeed, musician first-person accounts suggest that this was a key mechanism.[1]

Second, record labels were often associated with geographical locations (see Figure 2.1). To get a sense of how often record labels featured geographic information, I surveyed 78 rpm record labels by randomly sampling 10% ($N = 120$) of Sutton and Nauck's (2000) CD-ROM of 78 rpm record labels. I found that a majority (66%) of the labels I sampled had information on the geographical origin of the recording through conveying the city or country of the recording or manufacture. This would have facilitated future musicians' attempts to make inferences on the location of original recordings. The information on the label provided the location of production, which often coincided with where the music as actually recorded. This was especially true for the younger and smaller labels started after 1917. Older and larger labels such as Victor records often did not provide geographical information on their records. At the same time, labels were often exclusively associated with particular countries, and often the name of the label alone would provide information on the location of the recording—especially if it was a larger, more well-known label like Victor.[2]

Moreover, in some cases musicians could have also inferred the location from the language that appeared on the record label; non-English labels were more likely to be associated with locations high in disconnectedness. A record label printed in Swedish, for example, would reasonably lead members of the jazz community (musicians, instructors, collectors, aficionados, critics) to infer that the recording was from Stockholm. Indeed, as Paul Berliner and others have noted, records were very popular among aspiring musicians for much of the twentieth century, as they often used the recordings to learn a song by playing along. The information on a record label was thus one way that geographical information could have been dispersed.[3]

Third, most of the musicians who recorded in this period were located in major cities (New York, Chicago, and London),[4] which would have facilitated awareness of a song's geographical origins. For example, given musicians' touring routes and other geopolitical relationships, jazz emerging from Calcutta (part of British colonial rule until 1947) or Sydney (also a legacy of British colonial rule) could have been geographically identified by musicians in London even years after the recording. It is less likely, however, that musicians in Buenos Aires would have identified jazz from Calcutta. Indeed, my research revealed that the pattern of successful appeal overwhelmingly involved an initial early success in a highly central city like

FIGURE 2.1. A record label from 1923, "Milenberg Joys," with geographic information on the label (Richmond, Indiana) as one piece of evidence that musicians could use to infer the location of a recording.

Chicago, London, or New York, even for tunes and songs that had origins characterized by high disconnectedness. If a recording from outside these central cities did not get re-recorded in these cities within the first few years, the song or tune was likely to end up on the far edges of the jazz discographical universe.

This insight also called for the first modification to my initial thinking. In chapter 1 I implied that the origin of music from disconnected sources would be known as such to the global community of musicians—a recording from Richmond, Indiana, would be known as such to a musician in Hilversum, Holland. However, it is more accurate to say that the origin of recordings from disconnected sources was known as such *only* after musicians in more central locations made them salient. A musician in Holland would likely have known music originally recorded in Richmond only after it was re-recorded by musicians in Chicago, London, or New York. Indeed, as I examined the diffusion pattern of individual recordings, every successful case of music from disconnected sources involved an early re-recording of that music in Chicago, London, or New York. In the next section of this chapter I use "Milenburg Joys" to show that successful diffusion did not require that higher-profile musicians in the central cities record the songs from disconnected locations. Rather it appears that the endorsement of the tune could occur even if the central city musicians were considered "average" among the set of recording artists. This suggests that there is a particular sequence to positive long-run appeal—especially for music originating from disconnected locations. Early on, music from disconnected sources would be re-recorded by musicians in locations high in centrality. Following these early movers in highly central cities, the wider community of musicians re-recorded the music over time.

As I continued to examine the diffusion trajectories of individual records, additional insights emerged. I found out that most of the empirical support for my models of long-run appeal worked best before the early 1960s, before the free, avant-garde, and alternative music movements within jazz emerged alongside a sociopolitical transformation in American society. After the 1960s, the importance of an early jazz recording's origins seems to matter less for long-run appeal. Some of the songs and tunes that were re-recorded before the 1960s continued to be recorded often, but more and more this seemed to be due to the popularity of that piece of music independent of the context of its origin. Thus, while my many models explain appeal through 2004, they do so more powerfully before the 1960s (I explore this further in the final chapter). I thus revised my claim: the relevance of a recording's origin diminished during and after the major societal and musical shift of the 1960s.

The remainder of this chapter uses the (early) diffusion of "Milenburg Joys" as a case study to demonstrate a richer sense of the ways in which a tune from a source high in disconnectedness diffused in such a way that its geographical source would have been known to musicians during the decades after the original recording. I will show that a closer look (beyond simply reading the record label) gives a richer appreciation of the appeal of music from disconnected sources, as well as draw attention to other characteristics of recordings that made the geographical origins more salient. Namely, whenever the title of the recording or the name of the group has a geographical reference, disconnectedness operates more powerfully, as if these extra cues make it more likely that future musicians would notice the original location of the recording. In the case of "Milenburg Joys," these geographical cues exist with both the title ("Milenburg") and the group's name on the record label ("New Orleans").

THE EARLY DIFFUSION OF "MILENBURG JOYS"

The story in chapter 1 is built upon rich data on the origins of recordings but with less information on who is doing the adopting over time. Indeed, this type of analysis is more difficult to do on a grand scale given the data available. However,

I can glean some insights from my data. Figure 2.2 displays the early diffusion of one song with substantial long-run appeal, "Milenburg Joys" (Milenburg is a misspelled reference to Milneburg, a town formerly on the south of Lake Pontchartrain and now a part of New Orleans). It was recorded 338 times by 2004 (only 1.03% of all the songs in my data were re-recorded more than 300 times). The upper solid curve indicates the cumulative number of times each song was recorded in the first decade of its recording (1923–33). The lower dashed curve indicates the cumulative number of cities the song was recorded in. "Milenburg Joys" was first recorded in Richmond, Indiana (high in disconnectedness), as an unusual mixed-race collaboration between Chicago-based Jelly Roll Morton (pianist and the song's composer) and (the white) members of the New Orleans Rhythm Kings.[5]

Figure 2.2 shows that after the initial recording in 1923 the music was recorded again in 1924 in both Richmond and Dallas. In 1925 there was an explosion of recordings: "Milenburg Joys" was recorded by musicians in Buenos Aires, Chicago (two times) Hayes in the UK, Los Angeles, and New York (seven times). After 1925 re-recordings continued to increase in the cities where it had already been recorded, as well as diffusing more broadly to new cities from Sydney in 1926 to Hilversum in 1933.

I found the activity in 1925, when "Milenburg Joys" experienced a burst of recordings two years after the original recording, one of the most intriguing aspects of this figure because many other successful pieces from disconnected sources had a similar pattern of a burst of activity involving Chicago or New York within a couple of years after the original recording. In addition, the successful pieces from disconnected sources seemed to have broader and more diverse geographic diffusion patterns. By 1926, only three years after its initial recording, "Milenburg Joys" had been recorded in four continents: North America, South America, Europe, and Australia. This geographic breadth was typical of other songs from disconnected cities.

To get a better sense of the diffusion process that led to long-run appeal, I needed more detailed data on re-recordings from a city high in centrality. I began with identifying musicians who initially re-recorded "Milenburg Joys" (the early adopters). From 1925 to 1933 "Milenburg Joys" was re-recorded in Chicago by six different groups: Joseph Gish and His Orchestra (1925), Jimmie O'Bryant's Famous Original Washboard Band (1925), Rodney Rogers's Red Peppers (1927), Lil Hardaway's Orchestra (1928), Husk O'Hare's Wolverines (1928), and McKinney's Cotton Pickers (1928). In many ways these groups were typical of those in the Chicago jazz recording scene.[6] For instance, the early commercial success of songs by these six groups (captured as the number of times their recordings were reissued) was no different than the mean of all of the groups in my Midwest sample (2.97 versus the sample mean of 2.94). At the same time, all six of the groups were locally oriented, never recording outside Chicago. Five of the six groups were recording for the first time. This opens up the possibility that these groups recorded

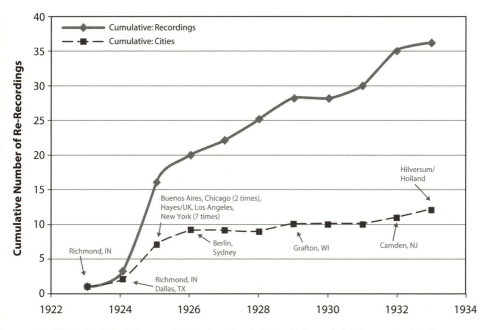

FIGURE 2.2. The diffusion of "Milenburg Joys": 1923–33 (recorded 338 times by 2004).

"Milenburg Joys" to make claims that they were a relevant and viable new entrant to the recording market.

Although the New Orleans Rhythm Kings (NORK) and Jelly Roll Morton recorded "Milenburg Joys" in Richmond, none of them lived in Richmond. In fact, Morton and NORK were residing in Chicago in the early 1920s. Thus some of the re-recordings may have been the result of musicians' learning the music by interacting with the originating musicians. For example, Jimmie O'Bryant, a clarinetist whose group recorded "Milenburg Joys" in 1925, played with Jelly Roll Morton in 1923. This exposure to the underlying network that collaborations might capture may have facilitated the 1925 re-recording. My models indicated that observable network ties (through collaborations on previous recordings) were a significant means by which appeal diffused. However, my findings on disconnectedness control for these network ties. In other words, after taking into account who collaborated with whom, my statistical analyses still yield positive effects for the role of a source's geographical disconnectedness (see Table A.3). Moreover, if this were simply a story of interpersonal network transfer by proximity then Morton's recordings made in Chicago would have had equal or greater appeal than his recordings made in Richmond. However, the median long-run appeal of his 1920s recordings in Richmond was substantially greater than the median long-run appeal of his 1920s recordings made in Chicago (52 vs. 5).[7]

In addition, the Richmond recordings were all done for a single label, Gennett; this is significant. There is no doubt that Gennett was idiosyncratic and has received a great deal of attention over time, making all of its 1920s recordings potentially more appealing (see Kennedy 1994). However, the advantage of my statistical approach is that I can isolate effects independent of the record label. In fact, my chapter 1 results that show the role of disconnectedness remained valid even after taking into account differences in firms and labels.

In sum, the example of "Milenburg Joys" prompts insights on how a successful tune from a disconnected source might diffuse by drawing attention to two distinguishing characteristics. First, there was a burst of recordings in major cities that appear to have been made by musicians who were talented but not famous. Second, music from disconnected sources seems to have had geographically broad diffusion patterns. When I looked at the patterns of music originating from cities high in centrality, the long-run pattern of appeal was not as geographically broad. It was more typical to see music from high central cities have an appeal more concentrated in those major cities; for example, the appeal of an original piece from New York was largely restricted to New York, Chicago, and London.

However, I still wondered whether what I observed for "Milenburg Joys" was the norm or an unusual case. Although it was difficult to construct a good quantitative test of the first distinguishing point (a burst of activity by talented but lesser-known musicians in central cities), I did have a way to check whether the second distinguishing characteristic was representative of early jazz recordings. I returned to the discographical data on jazz recorded worldwide and examined every original recording produced in 1929 ($N = 189$), the peak year of recordings, as well as every original recording from 1933 ($N = 114$) when recording was at a nadir due to the worldwide depression. I counted annual re-recordings of each song or tune through 2004.

I chose 1929 and 1933 because they represented stark contrasts in the economic environment for my observation period. Recording production peaked in 1929 and then dropped worldwide after the stock market crash, reaching its bottom in 1933. Using both 1929 and 1933 allowed me to take into account the otherwise unobserved economic activity surrounding the market for jazz. For example, in stable economic times, recordings would receive substantially more advertising and marketing, which would have drawn greater attention to the music. The market structure (the type of firms and competition between them) of the music industry was also radically different in 1929 and 1933. In 1929 there were myriad record companies and labels. Many of these labels went out of business or were acquired after 1929, resulting in a much more consolidated industry by 1933.[8] In addition, with the Great Depression and the beginnings of World War II in the 1930s came a dramatic decrease in the international travel of musicians, thus slowing the engines of diffusion.

Using cohorts of recordings also enabled me to conduct statistical tests that match the example in Figure 2.2 in that I can trace the annual appeal of every tune in each year. In other words, I tracked both the annual appeal of songs and tunes and the number of new cities that they were recorded in. Moreover, whereas the statistical analysis for chapter 1 estimates the long-run appeal by aggregating the total number of re-recordings since World War II, this chapter's focus on cohorts of recordings allowed me to code a song or tune's appeal in each individual year, as well as control for factors that might have made the entire cohort more or less appealing. For example, these cohort analyses would allow me to understand the volume and geographical breadth of appeal of a single tune from 1929 in 1979 controlling for the average appeal of all 1929 tunes in 1979.

For each song or tune originally recorded in 1929 or 1933 I coded the geographic network position (centrality and disconnectedness) of the original recording, information on the recording company (to rule out differences between record companies and labels), whether the song had a non-English title (in case disconnectedness was associated with the "foreignness" of the title), and the number of times the song was recorded in the initial year (songs recorded multiple times in the first year indicate particularly popular songs that many artists and record companies were striving to immediately record), as well as other variables discussed in chapter 1 and throughout this book, such as the experience of the band's leader, the age of the recording label, fixed effects controls for the labels and locations, period effects, the annual appeal of all songs in the same 1929 or 1933 cohort, and so forth.

Rather than focusing on the effect of disconnectedness on long-run appeal as in chapter 1, I wanted to verify that there was a positive association between music from disconnected sources and the geographic spread of appeal. Thus if my argument based on the "Milenburg Joys" illustration is correct, the variable for city disconnectedness would be positive and statistically significant in predicting the number of cities a song was re-recorded in over time, controlling for the total number of re-recordings. That is, I wanted to distinguish a song or tune that was re-recorded ten times across ten different cities from a song that was re-recorded ten times across only two different cities, where the former example of greater spread would be associated with high disconnectedness.

The findings were consistently distinct for the 1929 and 1933 cohorts, with different processes seeming to predict the long-run appeal of music from each cohort. As a consequence, I ran the results separately for each cohort (see Table A.5). The regressions show that disconnectedness was associated with a geographically broader appeal but that the effect is only significant for 1929 recordings (p = .004).[9] The results suggest that a one standard deviation increase in the source's disconnectedness increased the number of cities by about four. In other words, given two original songs or recordings with the same total appeal, the one from a more disconnected source has its total appeal spread out over a greater number of cities. At the same time, I found no effect for centrality, suggesting that the geographical breadth of the appeal of music emerging from a city high or low in centrality was independent of that centrality. This is not too surprising since we learned in chapter 1 that centrality had either a negative effect or no effect on overall appeal depending on the analysis run. The effect of disconnectedness as seen in this chapter, on the other hand, is a continuation of the robust role we noticed in chapter 1. When I ran the same model for 1933 recordings, the effect is positive but far from statistically significant ($p = .209$). In fact, very few of the variables in my model predicted geographical spread of the 1933 cohort of music. The short reason why this is so is this: during the height of the Great Depression, markets for recorded jazz became localized; producers recorded and released jazz for the local market and fewer musicians toured from city to city. Much of the international network of traveling bandleaders dissolved into local clusters that lacked the ties that previously bridged them.

Thus disconnectedness affects diffusion first through its attraction to musicians in central cities, which then spreads broadly to a wide array of cities. Many recordings emerged from Richmond, but those that were re-recorded in highly central cities early on in their trajectories experienced longer-term appeal. I could find no highly appealing early jazz tune from a source high in disconnectedness without early success in Chicago, New York, or London. If the source was disconnected, then long-run appeal required central cities as engines of diffusion. In this sense, the sequence of the diffusion process reflected my earlier conjecture. First, the music is picked up by musicians in a major city, presumably because it is difficult to categorize and thus a means for these musicians to differentiate themselves from one another. Second, the unique origin combined with the legitimacy of being recorded in a major city provided the fuel for the music to be not only appealing overall but also appealing in a geographically broad way. The information about the origin combined with its early appeal in central cities amplified its future appeal. The influence of geographical disconnectedness necessarily faltered when the macroeconomics of 1933 altered the geographical orientation of the market.[10]

GEOGRAPHIC REFERENCES AND THE DIFFUSION OF JAZZ

Another interesting aspect of "Milenburg Joys" is that it features a geographical reference to the New Orleans region. Initially naïve to the naming conventions of early jazz, I was drawn to the use of geographical references in song and tune titles, especially as I began to discover that the disconnectedness of the source was so powerfully associated with the tune's appeal. As I investigated geographical references I was impressed by how often they appeared in well-known tunes and in the number of ways in which they were used. When you are eighty years removed from a context, it is easy not to appreciate the simple but rich meaning the geographical references made at the time. Some of these were regional references, such as the "South" or "Dixie." Others referred to a particular street, such as "State Street Special" (in Chicago). The most re-recorded piece in my database is "St. Louis Blues"—itself a geographical reference. The more I investigated, the more possible it seemed that the role of space was relevant to understanding disconnectedness and the appeal of early jazz recordings. Might disconnectedness act most powerfully when the title of the song draws attention to geography? If so, would the geographical reference have made it more likely for a future musician to notice the source of the recording and thus have greater appeal if that source were high in disconnectedness?

I set out to answer these questions using the data on recordings originating in 1929 and 1933 from this chapter's preceding analysis to determine whether geographical mentions in song titles enhanced the role of disconnectedness. I used a 0,1 variable to code whether the music made a geographical reference to a country, region, city, street, neighborhood, or venue (9% of the titles made such a reference). Examples include the following: "The Blues Singer from Alabam'," "Harlem Rhythm Dance," "The Lure of the South," "Toogaloo Shout," "Hyde Park," and "He's Long Gone from Bowling Green."

The results (Table A.6) are consistent with my earlier models, the greater the disconnectedness, the more times in a particular year a song or tune was re-recorded over time.[11] I also used interaction effects to separate the effect of disconnectedness by whether or not the music's title made a geographical reference (see Figure 2.3). The bar on the left estimates the effect of having with no geographical reference in a recording's title; the bar on the right estimates the effect of having a geographical reference in the title using the mean level of disconnectedness. The results suggest that having a geographical reference provides around 0.93 more re-recordings annually. Over the approximately seventy years of tracking annual re-recordings, this amounts to a difference of sixty-five re-recordings. This alone would place the tune above the 95th percentile of the 1929 and 1933 cohorts of tunes. Disconnectedness thus enhanced appeal independent of the existence of a geographical reference, but that appeal was amplified when a geographical reference was made in the title. This suggests that geographical references were an additional way in which disconnectedness was highlighted, making it more likely that future musicians used the information on the recording's source in evaluating it as a candidate for re-recording.

Although this is interesting, it was not necessarily worth reporting. What made this result more compelling and surprising is that the specifics of the geographical reference did not matter, nor did it matter whether the reference was to the focal city. In fact, 75% of the geographical references in musical titles did not correspond to the actual location of the original recording. More often the title referred to a location that was geographically different than the origin of the recording. Moreover, I found no evidence that the relationship between disconnectedness, long-run appeal, and geographical references had anything to do with the specific geographical reference. Nor did it seem to matter that the location be specific. Regional references (e.g., the "South") seemed to generate the same effect as more specific references ("Alabama" or "New Orleans"). It only seemed to matter that the *any* type of geographic reference was made.

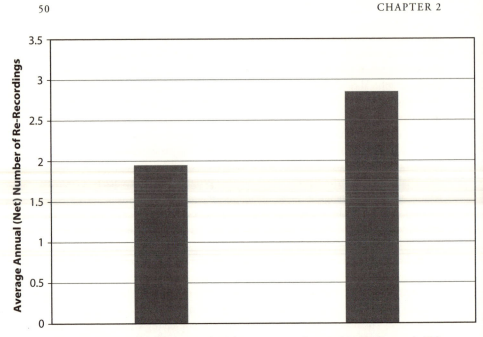

FIGURE 2.3. A recording's appeal for a city of mean disconnectedness according to whether there was a geographical reference in the song or tune title (using the 1929 and 1933 cohorts of original recordings).

I was not expecting these results. I assumed that the geographic references worked best when they were somehow congruent with the location. A recording from Sydney, I thought, would benefit from Sydney's disconnectedness if it referred to that particular location in the title (e.g., "The Sydney Stomp"). Seeking validation for this unexpected effect, I turned to my data on Midwest recordings from 1920 to 1929. In these data I had also kept track of each recording group's name, 15% of which made geographical references (e.g., New Orleans Rhythm Kings, Miami Lucky Seven, King Mutt and His Tennessee Thumpers), and used these data to run further regression analyses. Consistent with the analysis on geographic references in song and tune titles, the positive effect of disconnectedness on long-run appeal was amplified when the recording group's name had a geographical reference. And similar to my earlier finding on song titles, there was no evidence that the relationship between disconnectedness, long-run appeal, and geographical references had anything to do with the specific geographical reference in the recording group's name. Once again, I found that if the recording group's name made *any* geographic reference, the effect of disconnectedness on long-run appeal was amplified.

I was surprised by these results because congruence was such a powerful deter-
minant in chapter 1; I had assumed that it would neatly carry over to geographical
references. The quantitative analyses suggest a modification is in order. I misun-
derstood how the original location, especially for sources high in disconnectedness, became salient to future musicians who evaluated appeal over the years. The
evidence suggests that disconnectedness was made positively salient for any type
of geographical reference, whether the reference was local or non-local, specific or
general, or whether it was captured by the song's title or the name of the group. So
while geographical references are one way in which future musicians were drawn
to a recording's origins, I found no clear causal relationship between geographical
references and congruence. Geographical references operated at a more base level
and had the net effect of amplifying disconnectedness through the way in which
it made the original geographical information surrounding a recording salient. In
other words, my findings suggest that when "Milenburg Joys" recorded by the
New Orleans Rhythm Kings and Jelly Roll Morton made two geographical references (the title and the group's name), that amplified the salience of the source's
disconnectedness even though the recording was made in Richmond and not New
Orleans. It also may not have mattered that the references were to New Orleans;
for example, a hypothetical "Texas Joys" by the "California Rhythm Kings" might
have also amplified the salience of the source's disconnectedness.

IMPLICATIONS FOR THE SHAPING OF JAZZ

The investigation I reported here in chapter 2 suggests that there are many ways in
which musicians temporally removed would be have been aware of the location of
the original recording of a song, including the network of musicians with many of
them concentrated in a few cities, information printed on the record label, and the
geographic references associated with the original recording. I also developed a
better understanding of the process of diffusion that led to the long-run appeal of
early jazz from a city's disconnectedness. The case of "Milenburg Joys" allowed for
several insights for the shaping of jazz, with statistical support found using the
worldwide discographical data set of recordings from 1929 and 1933. Music from
highly disconnected sources tended to have a globally broader long-run appeal
than those originating from places like Chicago and New York. At the same time,
the role of these more central cities was critical to the success of music from disconnected sources, as the trajectory of a successful recording from a disconnected
source was often characterized by a tune or song emerging from a place high in
disconnectedness, then followed by re-recordings in one or more major cities in
the subsequent years after the original recording. Finally, recordings in geographically disparate places across the world would then follow the early adoption by the
major cities. The result is a unique three-stage diffusion pattern: (1) an original

recording emerges from a city high in disconnectedness; (2) early adoption by one or more central cities with high concentrations of musicians searching for music to re-record; (3) a broad, multicontinent diffusion of re-recordings. This three-stage pattern shaped a meaningful subset of the jazz canon.

While I am advocating for more attention to disconnectedness, the musicians based in Chicago, London, and New York were critical to understanding long-run appeal. The actions of these musicians drove the shaping of jazz, not necessarily in what they originated but what they found appealing and—through their actions of re-recording—legitimated. New York is widely known as a fountainhead of jazz. When it comes to the shaping of jazz, it often came down to what these musicians re-recorded, and it appears that one of the things they did was re-record music from disconnected sources. While higher-profile musicians did this as well, they appear to have done so less frequently. The middle-level musicians, through their actions (not necessarily their intentions), legitimated music through re-recordings.[12] I am suggesting that New York's primary role—at least in terms of shaping the discographical jazz canon—was one of evaluation, legitimation, and the construction of meaning around what is jazz.

The statistical models used for the analyses in the last two chapters are rich and detailed, providing a great deal of insight on the shaping of jazz. However, one city repeatedly failed to match my models: Berlin. Chapter 3 focuses on Berlin as a city that did not fit my theory or statistical analysis of how jazz unfolded. The more I examined the exception of early German jazz, the more I realized that it was sufficiently important to be investigated on its own. This meant that I needed to travel to Germany and draw on information and data that could only be found there. Chapter 3 represents the findings from that journey to incorporate this exception and better understand the shaping of jazz.

Chapter 3

SOCIOLOGICAL CONGRUENCE AND THE PUZZLE OF EARLY GERMAN JAZZ

with Gregory J. Liegel

It may interest our readers to know that the influence of American "jazz" music has made itself felt upon some well-known musicians abroad. When Mr. Whiteman was in Europe recently three leading figures in symphony orchestras there asked him for information regarding American "jazz" music. "That is the only distinctively American music that we can put our fingers on," they told him. "And it is the kind of music the public here is calling for."

—*Sheet Music Review*, FEBRUARY 1924

Krenek [composer of *Jonny Spielt Auf*] has also succeeded in mingling, to a certain extent, a degree of true novelty with these elements of jazz à la mode. . . . It is not a great opera . . . but stack *Jonny* alongside of the *Rhapsody in Blue* and it towers.

—ALFRED FRANKENSTEIN, "REVIEW OF REVIEWING"

In chapter 1 I showed that the long-run appeal of jazz music worldwide was related to the city of origin's network position. My model has good explanatory power with the exception of one city: Berlin in what was then Weimar Germany.[1] The long-term influence of most cities has been explained by their position in the network of bandleader mobility, alongside various controls for city, group, and record company differences. Berlin, however, is an anomaly that does not fit my model. Consider Figure 3.1.

Between 1923 and 1933, more original jazz recordings were produced in Berlin (156) than were produced in Paris (72), the city many associate with early European jazz. Berlin, as it turns out, produced more early jazz than any other city in Europe as the center of Weimar culture. And yet the lasting appeal of jazz music recorded in Berlin was notably less than that of other European cities. Recordings originating in Berlin (where essentially all of the jazz recordings in Germany were produced before 1933) were re-recorded over time substantially less often than were recordings originating in other cities. While discographical data provide clear evidence that a robust jazz recording industry existed in Berlin during this time period, they offer little insight into *why* jazz recorded in Germany ultimately had such little long-run appeal, especially in light of the amount of music it produced. In short, the countless statistical analyses I have run over the past several years can

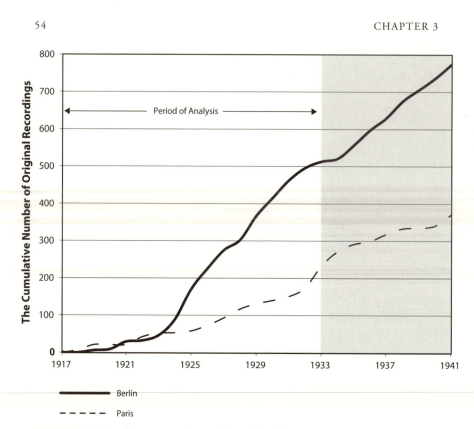

FIGURE 3.1. Cumulative count of original recordings from Berlin with Paris as a reference (1917–41).

account for every city's level of contribution to the jazz canon from New York to Paris and even Calcutta. Each time, Berlin seemed to be the one case whose depressed contribution to the jazz canon I could not statistically explain: the quest to understand the role of cities in the evolution of jazz had produced a clear, compelling, and potentially fruitful exception.

Rather than sweep this exception under the rug of empirical inconvenience, I decided to use this case as an opportunity for deeper theorizing. To explain this puzzle, I collaborated with Greg Liegel (of the University of Chicago sociology department) and Jennifer Omoregie (a multilingual research associate at the University of Chicago).[2] Our explanation of German jazz and the resulting theoretical advancement we developed are the subjects of this chapter.

To explain this puzzle, we oriented our thinking with insights from scholars who study the perception and reception of art, as well as those who study the legitimization of cultural products.[3] In particular, we drew heavily on scholarship that notes that the appeal of cultural objects requires a model that incorporates the social identity of those who receive or experience the cultural object. We also

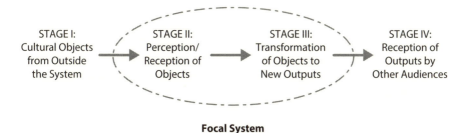

STAGE I:	STAGE II:	STAGE III:	STAGE IV:
Cultural Objects	Perception/	Transformation	Reception of
from Outside	Reception of	of Objects to	Outputs by
the System	Objects	New Outputs	Other Audiences

Focal System

FIGURE 3.2. A reception-production-reception model of cultural objects.

based our thinking on theory from the sociology of art that draws attention to the legitimation of genres and cultural products.[4]

Using this foundation, we developed a sequential relational model for understanding the fate of recorded jazz from Weimar Germany in which the locations of musical reception and production correspond to schemas that affect the tastes and the ways in which cultural objects are interpreted. In addition to the interpretation of cultural objects, our model considers the skills and technological capability available to (re-)produce cultural objects. Thus to understand the low long-term appeal of Weimar-era jazz, we began with the introduction of jazz into Germany, examined the reception and internalization of jazz by Germans, and then focused on why the music that subsequently emerged from Germany lacked long-run appeal (see Figure 3.2). We focused first on the types of jazz that came to Germany just as the post-inflationary period of post–World War I Germany began in 1923 (Stage I) then transitioned to the schemas used by Germans in receiving imported jazz (Stage II). We incorporated these findings with information on the type of jazz subsequently produced by German groups (Stage III) and completed our analysis by analyzing the reaction of those who experienced early German jazz to explain its low long-run appeal (Stage IV).

Though we had more data on the production than the reception of jazz in this period, implicit in our model is Griswold's notion of multivocality, whereby "cultural objects vary in their symbolic capabilities" such that multiple interpretations can coexist for the same object.[5] Jazz music, captured as cultural objects in the form of recordings, fits this notion of multivocality well. Meanings and value are fabricated using the relationship between characteristics of the object and the cultural schema of the recipient. This schema uses a set employed by social cues (including the identity of those that initially produce or provide the cultural object) to incorporate the cultural object in ways that attempt to preserve the receiver's social construction of the world.[6] Similarly, we draw upon Gombrich's emphasis on perception in art and how perception influences the production of art in particular through the process of "making and matching."[7]

Our model also builds upon the observation by Johnson, Dowd, and Ridgeway (2006, 54) that the legitimation processes, whether they pertain to the microprocesses of status hierarchies, to the more macroprocesses of organizational forms, or to cultural objects and genres, tend to reach successful legitimation through a staged process of "innovation, local validation, diffusion, and general validation." Even though ours is a case of the lack of appeal of music from Germany, their sequential model enables a formulation that captures both successful and unsuccessful legitimation.

After presenting the data and methods, we will sequentially navigate through our schema-based model on the reception of jazz and apply this model to jazz's introduction to Germany and then its integration, production, and subsequent reception by those outside Germany. As we progress, we will incorporate evidence and draw conclusions. After addressing the relationship between our data and the conceptual model, we turn to alternative explanations and then reengage the more general theoretical statement on shaping jazz.

A NOTE ON DATA AND METHODS

To elaborate and test our model, we gathered data from multiple sources in the United States and Germany. We needed to know the identities of key exemplars in the introduction of early jazz to Germany, to understand both popular interest and critical discourse about jazz within Germany, and to compare early German jazz recordings to those produced elsewhere. In the course of this research, we drew upon articles, oral histories, and autobiographies of 1920s musicians. We also examined 1920s publications from Germany such as *Der Artist*, a popular trade periodical for performing artists, as well as U.S. trade publications (*Musical Courier*, *Metronome*, etc.).

Much of these data came from the Jazzinstitut Darmstadt and the Berlin State Library (Music Department); some data also came from the Stanford University Archive of Recorded Sound and the Center for Jazz Arts' exhibit on early German jazz.[8] Newspapers and magazines provided critics' reviews, essays, and musician and venue advertisements, while oral histories and biographies supplied rich accounts of German and U.S. jazz during this period. In addition, we read digitized archives of the *New York Times* and other papers available from the Library of Congress's "Chronicling America" archive that mention and discuss jazz before 1922 (such as the *New York Tribune*, *Ogden (UT) Standard-Examiner*, *Morning Tulsa (OK) Daily World*, and *Cayton's Weekly* [Seattle]), all of which were important to solving the puzzle of early German jazz.

The Tom Lord discography database of jazz recordings continued to be helpful here for both constructing aural comparisons and running quantitative analyses, as were hundreds of recordings made available by collectors and archivists (e.g., Rainer Lotz and Horst Lange). These recordings allowed us to get a better sense of the style of jazz that was recorded in Berlin during this time and to better gauge its quality. In sum, the data provided unique insights into how jazz was perceived, received, and produced within Germany and were critical to developing our model of cultural reception and production.

WEIMAR GERMANY'S EXPOSURE TO JAZZ

Although World War I brought a style of jazz to Western Europe via black U.S. army bands led by James Reese Europe and others, it is difficult to discern precisely how and when jazz was first introduced to Germany.[9] The earliest exposure on a large scale likely occurred through imported recordings.[10] What is clear, however, is that jazz's popularity in Germany quickly spread following the 1923 currency stabilization, primarily through an increase in recordings and musician tours. This year also coincided with the rise of a different style of jazz: a symphonic form performed by larger orchestras that reached high levels of popularity worldwide, especially among white audiences, who represented disproportionate purchasing power. The synchronicity of these two events (Germany's currency stabilization and the rise of symphonic jazz) accentuated this popular entry of jazz into Germany. Germans would have been listening to symphonic jazz as one of the most widespread and legitimate representations of jazz at the time.

The more improvisational form of jazz, often performed in smaller groups (e.g., "hot" jazz), surely existed within Germany as well, but the key European tours for this "hot" style of jazz had come and gone by 1923 when touring economically fragile Germany was not feasible for most jazz groups. The first group to record music marketed as jazz, the four-member Original Dixieland Jazz Band (ODJB) in 1917, performed in England but never in Germany. Indeed there was a "hot" jazz group in Germany—the Original Piccadilly Four—but their existence is sufficiently short that historians lack substantial data on the group to correctly infer their demise. By 1923, when Germany was more viable as a destination, the ODJB had disbanded as this initial wave of jazz waned. Will Marion Cook's larger and all-black Southern Syncopated Orchestra (SSO), whose spinoffs included smaller groups like those in which Sidney Bechet performed, toured much of Europe from 1918 to 1923 (including Vienna), but we found no evidence that they toured in Germany. Howard Rye, who specifically examines where the SSO and its spin-off groups performed, found that they made their homes primarily in London (where the SSO was most influential) and Paris (where its most successful spin-off, the Jazz Kings, was based).[11] Rye has also identified some former members of the SSO in Berlin after 1924, but in each case they are either in vocal groups or musicians playing in German-based groups.[12]

The first well-known American jazz band to play in Germany was Alex Hyde's Romance of Rhythm Original Jazz-Band aus New York, a symphonic jazz group that first played in Hamburg in 1924.[13] Hyde's initial success was quickly followed up by Sam Wooding's orchestra, which accompanied the Chocolate Kiddies Negro revue and typically played in the symphonic style as well.[14] Eventually radio airplay would expose Germans to varieties of popular music that occasionally consisted of music labeled as jazz.[15] However, during the mid-1920s live performances and recordings were the primary means of exposure to jazz.

The first key to understanding the puzzle of early German jazz, then, is to appreciate the fact that the dominant touring groups were performing a particular type of jazz, one that was most often represented by Paul Whiteman. While today Whiteman is not commonly associated with the term "jazz," his name was synonymous with (symphonic) jazz at the time, especially for Europeans and white Americans.[16] From 1923 to 1933, for example, Whiteman was the name most associated with jazz in the *New York Times*. As Figure 3.3a shows, Whiteman was co-mentioned with jazz 140 times over this decade, whereas Duke Ellington was only mentioned five times by 1933 and did not overtake Whiteman until the late 1950s. Figure 3.3b shows the annual number of co-mentions of Whiteman and Ellington with "jazz" in the *New York Times*; Whiteman's association with jazz was more frequent than Ellington's until after World War II. Indeed, in 1926, Duke Ellington was hailed as the "Paul Whiteman of Colored Orchestras" in promotional materials for New England audiences.[17]

Much of Whiteman's extraordinary success can be linked to a May 1924 performance in New York, the Experiment in Modern Music concert, which culminated in a performance of "Rhapsody in Blue" and quickly became his (and composer George Gershwin's) signature piece. The performance initiated an international symphonic jazz tour, during which he was crowned the "King of Jazz." The March 1924 issue of *Sheet Music News* indicated that an overwhelming majority of critics had a favorable view of the performance. Outside of their overall evaluations, the reviews also serve as a helpful means for understanding how jazz was then defined by critics (many of whom used Whiteman's performance to guide their own definitions). From these reports, it is clear that much of Whiteman's acclaim was due to the fact that he was credited with having developed a legitimate, symphonic form of jazz as art.

It is this understanding of jazz that came to Germany when it finally became a lucrative destination for touring groups around 1924. Germans were interested in the music that was popular among their American counterparts. To many (white) Americans, Paul Whiteman was seen as the primary voice of jazz, which was interpreted as having originated with the "primitive Negro" but had been refined by Whiteman to yield jazz as a symphonic-derived form. This narrative was deeply rooted in the public discourse, often as a defense of jazz and as a counter to critics who thought jazz was not worthy of being considered music. As noted in the August 1922 edition of *Metronome*: "The bizarre 'blues' and maddening litanies of the old-style jazz band are dying in a vanishing diminuendo. Gymnastics and hula-hula are giving way to melody and orchestration. Credit for the revolution in jazz is generally attributed to Paul Whiteman. . . . He has literally applied a symphonic technic to syncopation" (Koenig 2002, 202). By 1924, especially after

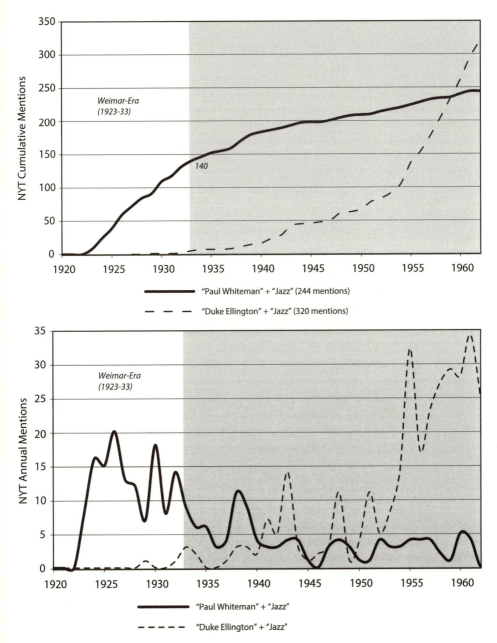

FIGURE 3.3. *New York Times* cumulative (a) and annual (b) counts of simultaneous mentions of Paul Whiteman and "jazz," compared to mentions of Duke Ellington and "jazz" (1920–62). By 1933 Paul Whiteman was co-mentioned with "jazz" 140 times.

Whiteman's performance of "Rhapsody in Blue," many writers were narrowly defining legitimate jazz as having an orchestral, symphonic sound.[18] In most cases, jazz's popularity was associated with the narrative that jazz was a legitimate form of music because it had been symphonically refined from its lowbrow, primitive (which for many was a synonym for "Negro") roots. For example, in the film *The King of Jazz* (1930), Whiteman described jazz through a refinement-of-the-primitive narrative both in the opening scene as well as in the part of the movie that introduces the performance of "Rhapsody in Blue." This scene is helpful in conveying the refinement narrative, especially since elements of this narrative are important to discussions in the remaining chapters in this book.

In the opening scene, the narrator, Charles Erwin, says the following: "[B]y the way you may be interested to knowing how he [Paul Whiteman] came to be crowned the King of Jazz. Once upon a time Paul, tired of life in the great City [New York], had a grand idea. He would go big game hunting. No sooner said than done, shooting the action camera, we find him a few weeks later in darkest Africa." The movie then switches to an animated sequence in which Whiteman, being chased by a lion and with depictions of dancing African natives, sings for the Lord to deliver him, pulls out his violin and begins to play, pacifying each of the African characters (the natives and jungle beasts), who dance and frolic to his violin playing. The "crown" (making him the "King") appears on his head after a monkey hits him with a coconut.

The refinement narrative reappears in the part of *The King of Jazz* that introduces "Rhapsody in Blue"—the signature tune of symphonic jazz. This time Whiteman speaks: "[T]he most primitive and the most modern elements of music are combined in this rhapsody, for jazz was born in the African jungle, to the beating of the voodoo drum." Whiteman's introduction is followed by a dark figure dancing on a drum to a simulated African beat (played on a Timpani drum), which then transitions to the clarinet introduction that signals the beginning of "Rhapsody in Blue." The symbolism is clear: proper jazz began with the "primitive Negro" but could not be clearly classified as music until it was refined with symphonic elements. While the movie was only mildly successful in the United States (released shortly after the 1929 stock market crash), it had greater appeal in Europe (we were not able to get German-specific data on the movie's success).[19]

Symphonic jazz was highly popular and recognized as a legitimate art form throughout Europe, but this was especially so in Germany. In fact, outside of records that the more avant-garde elite possessed and the reports brought back by those who traveled outside Germany, there is little evidence that Germans were widely familiar with musicians like Louis Armstrong or Sidney Bechet. Some of this was likely driven by the fact that Armstrong and Bechet were black; many Germans held deep anti-black sentiments in part because the post–World War I decolonization and subsequent occupation of Germany by French African soldiers (Senegalese) directly subverted German notions of superiority.[20] Thus for many, blacks in Germany were unwelcome, particularly in positions that afforded a degree of status. Even so, former members of the SSO did work in Berlin during this period as sidemen, and Arthur Briggs (an African American trumpet player) led a mixed-race jazz group (the Savoy Syncopators Orchestra, or the Savoy Syncops) and recorded in Berlin in 1927.[21] Moreover, one of the most successful touring groups in the 1920s was Sam Wooding's (all-black) Orchestra (see chapter 1). Wooding's group toured in Germany from July 1925 to October 1926, during which they performed almost daily and produced eighteen jazz recordings, more than any other American jazz group up to that point. They acquired a sizable fan base and experienced a consistently positive reception.[22] However, although they were black, their style of music was much closer to the symphonic jazz style associated with Whiteman. Indeed, members of the Sam Wooding Orchestra looked up to Whiteman as the best representation of their mutual form of jazz.[23]

In hindsight Germany's exposure to symphonic jazz was no surprise, as this was the form of jazz most often associated with popular social dances worldwide (e.g., the foxtrot, shimmy, Charleston, and tango). In contrast, Germany's relatively late attraction to jazz in 1924 meant that Germans received much less exposure to other forms of jazz. In cities such as New York, Paris, and London, multiple styles of jazz were more readily available, discussed, and performed throughout the 1920s. For example, as early as March 23, 1919, the *New York Tribune* interviewed James Reese Europe, an African American bandleader who was preparing to perform "seventeen species of jazz" at Carnegie Hall—a reference to the variety of music called jazz that already existed by then. Paris was exposed not only to Wooding's music but also to the music of Sidney Bechet, Eddie South, and other musicians from the New Orleans tradition. London was similarly exposed to a variety of forms of jazz, ranging from the ODJB to Sam Wooding's Orchestra to the SSO. In short, while jazz during this period encompassed multiple forms, Germany's exposure to jazz was more narrowly symphonic and was primarily performed by European or white American musicians.

Therefore, Germany was disproportionately exposed to and embraced a particular form of jazz, which I will argue also aligned with their own musical tradition. In general, Germans held broad and ambiguous definitions of jazz, many of which were more cultural references to a mix of modernity, Americanism, and Primitivism.[24] Critical discourse—often through the lens of Adorno's writings[25]—reflected a rich debate involving German cultural conservatives and the avant-garde. Some have argued that the tone and variability in this discourse around jazz were uniquely German, but we found little to support that argument. Our readings of American and French critical discourse in large measure mirrored the discourse and themes also observed in German discussions about jazz.[26] And in at least one case U.S. critics of jazz drew upon German critiques to support their own arguments.[27] Specifically, our readings of the discourse at that time show that advocates of the classical music community and members of religious organizations spoke out most strongly against jazz in ways that appeared to be independent of the critic's country of origin. As a consequence our analysis does not draw heavily from critical discourse and instead focuses on the entire process of how jazz was represented, perceived, and received, with a particular focus on the music that was captured through recordings.

GERMANY'S PERCEPTION AND RECEPTION

According to Susan Cook's analysis (1989) of Weimar-era jazz, Germany became more drawn to jazz than did any other European country. There are several reasons for this, including the fact that the post-inflationary society experienced a dramatic increase in discretionary spending. Moreover, the German cultural schema for music—its unparalleled tradition in classical music—made symphonic jazz attractive. German (and Austrian) musical identity, with its rich tradition of Bach, Beethoven, Brahms, Strauss, Wagner, and others, made Whiteman's version the closest match to this tradition. In addition, the ability to play symphonic jazz, which emphasized arrangements, sight-reading, and technical proficiency over improvisation, privileged skills that German musicians possessed.

Although there is evidence that German jazz musicians had poor improvisational skills (Danzi 1986), this was also true for classically trained musicians in the United States. Indeed, it was one reason why major record labels in the United States (e.g., Victor), well anchored in the classical tradition, often found it challenging to produce high-quality improvisational jazz (see chapters 4 and 5). In Germany, the tradition of classical music among the record companies (e.g., Deutsche Grammophone) was much more entrenched than it was in the United States. Moreover, the size of the German recording industry was greater than that of recording industries in the rest of Europe. For example, we identified eighteen Berlin-based record labels that released jazz in 1929, whereas London had fourteen and Paris had six. As a consequence, not only were musicians in Germany skilled in playing symphonic jazz, but the infrastructure for music production and reception (record labels, venues, record distribution channels) would have made the symphonic form of jazz something that the German music industry had the complementary assets to capture, the technology to produce efficiently, and the distribution and marketing infrastructure to promote. In fact, the complementarity between German national identity and industry infrastructure that was oriented toward symphonic music was unparalleled throughout Europe.

WEIMAR GERMANY'S PRODUCTION OF JAZZ

Jazz's importance in Germany is also suggested by the fact that it was home to the first institutionalized jazz instruction in the world: from 1927 to 1933 at Dr. Hoch's Conservatory in Frankfurt, students could enroll in a jazz curriculum. We focus on this conservatory not only as direct evidence of the production of symphonic jazz in Germany but also to gain insight into the debate surrounding the legitimacy of jazz in Germany. The criticism of the jazz curriculum had two primary components. First, there was a concern that instruction in jazz, as a representation of (Negro) American popular culture, would racially defile Germany. Second, since jazz at its best was rarely seen as a serious form of art, critics argued against a conservatory teaching "dance music," as the *Suddeutsche Musikkurier* argued on November 25, 1927:[28]

> Accursed jazz has ruled the hour . . . this is the "plague" that the musical world devoted to culture in Germany considered to be a miserable scourge . . . it is the laboratory for the transfusion of Negro-blood. . . . Anti-Germanism, in either its forms as atonality, internationalism, Americanism, pacifism, threatens our existence and the paramount role of our culture. The world of jazz represents minority, disharmony, and madness in contrast with high quality art music.

Equally instructive was the retort from Dr. Hoch's Conservatory's director, Bernhard Sekles. His response sheds light on how jazz was framed by German proponents and producers of jazz:

> The teaching of jazz is not only the right but the duty of every up-to-date musical institution. The majority of our musicians find themselves permanently or temporarily compelled to play in jazz ensembles. Aside from this practical consideration, a serious study of jazz will be of the greatest help to our young musicians. An infusion of Negro [blood] can do no harm. It will help to develop a wholesome sense of rhythm, which after all constitutes the life element of music.[29]

Sekles's defense has two parts. The first is practical: the popularity of jazz requires that German musicians learn how to play it. Second, he contends that learning jazz will teach German musicians "a wholesome sense of rhythm" that was attributed to "Negroes." This is most likely a reference to the role and type of syncopation that was widely thought to be a key component to most forms of jazz.

Dr. Hoch's Conservatory's jazz curriculum, led by Mátyás Seiber, had nine subjects: conducting, ensemble, instrumentation, and individual instruction on the piano, saxophone, trumpet, trombone, percussion, and banjo.[30] Two aspects of this curriculum are particularly compelling. The first is conducting, which was seen as a key component of jazz and is the first course listed in the curriculum. Indeed, our examination of the discographical data from this period revealed that the jazz from Germany was more likely to have someone listed in a conductor subrole ("arranger," "leader," or "director") than was jazz from any of the other major cities that we examined. Second, the instruments listed for instruction are those associated with jazz but on which German musicians lacked experience. While there was demand for German musicians who could play jazz on these instruments, many groups relied on American and British musicians to play them

11—12.00 Von Dr. Hoch's Konservatorium:
Erstes Konzert der Jazz-Klasse

1. „Dew-dew-dewy day" . . Johnson, Tobias und Sherman
2. a) Igloo Stomp . . . . B. Wirges
   b) Chips . . . . Th. Masmann
3. a) Valse Caresse . . . . R. Widhoeft
   b) Crazy Cords . . . . E. Henkel
4. Miß Annabelle Lee . . . . . Clare und Pollack
5. a) All alone Monday . . . . H. Ruby
   b) Cecilia . . . . Dreyer
6. a) Birth of the Blues . . . . Henderson
                        (bearbeitet für 2 Klaviere M. Seiber)
   b) „Aint she sweet?" . . . . Jellen und Ager
                        (bearbeitet für 3 Klaviere H. G. Schulz)
7. Virginia Stomp . . . . Geo S. Matthis
8. Kleine Suite für Orchester . . . . . . Igor Strawinsky
   Marche — Valse — Polka — Galopp
Ausführende: Heinz See (Saxophon), Bernhard Böse (Saxophon), Eugen Schmandt (Saxophon), Heinrich Lautz (Violine),
Marie-Luise Mönch (Violine), Elisabeth Sommer (Violine),
Joseph Seiber (Violine und Schlagzeug), Eugen Henkel (Banjo
und Gitarre), Heinrich Petri (Sousaphon), Fritjof Naumann
(Schlagzeug), Heinz-Günther Schulz (Klavier), Dr. Odilo
Furegg (Klavier) und die Oberklasse der Orchesterschule —
Leitung: Mathias Seiber

FIGURE 3.4. The playbill of the concert of the first cohort of Dr. Hoch's Conservatory jazz program in 1927. Source: "Von Dr. Hoch's Konservatorium" 1929.

and perform solos.[31] One of the conservatory's goals was to minimize the reliance on foreign musicians.

The playbill of Dr. Hoch's Conservatory's first student concert in 1929 is presented in Figure 3.4. For each of the musical selections listed, we researched in what style the song was played at the time and where the most popular recordings might have existed to establish a point of reference for the conservatory's first jazz performance. We found sufficient evidence for eight of the twelve musical selections. We could not find previous recordings of tunes written by members of the group or their instructor, Seiber (who also composed under the pseudonym Matthis).[32] For example, "Virginia Stomp" is a composition by Seiber. Another tune, "Crazy Cords," was by Eugen Henkel, one of the students listed as playing banjo and guitar. Most of the selections were popular songs from 1926 and 1927, recorded by New York–based groups in the symphonic jazz style.[33]

For example, our analysis (we listened to recordings of the songs and examined their sheet music) revealed that two of the songs, "Dew-Dew-Dewy Day" and "All Alone Monday," were popular as ballroom dance foxtrots, a common style played by symphonic (jazz) dance society orchestras. Two songs were different types of classical pieces: "Valse Caresse" is a waltz and "Kleine Suite für Orchester" is a classical modern composition by Igor Stravinsky. Three other tunes were popular symphonic jazz orchestra arrangements: "Miss Annabelle Lee," "Ain't She Sweet," and "Birth of the Blues." "Miss Annabelle Lee" was recorded widely in the year or two before this concert. Although there were many jazz orchestra arrangements of this tune that the jazz class could have drawn from, it possible that one of the influential recordings would have been Arthur Briggs's Savoy Syncops, who recorded the tune in Berlin during 1927. "Birth of the Blues" was performed across many jazz styles, but a very popular version of the song during the time of Dr. Hoch's Conservatory's existence was a recording by Paul Whiteman and His Orchestra. The Whiteman version featured an advanced arrangement with passages of "Rhapsody in Blue" integrated into the latter half of the recording. Finally, we identified "Igloo Stomp" as a ragtime tune composed in 1927 by Bill Wirges. The only audio version we could locate from that period was done as a traditional solo piano piece—the primary way in which ragtime was played. We assumed that the conservatory performance of "Igloo Stomp" was not performed in a symphonic jazz style even though Wirges led his own orchestral jazz group and was the pianist for the Harry Reser Band.[34] With that assumption, seven of the eight identifiable pieces of the conservatory's jazz performance were stylistically symphonic, and one was a ragtime performance. In short, the combination of the curriculum and the songs selected for the concert suggest the dominance of symphonic jazz, characterized as requiring a conductor and largely represented by music associated with society dancing and Paul Whiteman's approach to music.[35]

The playbill also listed the instruments used during the performance, which consisted of three saxophones, three violins, two clarinets, a sousaphone (a type of tuba), a drummer, a musician who played both the violin and the drums, and Henkel who played the banjo and guitar. This group was also accompanied by the conservatory's Oberklasse der Orchesterschule (or upper class of the school's orchestra). This information, along with what we learned about the tunes played, added to our evidence that early German jazz was a developed and serious effort that was engaging jazz that built off of the Germans' skills and traditions to produce jazz that would have comfortably fit in the category of symphonic jazz.

Although many German groups played and recorded jazz in a symphonic format, not all jazz groups in 1920s Germany were jazz orchestras. However, Whiteman influenced even top bandleaders in smaller, non-symphonic formats. For example, saxophonist and bandleader Eric Borchard traveled to New York in April 1927 to look for jazz singers and gain insight on how to better perform jazz. The description of Borchard's trip in the *New York Times* (April 8, 1927) concluded with the following: "Herr Borchard, who played for American soldiers in home camps during the war [World War I] and later on the Rhine, means to consult Paul Whiteman, who he smilingly calls the 'Borchard of America,' and Irving Berlin about his project."

Although our evidence showed that early German jazz was stylistically situated within a symphonic form that was consistent with Germany's cultural and technological infrastructure, we remained concerned that our information was not representative, falling prey to what remains in jazz archives and what is accessible as digitized music. Thus we turned to the discographical data, which more completely captures the universe of recordings from this period, and focused on the instruments used in jazz recordings. To the extent that instrument choices capture stylistic differences, we were able to compare jazz recordings from Berlin to those of other major cities, as well as compare major figures (exemplars) in early jazz. Specifically, we used data from 1929 (the year of peak production during the observation period) and examined how similar instruments used in Berlin recordings were to instruments used in New York, Chicago, London, and Paris recordings. We also compared the instrumentation of these Berlin recordings to 1929 recordings by three exemplars: Paul Whiteman, Duke Ellington, and Louis Armstrong. Over the years, most discussions of these three artists have suggested that Whiteman's symphonic sound and Armstrong's more improvisational New Orleans style were the most distinct, with Duke Ellington's music representing an innovative hybrid of the two.[36]

For the analysis, we extracted thirty-four different types of instruments and two types of roles ("arranger" and "leader"). Since discographic entries did not use consistent naming conventions and others aggregated instruments (e.g., "reeds" rather than specifying the type of reed instrument), we collapsed the instruments and roles into eight categories: brass, reeds, symphonic strings, drums, keyboard, vocals, guitar/banjo, and leader/arranger.[37] Using a matrix where each column was an instrument category and each row was a city or an exemplary jazz leader, we generated a non-metric multidimensional scaling (MDS) of the five cities and three exemplars. This MDS provided a two-dimensional representation of how similar each of our data points were with respect to instrumentation. The more similar the instrumentation, the closer the points (cities or exemplars) are on the MDS. Figure 3.5 presents the resulting diagram and accompanying distance matrix (using the MDS coordinates) to complement the map. The closer the distance on the MDS map, the smaller the value in the corresponding cell in the table in the map.

We first outlined the five cities (the crescent), with Chicago located in the top right and Paris at the bottom of the diagram, toward the center. Berlin is nearly at the midpoint between New York and London, although the distance table shows that it is actually closer to New York (0.69 vs. 0.84). We placed additional outlines to highlight the distance between Berlin, New York, and Paul Whiteman. From the MDS, we infer that jazz produced in Berlin, based on the instruments used in 1929 jazz recordings, was not unique. Similar to our qualitative evidence, it appears that Berlin's music was typical for the time period and more closely matched the music from New York (where musicians like Whiteman were based) than music from the other cities.

Also important is the relative distance between Berlin and the three key exemplars from this period. Berlin's instrumentation most closely matches the instrumentation of groups led by Paul Whiteman. To determine the source of this similarity, we found that both Whiteman's jazz and jazz from Berlin were more likely

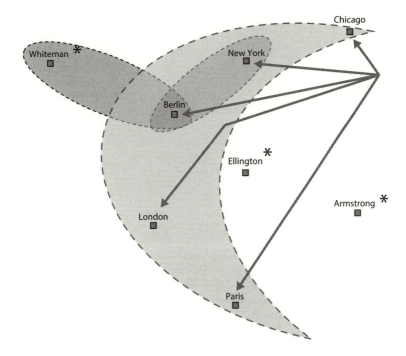

	Berlin	Paris	NYC	Whiteman	Ellington	Chicago	London	Armstrong
Berlin	0.00	1.49	0.69	1.05	0.69	1.49	0.84	1.61
Paris	1.49	0.00	1.81	2.29	1.01	2.22	0.86	1.21
NYC	0.69	1.81	0.00	1.55	0.80	0.83	1.42	1.42
Whiteman	1.05	2.29	1.55	0.00	1.73	2.37	1.44	2.66
Ellington	0.69	1.01	0.80	1.73	0.00	1.30	0.84	0.94
Chicago	1.49	2.22	0.83	2.37	1.30	0.00	2.10	1.33
London	0.84	0.86	1.42	1.44	0.84	2.10	0.00	2.27
Armstrong	1.61	1.21	1.42	2.66	0.94	1.33	2.27	0.00

FIGURE 3.5. Non-metric MDS of five cities and three key artists(*) using thirty-four instruments (collapsed into eight categories) in each recording of 1929.

to have a conductor, a common role in symphonic jazz. We also found that Whiteman's and Berlin's jazz were less likely to feature drums than the jazz produced in the other cities and by the other exemplars. Drums make up 3.9% of the instruments listed in Berlin jazz recordings, whereas in the other cities the average is 6.71%. The only data point that had a lower representation of drums was Paul Whiteman at 2.44%. Finally, we found that 48.1% of the German recordings had (pitched) instruments associated with a modern symphony orchestra: violin, viola, cello, contrabass, trumpet, trombone, tuba, clarinet, bass clarinet, bassoon, cello, contrabass, and xylophone. This was greater than that of any of the other cities and exemplars.[38] Recordings from Chicago contained the lowest percentage (30.4%) of symphonic instruments.

THE RECEPTION OF GERMAN JAZZ OUTSIDE GERMANY

Despite the volume of production and focus on symphonic jazz in Germany, we found little evidence of any attention outside Germany given to German-based symphonic jazz. American attention was instead given to another output from Germany, the "jazz opera," best represented by Ernst Krenek's *Jonny Spielt Auf* in 1927 (and later by Weill's *Threepenny Opera* in 1928). As music historian J. Bradford Robinson has noted, "The late 1920s were also the age of the so-called 'jazz-opera,' in which German dance music was not only quoted as a musical ingredient but entered the meaning of the work as a signifier."[39]

By current standards it is difficult to classify music associated with jazz operas in the late 1920s and early 1930s as jazz.[40] Even at the time of the operas' success, many observers questioned their connection to jazz music.[41] Indeed, Krenek himself noted, "*Jonny Spielt Auf* . . . created a tremendous sensation for reasons that I found entirely wrong. . . . It was labeled a 'jazz opera,' which I felt to be a misnomer." Krenek instead pointed to its use of jazz as a cultural construct and metaphor.[42]

At the same time, the classification of the work as a jazz opera was readily made by critics and promoters, which only increased its popularity. Americans in particular referred to *Jonny Spielt Auf* as German jazz or as "the principle [*sic*] example of Teutonic jazz."[43] For example, the headline in the *New York Times* on January 20, 1929, for the Metropolitan Opera Company's performance of *Jonny Spielt Auf* was "The Opera's King of Jazz." Another critic proclaimed it "a stroke of genius."[44] That said, the classification of jazz opera seemed to be independent of the critics' evaluation of the opera's quality, with both supporters and detractors classifying the opera as German jazz. The classification of *Jonny Spielt Auf* as a jazz opera and as an authentic German export also occurred because the opera was widely successful in Germany before arriving in the United States and was billed as such. Thus, to Americans, this was a German exported jazz opera, written by a German (Austrian) and endorsed by the German populace.

Moreover, many members of America's arts community were desperately looking for a legitimate synthesis of jazz with various highbrow musical forms. In 1924, following the success of "Rhapsody in Blue," called by some a "jazz symphony" or a "jazz concerto,"[45] there were calls for the development of "jazz operas" by Otto Kahn (chairman of the Metropolitan Opera) and "jazz ballets" by ballet master and choreographer Mikhail Morkdin. Kahn in particular asked several

U.S. composers (e.g., Irving Berlin, Jerome Kern, and George Gershwin) to create a jazz opera, but many questioned whether there was an American capable of adequately accomplishing the task. Irving Berlin, for example, stated that "he would 'give his right arm' to compose a syncopated opera suitable to the reparatory of the Metropolitan" but "did not feel that he was technically qualified for such a work."[46] The same article stated that Kern had attempted to create a jazz opera and failed a few years earlier. Gershwin, in the wake of his "Rhapsody in Blue" performance with the Whiteman Orchestra, was seen as the most likely composer to develop a jazz opera, although he had already written a one-act opera in 1922 (*Blue Monday*) that was a failure. Indeed, reexaminations of operas during the period point to previous operatic works—such as Ravel in France who debuted *L'Enfant et les Sortileges* in 1925—that drew at least as much from jazz as *Jonny Spielt Auf*, but none of these other alternatives was from a German or an Austrian.[47] It was Ernst Krenek, the more authentic German operatic composer, who was lauded as someone who finally created the synthesis in 1927, followed by Kurt Weill in 1928.

Despite the attention jazz operas received, there were very few jazz operas ever produced in Germany. That is, Germans actively produced jazz, but the form of jazz most often recorded in Germany, symphonic jazz, resides on the sidelines of our collective memory. The rarer jazz opera—with even fewer musical connections to jazz—was instead seen as authentically German by American audiences. And herein lies the more complete reason why the analyses in chapter 1 did not explain music from Germany. Germany's jazz output was dominated by (what would become) marginalized symphonic jazz with few other types of jazz such as Dixieland or other more improvisational or ethnically diverse forms (such as the Gypsy style developed in Paris). In addition to this, the type of music that was exported was the jazz opera, which remained (by construction) well beyond the boundaries of traditional jazz.

Indeed, the biggest contribution to the jazz canon from early Germany jazz is "Mack the Knife" from the *Threepenny Opera*, which the discography data show was recorded 325 times by 2004. Interestingly, the inclusion of "Mack the Knife" into the category of jazz did not occur until the 1950s, when it was recorded by Louis Armstrong (1956); Bobby Darin (1959) and Ella Fitzgerald (1960) also recorded it. Their very successful renditions of this song (Darin's version was #1 on Billboard, and both he and Fitzgerald won Grammy Awards for their recordings) made it a staple for many jazz musicians that continues today.

Figure 3.6 reintroduces our model from Figure 3.1 with a summary of our evidence thus far. We have indicated that symphonic jazz came to Germany just as the post-inflationary period for post–World War I Germany began in 1923 (Stage I) and was accepted as legitimate jazz in part because it matched the schemas of tastes, skills, and industrial orientation of the German musical tradition (Stage II). We then showed that these factors led to the production of symphonic jazz, using as evidence music from Dr. Hoch's Conservatory and instruments used in recordings from 1929 (Stage III). Finally, we analyzed the reaction of those who experi-

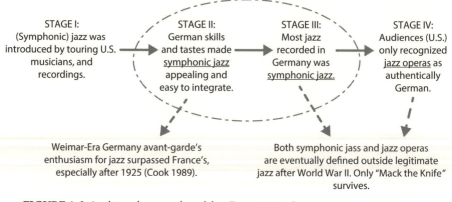

FIGURE 3.6. Applying the general model in Figure 3.1 to German jazz.

enced early German jazz in the United States to explain that its low appeal is rooted in the waning popularity of symphonic jazz, as well as a disconnect between the type of jazz most commonly produced and the jazz opera that came to signify "German jazz" (Stage IV) to U.S. audiences.

EVIDENCE OF THE MODEL'S VALIDITY

We argue that Germany produced a great deal of music that was legitimately jazz at the time and was similar to the music of Paul Whiteman. However, this form of jazz eventually lost its legitimacy as an authentic representation of jazz. This claim suggests a falsifiable test using the discographical data to shed light on our model's validity. Specifically, if our claim about German jazz's mirroring of Whiteman's legitimacy is accurate, we would expect to see the appeal of early German jazz positively associated with Whiteman's appeal.

To conduct this test, we again examined songs in 1929 (from chapter 2) to determine whether Berlin-based music was more likely to be re-recorded (or have appeal) during periods of high legitimacy for Paul Whiteman. Specifically, we tested whether early German jazz had higher appeal during years in which Whiteman was popular as a jazz artist in the public discourse. To capture Whiteman's legitimacy and salience as a representative of jazz, we calculated the annual proportion of *New York Times* mentions of "jazz" that also included "Paul Whiteman" and inserted the variable *PW Jazz* in regressions controlling for indicators of the city-level production of jazz and mobility of recording musicians in and out of Germany.

The historical evidence suggests that early German jazz would have more appeal during the same years in which Whiteman was legitimate as a jazz musician (*PW Jazz* > 0). For example, if Whiteman received a substantial amount of attention as a jazz artist in 1938, then the salience or appeal of Whiteman's style of jazz should also positively affect the appeal of music from Germany in 1938. Building off of the MDS in Figure 3.5, we also examined how the annual appeal of German jazz varied with the legitimacy of Duke Ellington and Louis Armstrong. If our interpretation of the historical record is correct, then German jazz should have less appeal in the years in which Ellington and Armstrong received more attention as jazz artists in the *New York Times*.

The results from the regressions (see Table A.7) build off of the models from chapter 2 with the same set of control variables. The regressions predict the number of times, in year y, that a song that originated in 1929 or 1933 was re-recorded until 2004. The key to these analyses are interaction effects representing the proportion of mentions of "jazz" in the *New York Times* in year y that also mention Paul Whiteman, Duke Ellington, and Louis Armstrong, respectively. The earlier evidence suggests that music originating from Berlin should be re-recorded more often when Whiteman is linked to jazz but less often when Ellington or Armstrong is linked to jazz. These regression results verify that these patterns are statistically significant. The more Whiteman is associated with jazz in year y, the more appealing are recordings from Berlin in that year. However, the more Ellington or Armstrong is associated with jazz in year y, the less the appeal of Berlin-based music.

The results of these statistical analyses, combined with our knowledge that over the course of the twentieth century Whiteman's legitimacy waned as that of Ellington and Armstrong grew (Figure 3.3), help provide further evidence of the validity of our German jazz explanation. In recording symphonic jazz associated with Whiteman's style, the Germans made an extensive investment in re-producing a style of jazz that had contemporary appeal but waned over time.[48]

However, it is difficult to determine whether early German jazz's fate was due to Whiteman's symphonic style or his race—both of which substantially faltered as authentic markers of jazz during and after the 1940s.[49] To test whether the effect was due to Whiteman's race or symphonic style, we examined the co-mention of different exemplary white artists in early jazz to determine whether their legitimacy also affected the annual appeal of music from Germany. In particular, we examined the New Orleans Rhythm Kings (NORK) and the ODJB as the two most prominent white "hot" jazz groups in early jazz and the groups most noted for the spread of hot jazz to Europe in the early 1920s. The analyses of NORK and ODJB revealed that their legitimacy was *negatively* associated with the annual appeal of songs from Berlin, although only the regression term for NORK was statistically significant ($p < .01$). In other words, the appeal of Berlin-based jazz diminished when NORK was associated with jazz in the *New York Times*; it was only when Whiteman is associated with jazz that the music from Berlin has an increase in appeal. Given that we find diminished appeal when the all-white NORK is co-mentioned with jazz, we suggest that much of the Whiteman-Berlin effect is due to symphonic style and cannot easily be accounted for with simple notions of race.

OTHER EXPLANATIONS

While the bulk of our evidence speaks to the role and evolution of symphonic jazz's legitimacy for early German jazz, we also believe that other factors were relevant. For example, there is evidence that the high volume of German jazz recordings may have disproportionately served the local market and may not always have been produced for external consumption. Compared to other European countries, Germany had more labels that were more exclusively oriented to the German market. Of the eighteen labels based in Germany upon which jazz music was recorded from 1923 to 1933, fourteen, or 78%, were focused solely on the German market. This was much higher than the proportion of locally oriented labels in London (43%) and Paris (50%).

Even with the results that suggest that the Whiteman-Berlin effect cannot be fully accounted for by race, the fear of and prejudice against the cultural influence of "Negros" in Germany before World War II is well documented[50] and was likely a component in Germany's preference for jazz associated with Paul Whiteman over the jazz associated with Louis Armstrong.[51] Indeed, even when the Nazis explicitly banned jazz in 1933, the edict was a ban on "Negro Jazz,"[52] jazz that was associated with blacks and Jews, but not necessarily all forms of jazz, as evidenced by the continuing popularity of a form of jazz (i.e., swing) throughout the Nazis' reign. Michael Kater has shown (2003), for example, that even during the peak of Nazi power, symphonic jazz and forms of swing flourished. Thus, even though our quantitative evidence finds less of an effect for race, there is a substantial volume of historical and qualitative evidence that shows the relevance of race and the evolving authenticity of jazz among sociologists, historians, and musicologists.[53]

That said, the sum of our evidence adds to our understanding of why Germany produced a high volume of jazz that did not have the lasting appeal of jazz produced in other cities. The evidence suggests that the German public was interested in German symphonic (dance society) jazz and jazz operas. The rest of the world—or at least the critics and consumers in New York—seemed interested in only the latter.

As we researched the answer to this chapter's puzzle, we realized that the explanation we uncovered conflicts with other alternatives. For example, the Nazis were well-known for suppressing many forms of cultural expression and paid particular attention to jazz music. One may expect, then, that their pre–World War II efforts or stigmatized post–World War II reinterpretations of German culture by others affected the appeal of jazz music from Germany.[54] However, we restricted our observation period to the time before the Nazis gained power. Ours is the period of active avant-garde cultural activity, the period in which Germany became the first country to institutionalize jazz instruction with Dr. Hoch's Conservatory. Moreover, a theory of cultural suppression would have to take into account the fact that other art forms during the Weimar era, most notably German Expressionism in cinema[55] and Bauhaus architecture and design,[56] were also seen as problematic by the Nazis yet unlike early German jazz had substantial long-run appeal. Kater's (2003) work on jazz in Germany casts further doubt on this alternative, as he documents a rich volume of jazz recorded in Berlin *after* 1933. Thus we forgo a more general cultural argument for a model and evidence that center more exclusively on the market for jazz music. Our conclusion is that, at best, an explanation that centers on the role of the Nazis is overdetermined—even if the Nazis had not taken power, the similarity of early German jazz to Whiteman's symphonic style would have dramatically diminished its long-run appeal.

Another alternative explanation made by scholars of Weimar-era music is that German jazz did not have long-term appeal because it was not *really* jazz. The critique here is that the music we draw upon is misclassified as jazz and is better understood as dance or society orchestra music.[57] For example, J. Bradford Robinson has argued that "The rare and isolated appearances of legitimate jazz in Weimar culture were overwhelmed by the great mass of commercial syncopated dance music, especially Germany's home-grown product" (1994, 113).

However, we believe that this interpretation neglects the fact that Germans were engaging in a form of jazz that not only was consistent with their narrow view of music but also mirrored a version of jazz that was dominant worldwide at the time, led by the United States. In 1923–33, most European and white Americans would have easily classified the symphonic style as authentic jazz (even Sam Wooding and Duke Ellington praised Whiteman publicly as a jazz musician),[58] and Whiteman was by far the musician most associated with jazz in the *New York Times, Musical Courier, Metronome,* and other popular trade publications. Consequently, even scholars like Robinson who argue for the exclusion of German music as jazz ultimately concede that the music was a form of jazz *as recognized at that time*: "German commercial musicians invented their own brand of jazz, based on a certain amount of lore regarding the fabled music from America, and grafted it onto their own tradition" (1994, 114–15).

IMPLICATIONS FOR THE SHAPING OF JAZZ

In shedding light on the puzzle of German jazz, we can now better understand the relationship between the geographic origins of recordings and their incorporation into the discographical canon. Standard notions that emphasize the role of reception apply in this case, but less often is the study of reception coupled with production in a multistage approach.[59] Without such an approach, an understanding of jazz would be compromised. The first more general insight is that as jazz diffused it was received in a variety of ways; every country was not introduced to the same style. Even neighboring countries like France and Germany were exposed to jazz in different moments of its evolution and thus received different styles and varieties. Second, the capacity to (re-)produce jazz varied widely—Germany was an extreme case in terms of the combination of local tastes, skills, and technological capability to produce symphonic jazz, which led to the high volume of jazz that characterized this chapter's opening puzzle. A third point for theoretical advancement is that the German case suggests that any model of cultural diffusion requires that the units or nodes in question are not somehow restricting their cultural objects to local consumption. This isolation may have facilitated the attribution of the jazz opera as Germany's contribution to jazz. If consumers and critics outside Germany were less familiar with the volume of symphonic jazz Germany produced, the more rarely produced but heavily marketed jazz opera could be successfully framed as Germany's representation of jazz.

In either case, whether one examines symphonic jazz or jazz operas, neither truly survived as the boundaries of authentic jazz evolved (with the exception of "Mack the Knife"). Early German jazz's long-run appeal and influence are wedded to the time-varying authenticity of symphonic jazz, which we captured using the attention given to Paul Whiteman in the public discourse. During periods when symphonic jazz was given attention, such as when there was increased interest in Whiteman as a jazz artist, the music from Germany has had increased legitimacy. But these moments were few, and diminishing at that. With respect to jazz operas, their connection to jazz represents Germany's key contribution in the evolution of the discographical canon.

I close, then, with observations that abstract from this case. First, to the extent that a genre has an evolving narrative, the historical facts associated with the genre's development can be lost or reinterpreted; in this I concur with scholars such as Gladys Lang and Kurt Lang, Jennifer Lena, and others. It is incorrect, for example, to label symphonic jazz in 1920s Germany as lacking authenticity in situ. Doing so ignores the diversity of styles that often exist as a genre is emerging. It is more accurate to state that symphonic jazz music currently lacks legitimacy as a representation of jazz.

Second, the research in this chapter suggests that there is a positive association between the diversity of the subtypes of jazz a locale sustained and the likelihood that the locale was prominent as jazz evolved. Germany's attraction to a form of jazz that was close to their own musical tradition and their opposition to jazz that was too closely associated with "the Negro" may have caused Germans to be drawn to and produce a small subset of jazz styles. This would help explain why German jazz did not have substantial worldwide influence while other cultural products from Weimar-era Germany, such as film and architecture, did.

More broadly, this chapter has important implications for better understanding the emergence and shaping of jazz. First, sources that produce music that is exceptionally unoriginal *and* narrow are less likely to have shaped jazz. We know from the first chapter that cities high in disconnectedness had lower originality in terms of their recordings, but Berlin was unoriginal even by this standard. Germany was unique within Europe as it had the most advanced and intensive record production, but the bulk of the jazz produced from this system stylistically replicated the symphonic jazz from places like New York and London. Recalling the relationship between sociological congruence, the geographic source, and the music's ease of categorization, we have a clearer sense of why music from Berlin did not seem to fit my initial expectations. In essence, Berlin produced a lot of stylistically narrow music that was not congruent with Berlin's disconnectedness in part because it was too easy to categorize as jazz at the time. And indeed, the Germans were so advanced in this effort that they founded the first school for the formal study of jazz. At the same time, music that was easy to categorize was appealing when it originated in central cities located in the core of the network (see chapters 1 and 2). In other words, if in 1929 I wanted good symphonic jazz, there was little reason to go beyond groups based in New York, London, or Chicago. Moreover, there was little to no stylistic innovativeness or variability in Germany, at least in terms of recordings. The bulk of German offerings were straight-ahead symphonic jazz, more distinguished by quality than type or style.

The example of Germany also suggests that my model of sociological congruence works best when the musical identity of a location is not so strong that its actual output is overwhelmed by the perceived output from a location. The strong association between Germany and classical music had both a production and a reception effect. Germany's national identity drew its musicians, bandleaders, and record companies to symphonic jazz; this also meant that only certain types of jazz would be considered appropriate by external audiences. Even if there were successful hot jazz groups in Germany they would have had a difficult time getting recorded, and if they did, few external to Germany would have found the hypothetical German "hot" jazz congruent with Germany's strong identity. Of the sixty-seven sources of recordings in my sample, Germany (Berlin) encountered jazz with perhaps the strongest musical reputation. This identity was sufficiently strong that the handful of jazz opera pieces—where the opera linked directly to Germany's national identity—were the only ones that survived and shaped the jazz discographical canon.

Third, this case shows that one of my implicit assumptions in chapter 1—that all locations were exposed to jazz at the same time—is incorrect. Germany discovered jazz at the particular moment when it was most often exported as symphonic jazz. If jazz had entered Germany just a few years earlier, its influence might have been different. It is unlikely that even if jazz had come to Germany in the early 1920s that its attraction to black musicians would have been different, but their attraction to hot jazz by artists like NORK and ODJB might have broadened their exposure to (and thus perhaps their production of) the varieties and evolution of jazz music. On the contrary, Germany was underexposed to this style.

Finally, Germany did not fit my initial model in part because jazz itself changed. If, for example, Paul Whiteman had retained even a quarter of his legitimacy as a jazz figure, Germany's influence on jazz would have been greater and more broadly known as such.[60] Bernhard Ette (the "Paul Whiteman of Germany"), Mátyás Seiber, Lud Gluskin, Efim Schachmeister, Oscar Joost, Billy Bartholomew, Eric Borchard, and others would be more familiar names to twenty-first-century consumers of jazz. Moreover, some of the tunes they wrote and arrangements they developed might have had more of an influence on the jazz canon. The social, economic, and artistic forces that modified our understanding of jazz across the twentieth century (most of which are beyond the scope of this book) are also part of understanding Germany and the shaping of jazz.[61]

Chapter 4

SOCIOLOGICAL CONGRUENCE AND RECORD COMPANY COMPARATIVE ADVANTAGE

Tastes are created by the business interests. How else
can you explain the popularity of Al Hirt?

—CHARLES MINGUS (MUSICIAN AND COMPOSER)

Record companies . . . exercise great power simply because they offer
record contracts to a few groups among many within the jazz community.
In some instances, a company actually creates bands, fashioning them
according to budgetary concerns and the tastes of its producers.

—PAUL BERLINER, *Thinking in Jazz*

On the other hand, ideas originating with the production staff
. . . may produce positive results . . . [Coleman Hawkins]
related that he was not interested initially in either playing or
recording "Body and Soul", an eventual classic.

—PAUL BERLINER, *Thinking in Jazz*

The epigraphs point to the fact that both musicians and scholars recognize the influence of record companies on what occupies the market for jazz—even in a genre where the artist has greater control over what they record than most other musical genres. With this in mind, my colleague David Owens and I came across a very curious discovery that did not quite fit our sense of how competitive markets worked. It was a discovery that had substantial implications for how jazz was shaped.

First we need a little context. Josef Schumpeter (1942) has fueled decades of research in economics, sociology, and management scholarship, in part by making the following observation: radical innovations are pursued by market entrants to the detriment of incumbent firms. These incumbents hold market power yet do not take advantage of or respond to the new innovations. I suspect that even if you have not heard of Schumpeter, this notion of the larger, technologically disadvantaged firm is not new to you. Either way, scholars on this topic typically provide one of three explanations for this observation. The first highlights cases where incumbent firms recognize a radical innovation but find it too costly or risky to pursue and, as a consequence, ignore the innovation altogether or attempt to thwart the innovators.[1] When the competitiveness of the innovators or the actual value of the innovation is underestimated, incumbents suffer. A second explanation argues that incumbents may produce the innovation but are less successful than their challengers owing to inertia associated with organizational age or size.[2] A third explanation notes that new knowledge associated with the innovation may render an incumbent obsolete and thus incompetent in its production.[3] In this case it is typically thought that the incumbent may not even anticipate the innovation.

I expected to see one of these explanations easily apply to the market for recorded jazz in the 1920s. I was mistaken, however, in part because the real story—rooted in a better understanding of the context—involves pieces of these three types of explanations as well as factors not associated with any of them. First, it turns out that incumbent firms were first movers in recording "illegitimate" (but profitable) jazz in 1917. The initial jazz recordings were by the Original Dixieland Jazz Band (ODJB). These first ODJB recordings were extraordinarily successful, ushering in a new market for popular music that would soon overtake all other markets. That is not at all unusual and is consistent with some of the ideas associated with Schumpeter. But here is the puzzle: these same incumbents who were first movers soon distanced themselves from the ODJB type of jazz that they successfully introduced into the market and instead began to produce a more symphonic, hybrid form of jazz that peaked with Paul Whiteman (whom I discussed in chapter 3 as an exemplar of 1920s symphonic jazz). I will show in this and the next two chapters that early record companies' decision to focus on symphonic jazz had profound implications on how the market for jazz evolved by contributing to the rise of big bands and seeding the swing era. That is, the actions by the incumbents did not necessarily result in their producing jazz with long-term appeal, but their actions did affect the trajectory of the market and genre, making it both more symphonic and thus more stylistically diverse than it otherwise might have been. As I note in chapter 3, these symphonic jazz recordings were produced in high volume and exported to the worldwide market, leading many to recognize symphonic jazz as the most representative form of jazz.

Although this change in the type of jazz that was recorded had a long-run impact on the shaping of jazz, it was less clear to me why these incumbents switched to symphonic jazz in the first place. This chapter seeks to solve this puzzle by suggesting that the incumbents shifted in order to produce the form of jazz that was most congruent with their organizational identities and competencies, which were not fully evident until *after* the first set of jazz recordings of 1917. That is, incumbents reacted after influential anti-jazz critics and new entrants shaped the emerging market and caused the incumbents to reconfigure their offerings with respect to their evolving positions in both product and identity space.[4] In the next chapter I extend this argument by suggesting that incumbent firms even manipulated their marketing and catalogues through pseudonyms to align their products (records) with their identities in the marketplace.

In this chapter I focus on how incumbents, after releasing the earliest jazz recordings (in 1917–18), reoriented the production of jazz music to align with their
identities as producers of symphonic music amid mounting elite anti-jazz pressure. While it was technologically easier to produce symphonic jazz, a focus on
incumbents' competence in producing symphonic jazz (which I have previously
explored with David Owens [2004]) can distract from the larger underlying issue:
that incumbent firms' primary constraint was one of a congruence mismatch between their identity and the type of jazz they sought to produce. The issue of
identity provides a more fundamental rationale for the reorientation of inserting
"legitimate" elements into the original form of jazz. While the incumbent firms
were more aligned with symphonic music, this alignment only mattered after the
market was reshaped by the entry of new competitors on the one hand and negative jazz sentiments and an elite understanding of jazz as "primitive" on the other.
I will provide evidence that compared to the newer entrants (jazz-era firms), incumbents (Victorian-era firms) sought to deflect pressure from cultural arbiters by
minimizing experiments with jazz and recording white jazz orchestras. It became
evident that there were greater social costs for these incumbents when recording
groups that were black, more improvisational ("hot" or Dixieland-style jazz), and
otherwise more innovative.[5] The immediate effect on jazz was that record company identities and the competition between incumbents and newcomers facilitated the bifurcation of early jazz into a more symphonic ("sweet") style on the
one hand and a more improvisational ("hot") style on the other. And while there
were black and white musicians performing both forms of jazz, sweet jazz was
more associated with white musicians while hot jazz was more associated with
black musicians. Hot jazz was publicly associated with African Americans so much
so that the ODJB was advertised as group of black musicians when their now
historic recording was first introduced.

Two images from 1917 can help us better understand the relationship between
jazz, race, and Victorian-era firms (Figure 4.1). The first image is a promotional
photograph of the ODJB. However, the second image shows that in newspapers
such as the *Los Angeles Times*, the group and their music was advertised as black
(or "Negro"). In particular, the advertising from Victor Records used black musicians to describe to readers of the *Los Angeles Times* what a "Jass Band" was: the
music of (stereotypical) Negroes. Also important at the bottom of the *Los Angeles
Times* ad was the statement that "jass" is directly associated with dances such as the
fox trot since its first recording—an association that would be maintained with
symphonic ("sweet") jazz.

Building off of these early associations between race and style (see also chapter
3), I will employ a combination of race (black versus white) and musical style
(small and improvisational versus symphonic or orchestral) as an important typology.[6] With respect to race, I examine a key source of jazz's illegitimacy with
respect to cultural elites: its association with African Americans.[7] In terms of

FIGURE 4.1. Although the Original Dixieland Jazz Band was white, they were often advertised as being African American: (a) a promotional photograph of the actual Original Dixieland Jazz ("Jass") Band; (b) an ad for the Original Dixieland Jazz Band in the *Los Angeles Times*, April 20, 1917.

style, I focus on the extent to which jazz groups were identified as "orchestras"—an identifier that signaled a cultivated sound valued by elites.[8] In this way the *Los Angeles Times* ad represented a double violation for the elite. Not only was this style of music not highbrow (e.g., symphonic or operatic), but Victor Records was stating that the music and its representative musicians had "Negro" origins. To the extent that this was a mistake on Victor's part, it was commercially successful but one that they quickly corrected. This gets to the heart of my argument: incumbents such as Victor initially introduced a product that was not congruent with their organizational identities. Not only were Victorian-era firms less likely to subsequently record "lowbrow" jazz when negative jazz sentiment was high, but they were generally more conservative and favored white symphonic jazz (jazz orchestras).[9]

In the remainder of this chapter, I focus on the role of the cultural elite and its negative reaction to jazz and its producers. The same firms that introduced recorded jazz feared being penalized (losing status and legitimacy) in the eyes of the

Have You Heard the New "Jass" Records?

"A Jass Band"

Hear These Two Selections on Your

Victrola

No. 18255—75c

"Dixieland Jass Band," One-step, and "Livery Stable Blues," Fox Trot. by the original Dixieland "Jass" Band.

FIGURE 4.1. (cont.)

cultural elite. Using both qualitative historical and quantitative analyses, I show that these firms responded by minimizing their production of "original" jazz recordings in order to limit their public association with jazz's low-status racial and stylistic elements. In short, the illegitimacy of jazz among elites was a significant constraint for firms that had been catering to the elite prior to the commercialization of recorded jazz.

FIRMS AND THE MARKET FOR EARLY JAZZ RECORDINGS

The market for early jazz recordings was different from modern cultural markets. Early commercialized music was an emerging market in which firms' identities were less stable than they would be later in more mature markets. Many of the firms founded before the commercialization of jazz had initially crystallized their identities in the market for phonographs, which were marketed as sophisticated living room furniture designed to compete with pianos.[10] Initially recordings were sold as secondary products to support phonograph sales. Beginning around World War I and continuing with the rise of jazz, the market for recordings overcame the market for phonographs. With this change came an accompanying shift in the basis for understanding firm identities.

In addition, firms during this period were less organizationally sophisticated than the typical modern corporation, with structures derived from owner-capitalist models consistent with the dominant organizational logic at that time.[11] This is key because more modern tools for decoupling illegitimate products from a parent firm were not as salient to record companies at the dawn of jazz's commercialization. For example, whereas contemporary record companies may use their multiple labels to segment the market and disassociate the parent from a particular market segment,[12] the early firms that sold to multiple segments often did so under the same parent name.[13] Any inconsistency between the identity of a firm and its products was more often transparent to constituents.

The ways in which records were sold to consumers were also very different from the ways in which they are distributed today. For example, the strategies of distribution and sales that emerged in this early period did not have the structure of large distributors we see in today's industry. Records were sold through mail order, music departments of urban-centered stores, and small-town all-purpose stores. In each of these cases, the company's catalogue of recordings played a central role. Consumers ordered a large proportion of their records by directly consulting record companies' catalogs (which for larger companies may have included more than one of their labels).[14] In stores, customers not only bought what was in stock (which was usually very limited) but also ordered out-of-stock recordings by consulting record company catalogues. In addition, the role of (end-user) consumer demand often trumped that of the other market intermediaries (such as stores' sales departments). Thus while some stores may have pushed one type of recording over another, consumers had more direct influence on the demand for popular music through mail ordering.[15]

Because of my emphasis on individual recordings, two additional features of this setting require mentioning. First, the early market for commercialized music was organized around singles rather than albums. In fact, albums would only emerge after the successful introduction of the LP after World War II.[16] Second, there was little variation in the price of recordings within the genre of jazz. For example, when I examined advertised record prices in display ads in the *Chicago Defender, Chicago Tribune, New York Times, Wall Street Journal,* and the *Washington Post,* I found no price variation by type of jazz during the 1920s. For most of my observation period, jazz records were $0.75.

ORGANIZATIONAL IDENTITIES IN EARLY JAZZ

The early U.S. recording industry was dominated by three firms: Edison Phonograph Company and Works (founded in 1887), Columbia Phonograph Company (founded in 1891 as American Gramophone Company), and Victor Talking Machine Company (founded in 1901), where each of these record companies would come to issue recordings under multiple labels (e.g., the "Victor Red label" featuring Victor's classical music, the "Victor Black label" featuring Victor's popular music). Although there was a rise in the number of firms entering the market before 1917, the commercialization of jazz in 1917 ushered in a distinct set of new firms that were founded to take advantage of the burgeoning market. Among the most well-known new entrants were Gennett Records (founded in 1917), Okeh Records (founded in 1918), and the Brunswick-Balke-Collender Company (founded in 1919). Musical recordings became a distinct market after World War I. The larger market for recordings coincided with jazz music's emergence from New Orleans and came to the Midwest with musicians—both African American and lower-class (typically non-Anglo) whites—who migrated from Louisiana and the rest of the South.[17] Though New Orleans was the birthplace of jazz, Chicago and the Midwest were the primary home of recorded jazz until the late 1920s.[18]

The first firm to commercialize recorded jazz was the market leader, the Victor Talking Machine Company. The Victor recordings of the ODJB purportedly sold in the millions and surpassed such contemporary top sellers as Enrico Caruso and the John Phillip Sousa Band.[19] Although Columbia recorded the ODJB before Victor, they chose not to release the recordings out of fear of being attacked by elites. Apparently Victor would later concur with Columbia. As William H. Kenney notes,

> Despite introducing the Original Dixieland Jazz Band [ODJB], the company [Victor] had not followed up on its popular success, disassociating itself from jazz. . . . As *Talking Machine World* put it, two full years after Victor's introduction of the ODJB: "The future of our industry lies in encouraging the sale of high-priced goods and the best records. It does emphatically not lie in pushing cheap machines and jazz records."[20]

Classical organizational scholarship such as Stinchcombe's imprinting hypothesis and Landes's research on the role of segmented consumers in industry evolution would suggest that firms founded before the commercialization of jazz were fundamentally different than the firms founded to take advantage of the growing market in jazz.[21] Indeed, firms founded before jazz's emergence, such as Victor Records, had established an identity emphasizing cultural production that sought to morally uplift consumers using strong associations with highbrow (classical) music.[22] This emphasis on highbrow music before jazz's emergence in 1917 was certainly rational as firms such as Victor and Columbia were selling records to complement their production of phonographs (or gramophones). I refer to these firms as Victorian-era firms based on the fact that they were all founded before 1917.

The founders and executives of Victorian-era record companies were typically members of the elite and nouveau elite.[23] For example, the corporate officers of firms such as Victor and Columbia were strongly affiliated with the American elite class through educational, matrimonial, and financial ties. Eldridge Johnson, the founder and president of Victor, was the top financial contributor to the Republican Party in 1928, whose list of top contributors also included the Mellons, Rockefellers, and Guggenheims. In addition, Johnson sat on boards alongside members of the financial and industrial elite such as Pierre S. duPont.[24] Victor's own board had members of the elite who were linked to sources of anti-jazz sentiments.[25] For example, an executive of the company that published *Ladies Home Journal*—well-known as an outlet for jazz criticism—was a board member of Victor Records.[26] Leon Douglass, Victor's vice president, married into the prominent Adams family that produced two presidents. Thomas Edison, founder of Edison Phonograph Company and a well-known member of the business elite, was married to Mina Miller, an active member of the Daughters of the American Revolution.[27] The founders and executives of Columbia Phonograph included influential attorneys, graduates of prestigious universities, and financiers associated with the U.S. Supreme Court and U.S. House of Representatives.[28]

To understand Victorian-era firms' desire to invoke a highbrow identity, I examined their newspaper and magazine ads. Advertisements were critical to the marketing and sale of records, as they were the primary means of mass marketing the weekly release of new records.[29] Figure 4.2a features an advertisement in *Ladies Home Journal*, the aforementioned publication often cited as advocating against jazz and for more "cultivated" music.[30] Advertisements such as these were commonly used to link Victorian-era firms' records to popular high-status classical stars (e.g., Sergei Rachmaninoff, Enrico Caruso) and to demonstrate companies' commitment to "high-class music" that "appeals to the best class of people."[31] Victorian-era firms' advertisements supported the cultural elite's contention that the type of record purchased signaled one's social standing.[32] During the 1920s, ads like that depicted in Figure 4.2a often appeared prominently on the inside cover of the first page of a magazine, sometimes spreading over two pages. Victor Records was not the only firm to construct highbrow identities through their advertisements. Within the same issue of these magazines were advertisements from competing Victorian-era firms (such as Columbia) that made similar claims of producing "the best music" and provided pictures and names of classical musicians as evidence of their highbrow identity. Although these firms also advertised more popular music, the ads exhorting a highbrow cultural identity were invariably larger in size, more frequent, and more prominently placed during the early to mid-1920s.

Figure 4.2b shows a *New York Times* advertisement of some of Victor Records' jazz offerings, centering on Paul Whiteman and His Orchestra. It is important to note that within the same ad listing of jazz recordings that the Virginians were a subset of the musicians from the Paul Whiteman Orchestra. The International Novelty Orchestra and the Great White Way Orchestra were Victor Records house bands. I was unable to locate additional information on the Serenaders. To signal the highbrow nature of Victor Records and its jazz recordings, not only are many of the groups referred to as orchestras, but they are also included in the same advertisement as Victor's in-house symphony, the Victor Symphony Orchestra (see the first recording listed).

Also of note in this advertisement is the prominence of the record catalogue. This magazine advertisement encourages consumers to purchase the special issue of Victor Records offerings rather than directing customers to a retail outlet or other forms of distribution. This is consistent with other evidence suggesting that although music was sold in large, urban-centered, department stores, the catalogue was a prominent means of conveying song offerings.

Firms founded after the rise of recorded jazz in 1917, or what I term jazz-era firms, typically constructed different identities through advertisements as they were oriented more to the mass market than to the cultural elite.[33] These firms took advantage of spaces in the market that were unoccupied as a result of the incumbents' alignment with the cultural elite. For example, Okeh Records, part of one of the dominant jazz-era firms, also advertised the quality of the sound in their ads, and like many of the recordings advertised in the *New York Times*, they mentioned jazz groups as orchestras, although not with the same emphasis that Victorian-era firms did.[34] In its advertisements, Okeh (an independent label with the General Phonograph Corporation until 1926 when it was reorganized as the Okeh Phonograph Corporation until 1933) also signaled its identity by using the graphics and language of popular music with themes of dancing or partying, all of which lacked the highbrow status of Victorian-era firms. Jazz-era firms were also more often associated with smaller, local, less prestigious retail outlets than with large department stores (which often had financial ties to Victorian-era firms). At the same time, song catalogues (which consumers used to mail order records) were key elements of jazz-era companies' advertising and sales.[35] Moreover, the language of these catalogues was often geared to the average consumer: "What does the public want? . . . What will you have? If your preferences are not listed in our catalog, we will make them for you, as Paramount must please the buying public."[36]

FIGURE 4.2. (a) Victorian-era firm full-page ad, *Ladies Home Journal*, March 1921; (b) Victorian-era firm full-page ad, *New York Times*, January 17, 1923.

"HIGHBROW" AND "LOWBROW" IN EARLY JAZZ

Naturally, *there is both good and bad jazz . . . but in this article I have in mind only the better type of jazz*; that which is composed by understanding musicians, that which is conceived and written according to ordinary esthetical and technical standards. . . . *Many of the orchestral arrangements are very clever indeed.*

—EDWIN J. STRINGHAM, *Musical Quarterly*, 1926 [EMPHASIS ADDED]

While elites were concerned with separating high and low culture in general, they paid special attention to distinguishing between highbrow jazz and the more original lowbrow jazz. Much of the resistance to lowbrow jazz came from the elite music press, although publications such as the *New York Times* also expressed resistance to this "lesser" form of jazz. These critics associated jazz with the downfall of civilization, treated it as a health risk, and claimed that jazz was too "primitive" to be classified as any form of music at all. As the prominent classical music conductor and British cultural critic Sir Henry Coward noted, jazz was a "gigantic black man striding over the world with a banjo in one hand and a saxophone in the other, disintegrating the British Empire" (Laubenstein 1929, 622). Sir Coward's critique, similar to Stringham's definition of good jazz, the rhetoric around early German jazz in the previous chapter, and several other critiques by the elite that we found, classified jazz as either (symphonic) highbrow or ("hot") lowbrow depending on the race of the performers and the instruments used in the recording.

Thus, although producing hot jazz was profitable for record companies,[37] the music was deemed illegitimate by elites largely because of its association with Af-

Not only the best but the newest in music

Special issues of Victor Records serve to illustrate the extent of the service performed by the Victrola and Victor Records. Not only are Victor products and Victor processes supreme in the great art music of the world, but in music which follows the popular vogue and is of timely appeal there is a clearness of tone production, a brilliance and a finish which are obtainable from no other such sources. In all cases however it is well to realize that the nearest approach to perfection is possible only when Victor Records are played on Victrola instruments.

Special issue of Victor Records out today

Faust—Ballet Music, Cleopatra and the Golden Cup Faust—Ballet Music, Dance of Cleopatra and Her Slaves	Victor Symphony Orchestra	35719 12-inch $1.25
When Hearts are Young—Fox Trot Journey's End—Fox Trot	Paul Whiteman and His Orchestra	18985 10-inch 75c
Lost (A Wonderful Girl)—Fox Trot Great White Way Orchestra Where the Bamboo Babies Grow—Fox Trot The Virginians		18986 10-inch 75c
My Buddy—Fox Trot International Novelty Orchestra When Winter Comes—Fox Trot Great White Way Orchestra		18995 10-inch 75c
Thru' the Night—Waltz The Serenaders Red Moon—Waltz The Serenaders		18996 10-inch 75c

Victrola

Important · Look for these trade-marks. Under the lid. On the label.

Victor Talking Machine Company, Camden, New Jersey

FIGURE 4.2. (cont.)

rican Americans and illicit activity that supposedly accompanied its performance.[38] Table 4.1 provides a sample of sources that publicly spoke out against jazz music, jazz dancing, and those responsible for producing it.[39] Negative and anti-jazz sentiment emanated from government agencies, periodicals, Ivy League academics, and representatives of leading business interests. The New York state legislature even passed a bill to regulate jazz.

Table 4.1 reveals that elites (along with many in the upper-middle class) worked against jazz through music and dancing clubs, women's organizations, and public health agencies.[40] In 1921 Philadelphia's mayor and in 1922 New York's police department each established special jazz music-and-dancing police units to regulate the music.[41] These moves were not just symbolic; in 1924 the mayor of Philadelphia revoked the license of a theater for playing "bad jazz."[42] Prominent individuals such as Thomas Edison publicly expressed their disdain for jazz, as did the wives of the leading industrialists and financiers of the period (Morgan, Harriman, and Phipps), who represented elite cultural and moral interests.[43] In addition, many religious organizations (e.g., Catholic Church, Salvation Army) and clergy fought vigorously to suppress the rise of jazz.[44]

Anti-jazz sentiment peaked in the early 1920s. *Etude* even published an annual issue on the "Jazz Problem" during the early 1920s in which prominent cultural representatives spoke out against jazz. Most of the laws against jazz were passed in the early 1920s. This is not to say that anti-jazz discourse did not persist into the late 1920s and beyond; it certainly did. However, after 1925 it was widely acknowledged that all forms of jazz were not the same; some forms of jazz were indeed legitimate. In fact, by 1930 Louis Armstrong was recording for a Victorian-era firm with his jazz orchestra.

The class status of the record company leaders determined how they responded to this anti-jazz sentiment. The closer a firm's leadership was to the cultural elite, the more likely such a firm would try to make a trade-off that was palatable to the cultural elite but still enabled the firm to garner a sufficient share of the thriving market for jazz. Thus, while anti-jazz sentiments would have been relatively meaningless to jazz-era firms or might have increased the intrigue around jazz as a taboo, Victorian-era firms felt pressure to minimize their association with jazz. The identities of the dominant record companies were too intimately rooted in the values and agenda of the American elite in a period when elites paid close attention to the relationship between social status and the arts.[45]

The problem facing Victorian-era firms was one of incongruence between the location of these firms in an organizational identity space and the optimal position in product space. In terms of identity space, Victorian-era firms were more congruent with symphonic and operatic music, especially at the onset of the 1920s. Occupying that position in identity space met the expectations of their traditional audiences (whether they were critics or consumers). In contrast, in terms of product space, the optimal market position meant producing a great deal of jazz that

TABLE 4.1. Sources of Negative or Anti-Jazz Sentiment in the 1920s

Nonreligious institutions/ organizations	Federal Interdepartmental Social Hygiene Board; General Federation of Women's Clubs; Health Commissioner of Milwaukee; National Association of Masters of Dancing; National Federation of Music Clubs; New York City Police Department; New York State Legislature; Public Welfare Department of Illinois; United States Public Health Service
Trade press	*The Baton; Etude; Melody; The Metronome; Musical Courier; Musical Leader; The Musician; New Music and Church Review; Talking Machine World*
Popular press	*Ladies Home Journal; Literary Digest (Reader's Digest); New York Herald Tribune; New York Times*
Prominent individuals	University of Wisconsin professor; Henry Ford; Thomas A. Edison; Harvard University professor; Princeton University professor; Yale University professor; Mrs. J. P. Morgan; Mrs. Borden Harriman; Mrs. Henry Phipps; Mrs. James Roosevelt; Mrs. E. H. Harriman

Sources: Berger 1947; Leonard 1962; Koenig 2002.
Note: Most publications listed in the table have multiple articles on jazz. For example, *Etude* has more than a dozen articles on jazz from 1923 to 1945.

would have been considered lowbrow because the mass market consumer found this form of jazz appealing. Consumers in clubs and dance societies often requested the original (lowbrow) jazz songs, artists, and styles considered sacrilegious by the elite. Even middle-class white consumers (who occupied an overlapping position between the elite and the "masses") seemed to have a wider scope of musical taste than did the cultural elite, often preferring a more lowbrow form of jazz. W. H. Kenney's description of Chicago's jazz market notes that the middle-class breadth of taste required white jazz orchestras to also play the more lowbrow form of "hot" jazz: " 'when required' Lombardo's dance band of the twenties [Guy Lombardo and His Royal Canadians] could 'play as "hot" as any of their contemporaries.' . . . But Lombardo [who typically recorded with Victorian-era firms] was more likely to record waltzes . . . and a broad range of mawkish vocal numbers."[46] Kenney notes that the actual tastes of the average consumer were also expressed in the trade journals, which noted, "If it were not for the flapper, the Victor people might well go out of business. They buy ninety percent of the records."[47]

The constraints on the incumbents diminished during the mid- to late 1920s when jazz's legitimacy began to grow and when dominant incumbents themselves produced recordings of jazz "orchestras" that they could claim cultivated and enriched jazz. Especially notable was the crowning of Paul Whiteman as the King of Jazz in 1923 by the trade publication *Talking Machine World*—the same publication that had scolded Victor for producing jazz six years earlier—and by the *New York Times*.[48]

But this also means that Victorian-era firms helped bifurcate jazz into subtypes that mapped onto the social hierarchy of the period. One of the ways that record companies shaped early jazz was through the production and advertising of symphonic jazz in part to reconcile their identity space with the optimal location in the product space. These companies, with greater distribution systems, marketing investments, and access to endorsements, helped make symphonic jazz—and the dance society songs associated with symphonic jazz—a force that altered the trajectory of the genre.

SOME QUANTITATIVE EVIDENCE: RECORD COMPANY IDENTITY AND RECORDING BEHAVIOR

The core insight to solving this chapter's puzzle of why Victorian-era firms switched to symphonic jazz is that pressure from the elite highlights an incongruence between Victorian-era firms' identities and their products. This incongruence made it difficult for incumbent Victorian-era firms to maintain an active focus on jazz in its original form. Even if symphonic jazz did not always fare well in the marketplace, it was easier for Victorian-era firms to produce and market. Moreover, the fact that symphonic jazz ultimately faltered is something we know only in hindsight. During the 1920s, the fate of symphonic jazz versus hot jazz was much less clear. We will see that Victorian-era firms were able to become more publicly associated with symphonic jazz but also that they never completely abandoned the original form.

Using quantitative data, I conducted three studies to better understand what Victorian-era firms recorded and how their actions were associated with anti-jazz sentiments. In Study 1 I examined whether recordings from Victorian-era firms were more innovative and experimental during the early years of jazz and whether this innovativeness diminished over time as they focused more on recordings that would align with their highbrow identities. My study of the qualitative evidence suggested that jazz in the 1920s would have been more stylistically experimental when coming from jazz-era firms. For example, the first mixed-race recordings were by a jazz-era firm (Gennett Records) when Jelly Roll Morton recorded with NORK (see chapter 2).[49] In Study 2 I tested for quantitative evidence that during the 1920s Victorian-era firms were more likely than jazz-era firms to record white jazz orchestras and less likely to record black (African American or "Negro") hot jazz groups. In Study 3 I considered whether the propensity to both experiment as well as record the different subtypes of jazz (classified by race and style) was influenced by the elite's negative public discourse. The more negative the discourse, the

TABLE 4.2. Differences between Victorian-Era and Jazz-Era Firms

	Victorian-era firms[a]	Jazz-era firms[b]
Firm age (years)	14.83**	8.48
Number of labels	4.28**	3.20
Founder's industry experience (years)	15.58**	10.87
Proportion of *Chicago Tribune* display ads on jazz records	4.21%	18.41%
Proportion of *Chicago Defender* ads on jazz records	31.03%	33.33%
Cases	1,114	881

Note: Means are subjected to *t*-tests across rows.
[a]$N = 1,114$ recordings from 4 firms
[b]$N = 881$ recordings from 8 firms
**$p < .01$

more likely that Victorian-era firms should have avoided experimenting and shunned what was seen as the lowbrow form of jazz. Instead, these firms would have reacted conservatively by disproportionately producing recordings of the symphonic form. At the same time, the anti-jazz sentiments may have been a source of competitive advantage for jazz-era firms if it allowed them to sell to the mass market with buffered competition from Victorian-era firms. Although it is not clear that jazz-era firms were explicitly attracted to lowbrow recording during periods increased anti-jazz sentiment, they at least should not have avoided these recordings when anti-jazz pressure increased.[50]

The empirical evidence for this chapter utilizes the discographical and recording industry data for the Midwest sample recordings used in chapter 1.[51] These Midwest data confirm that Victorian-era firms were distinct from jazz-era firms and that they recorded different types of groups. Table 4.2 compares several characteristics of Victorian-era and jazz-era firms using my more detailed Midwest data: firm age, firm size and scope (number of labels), the founder's industry experience, and their explicit use of jazz ads in the *Chicago Tribune* and the *Chicago Defender*.

Victorian-era firms, by construction, were older companies with founders who had a greater amount of industry experience. Victorian-era firms also had more labels—an indicator of a record company's size and scope. I examined the advertisement placements of each type of firm by comparing ads in the *Chicago Tribune* with ads in the *Chicago Defender* during the 1920s. The goal was to see what proportion of the total number of ads was devoted to jazz records versus some other genre of music (the word "jazz" had to explicitly appear in the ad). I selected Chicago since it was a metropolitan market with data I could digitally capture using the more middle-class and elite (white) market of the *Tribune* and the *Defender*'s African American readership, while controlling for the fact that they were in the same region. The pattern of advertising suggests that about a third of both Victorian- and jazz-era firms' *Chicago Defender* ads were devoted to jazz. The big difference appeared in the *Chicago Tribune*, where Victorian-era firms mentioned jazz in only 4.21% of their ads but jazz-era firms mentioned jazz in 18.41% of theirs. Someone who read only the *Tribune* would think that Victorian-era firms produced little jazz, where what jazz did exist was usually from jazz-era firms. However, more jazz recordings came from Victorian-era firms than from jazz-era firms (1,114 vs. 881). Victorian-era firms were indeed very active in the market for jazz recordings despite the message their marketing conveyed.

A Typology of Early Jazz Groups: Race and Style

David Owens and I (2004) used the discographical data to distinguish the key dimensions along which early jazz was arrayed. We were able to use the group's name as listed in the discographies to determine whether a jazz group was identified as an "orchestra," and we were able to determine the race of most of the groups from jazz pictorials.[52] We then constructed a typology of four different types of early jazz recording groups: (1) white orchestras, (2) white non-orchestras, (3) black orchestras, and (4) black non-orchestras.[53] White orchestras were the strongest signal of highbrow identity. In contrast, the work of black non-orchestras epitomized lowbrow or "illegitimate" music from the perspective of the cultural elite. This typology is helpful in understanding the puzzle of this chapter and in gaining a better perspective on the role of record companies in shaping the early market for jazz. For example, anti-jazz sentiments, while at times pertaining to all forms of jazz, were reserved most often for black non-orchestras because this group represented the greatest challenge to legitimate music from the perspective of the elite.

Table 4.3 uses *t*-tests to compare the proportion of each of the four types of groups recorded by Victorian-era firms to the proportion recorded by jazz-era firms. Row-wise, 18% of Victorian-era firms' recordings are of white orchestras, compared to 8% of jazz-era firms' recordings. Of the more popular black non-orchestral jazz groups, the proportion recorded by Victorian-era firms was less than that of jazz-era firms (50% versus 65%). Of the two remaining types of groups, black orchestras make up a similar proportion of Victorian- and jazz-era firms' recordings. White non-orchestras make up a larger proportion of Victorian-era firms' offerings than jazz-era firms' offerings.

There are two important insights to be gleaned from Table 4.3. First, a row-wise examination shows that Victorian-era firms devoted a greater proportion of their jazz recordings to both white orchestras and white non-orchestras. In contrast, jazz-era firms devoted a greater proportion of their jazz offerings to black non-orchestras. Second, a column-wise examination shows that while a majority of jazz-era firms' recordings were by black non-orchestras, Victorian-era firms offered a wider range of recordings. Many of the Victorian-era firms' releases were of

TABLE 4.3. Victorian- and Jazz-Era Firms' Allocation of Recordings across Subtypes of Jazz Group

	Victorian-era firms	Jazz-era firms
White orchestras	0.18**	0.08
White non-orchestras	0.16**	0.11
Black orchestras	0.17	0.16
Black non-orchestras	0.50	0.65**
Cases	1,114	881

Note: Means are subjected to *t*-tests across rows.
**$p < .01$

the lowbrow form (which was the center of the mass market after 1917). To a member of the 1920s cultural elite, this pattern would have been disturbing. Not only do Victoria-era firms produce more than half of the jazz recordings (Table 4.2), but 50% of the Victorian-era firm recordings are of black non-orchestras (Table 4.3). Thus, with respect to what was produced, Victorian-era firms were generalists. Most of the evidence on the audience for jazz, however, points to the fact that the elite were not fully aware of Victorian-era firms' actual position as generalists in the product market space for jazz—a point I will elaborate on in the next chapter, which builds off evidence presented in Table 4.2.

Study 1: Record Company Identity and Experimentation in Recording

Study 1 uses the Midwest data from the 1920s to ask whether Victorian-era firms were less experimental and innovative than jazz-era firms during the 1920s by using an indicator of how unique the combination of instruments was in the recording. For this indicator I constructed a recording-by-instrument matrix for the entire observation period. I used this matrix to calculate a Euclidean distance measure for each recording and to index its average distance from all other recordings. The more unique the instrumental combination, the more experimental or innovative the recording.

The instrumental combination uniqueness measure is driven by two factors: rare instruments and unusual combinations of common instruments. In the regression analyses I controlled for the existence of rare instruments to isolate the effect of unusual combinations of instruments. To give a sense of the consequence of this operationalization, while a trombone often appears on a recording with a trumpet, it was statistically unusual for a recording to feature a trombone and a vocalist. My calculation (the log of the Euclidean distance of a recording based on the combination of instruments used) would assign a group with a trombone and a vocalist a higher uniqueness score, and the regressions I ran adjusted for the independent likelihood of trombones, trumpets, and vocalists appearing in the recordings. The prediction in this hypothetical would be that this unusual trombone-vocalist pairing would occur more often with jazz-era firms than with Victorian-era firms. The objective is to use this measure not only as a proxy for innovativeness and experimentation in terms of instruments but also as a proxy of other unobserved aspects of the music. Thus if a recording has a unique combination of instruments, I would expect that other aspects of the recording's aesthetic experience that I cannot measure with the available data might also have been unique. The statistical test is to see whether Victorian-era firms were less experimental and innovative than jazz-era firms and if this difference varied across the 1920s.

Study 2: Record Company Identity and Type of Group Recorded

Study 2 examines whether Victorian-era firms were more likely than jazz-era firms to record white orchestras and less likely to record music by groups who were both black and non-orchestral, even though we know from the historical record that (a) Victorian-era firms successfully introduced the "hot" style of jazz and (b) the "hot" style of jazz had great market appeal. Accordingly, I use two logistic regression models to test the tendency of Victorian-era firms to record white orchestras and avoid groups that were black non-orchestral.[54]

Study 3: Record Company Identity and Responses to Anti-Jazz Sentiments

Study 3 examines whether innovativeness and the likelihood of recording different types of jazz were affected by negative jazz sentiments within the public discourse. This is an important study for this chapter, since there are many alternative explanations for the theories of Studies 1 and 2. For example, one could argue that the recording choices of Victorian-era firms were based solely on their technical competence (they were recording what they were efficient at doing), independent of any anti-jazz pressure. Indeed, Owens and I (2004) have shown that technical competence was an important factor, but we also argued that it was was an incomplete explanation. The goal of Study 3 was to find more complete explanations.

For Study 3 I relied heavily on the *New York Times* for several reasons. First, the *New York Times* was a key source for understanding discussions of jazz outside trade magazines. When compared to other sources of public discourse that also discussed jazz (e.g., *Ladies Home Journal*), the *New York Times* has a relatively high volume of content related to jazz with both positive and negative views. Second, the *New York Times* is digitized and easily searchable. My comparable search by hand of other sources like the *Literary (Reader's) Digest* and the *Ladies Home Journal* was done in the archives of various libraries with all of the disadvantages that came with that slow, non-random, and manual approach. Third, record companies advertised consistently within the pages of the *New York Times*, so much so that I was even able to use the frequency of their advertisements as a control variable to capture their sensitivity to the values of the *New York Times* readership.

Finally, the *New York Times* was an organ of many in the cultural elite such that my use of the count data is something I viewed as a reflection of the sentiment of the elite (rather than something that drives the sentiment of the elite). Often the anti-jazz discourse was written by elites as a way of trying to convince other (non-elite) Americans of jazz's ills.

I used the *New York Times* to construct a monthly count of how many times jazz was directly portrayed as "primitive" during the 1920s by finding and reading every co-mention of "jazz" and "primitive." This variable ranged from 0 to 9, with a mean of 4.06. Because having zero mentions is qualitatively distinct, I also created a separate indicator variable that captures the 22% of cases where there were no co-mentions of "jazz" and "primitive." The association of "jazz" and "primitive" is a good indicator of the pressure Victorian-era firms faced to move away from "bad" jazz (the "hot" style associated with African Americans) and toward the "good" symphonic jazz popularized by Paul Whiteman. Below are two excerpts drawn from the *New York Times* that represent the type of article I coded as having an explicitly negative portrayal of jazz as "primitive" (all emphases were added):

> *Jazz* may be analyzed as a combination of nervousness, lawlessness, *primitive* and savage animalism and lavishness. (*New York Times*, March 3, 1922)

> *Jazz* must be banned by the white races if they wish to maintain their prestige. . . . *Jazz* is a low type of *primitive* music founded on crude rhythms. . . . It debases both music and instruments by making both farcical. (*New York Times*, September 19, 1927)

The number of negative portrayals in the *New York Times* became a key variable in my analysis, as I examined whether Victorian-era firms recorded different kinds of records when jazz was portrayed as "primitive" in the preceding month as compared to the months when there were no similarly negative portrayals. That is, the evidence for my answer to this chapter's puzzle is stronger if I can show that in response to recent (within the last month) negative portrayals of jazz, Victorian-era firms altered their recordings so that they were: (a) less instrumentally experimental or innovative; (b) more likely to record white orchestras; and (c) less likely to record black non-orchestral groups.

RESULTS OF THE QUANTITATIVE ANALYSIS

Study 1: Identity and Innovativeness over Time

The results of the analysis for Study 1 are presented in Figure 4.3, where a high instrumental combinatorial uniqueness score indicates that the combination of instruments is particularly experimental or innovative (see Table A.8). To best represent the effects I coded three different time periods: 1917 to 1925; 1925 to 1927; and 1927 to 1929. The years from 1917 to 1925 capture the period in which the volume of anti-jazz discourse in the *New York Times* became prominent. In addition, the technology for recording changed in 1925 with the introduction of electric recording (versus recording on warm wax). This new technology altered the cost and manner of production and likely did so differently for Victorian-era versus jazz-era firms. Moreover, jazz's legitimacy was greatly impacted by the rise and global appeal of Paul Whiteman in 1923–24. I also captured the period from 1925 to 1927, during which the market for jazz expanded but had to compete more vigorously with radio. In 1927 Victor was sold to new investors who—without the same ties to the cultural elite—began producing recordings that would have been formerly too illegitimate to produce. My reference category 1927–29 characterizes the period in the 1920s in which there was the least number of anti-jazz references, the greatest number re-recordings, and almost no new entrants. Similar to the statsitical models in chapter 1, the analysis for this chapter includes dozens of time-varying and invariant controls and fixed effects at the market, firm, group, and recording levels.

There are several things to be gleaned from Figure 4.3. First, the innovativeness of Victorian-era firms (the darker bar) is substantially less in the early 1920s as jazz-era firms (the lighter bar) entered the market with new combinations of instruments. In fact, Victorian-era firms' innovativeness was never significantly different than zero in any of the models for any of the time periods. In other words, their recordings had little relative innovativeness and held a consistent level of innovativeness across the 1920s. The innovativeness of jazz-era firms was high in the early 1920s when they first entered the market and then diminished over time with levels that were statistically greater than zero for the first two periods. In the third period, after 1927, the market had reached what looks to be a point in which firms' recordings were no longer distinguished by my measure of innovativeness, as neither type of firm had a net level of innovation that was significantly greater than zero. Overall, it appears that although Victorian-era firms initiated the market with the innovative recording of the Original Dixieland Jass Band and other similar groups in 1917, this innovativeness was quickly overshadowed as jazz-era firms entered the market experimenting with different forms of jazz. This difference had completely erased by 1927 as jazz gained cognitive and social legitimacy, marking the recording industry's convergence to consistent combinations of instruments that represented the market for jazz music.[55] At the same time, while this looks like a strong case for convergence, we need to be cautious. In 1929 the recording industry was completely upended by the stock market crash; thus there is not enough evidence to make certain claims about long-run trends. Still the available evidence is certainly suggestive of the diminishing innovativeness of the jazz-era firms.

To elaborate further and build upon my hypothetical example of the trombone featured alongside the trumpet versus a trombone featured alongside a vocalist, I examined two recordings (one from each type of firm) from 1926 (Table 4.4). Here the recording from the jazz-era firm had a greater uniqueness score than the

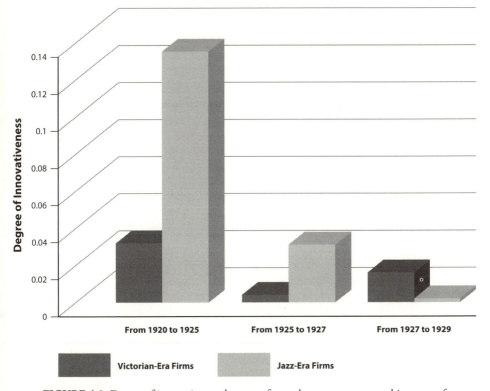

FIGURE 4.3. Degree of innovativeness by type of record company, measured in terms of the combinatorial uniqueness of instruments used. The dark bars for Victorian-era firms are not statistically significant.

recording from the Victorian-era firm even though there are more instruments in the Victorian-era firm's recording (my regressions control for the total number of instruments). The difference is because the combination of instruments in the Victorian-era firm was more common than the combination in the jazz-era firm's recording, even though none of the instruments is unique. The eight instruments in the Victorian-era recording were a relatively common combination. At the same time, the jazz-era firm's recording was unique not only because the particular combination of four instruments was relatively uncommon but also because this combination excluded drums—something that met my criteria of being experimental and innovative. Not only did this involve a rare arrangement, but it is likely that musicians would have played jazz differently without drums, adjustments in the studio would have been made to record this unique combination, and consumers would have ultimately experienced the "drumless" jazz recording as something that was unique. That said I was a bit surprised that Victorian-era firms did not become less innovative over time; their innovativeness was un-

TABLE 4.4. Two Recordings from 1926 with Different Combinatorial Uniqueness Scores

Type of firm	Instrumental combinatorial uniqueness	Number of instruments	Instruments
Victorian era	162.71	8	Alto sax, banjo, coronet, drums, piano, soprano sax, trombone, vocals
Jazz era	192.94	4	Alto sax, banjo, vocals, violin

changed. At least in terms of instrumental combinations, the results suggest that Victorian-era firms merely maintained their level of combinatorial uniqueness. The invariance suggests that instead of exploring new combinations of instruments, they might have been exploiting their existing resources and expertise by replicating the same level of combinatorial uniqueness when recording. It was jazz-era firms, on the other hand, that were less innovative over time.

STUDY 2: IDENTITY AND TYPE OF GROUP RECORDED

I next examined the likelihood of each type of firm to record white orchestras and black non-orchestral groups. I predicted that Victorian-era firms were more likely to record the first and less likely to record the second type of group (I also tested for the other types of race/style combinations but none was statistically significant). The result of this analysis is strong, statistically significant, and relatively straightforward (see Table A.9). Compared to jazz-era firms, Victorian-era firms were much more likely to record white orchestras. Moreover, they were less likely to record black non-orchestral groups. Both of these findings are consistent with and reflect the constraints faced by Victorian-era firms to produce music that was congruent with their organizational identity as highbrow producers. In supplemental analysis I confirmed that jazz-era firms were more likely to record black non-orchestral groups than any other type of group. Jazz-era firms were not less likely to record white orchestras compared to other kinds of groups.

STUDY 3: IDENTITY AND RESPONSES TO ANTI-JAZZ SENTIMENTS

We now know that part of the solution to this chapter's puzzle lies in the findings from the first two studies. First, it appears that Victorian-era firms maintained the same level of experimentation while jazz-era firms entered with lots of innovation but that decreased over the 1920s—a finding that would not be surprising if it were not for the fact that it was Victorian-era (not jazz-era) firms that introduced the innovative "hot" jazz style in the first place and then backed away from further experimentation. Second, Victorian-era firms were more likely to record white orchestras and less likely to record black non-orchestras. In large part, then, the results of Studies 1 and 2 are consistent with the historical record and analyses. However, what is left unsettled is whether these patterns were related to pressure from the cultural arbiters who publicly fought against jazz. Study 3 used the aforementioned variables that count the associations of "jazz" and "primitive" in the *New York Times* in the month that precedes each recording. This variable is a proxy for the contemporaneous discourse around jazz during the recording, and I predicted that this discourse influenced real-time recording decisions by Victorian-era firms (especially when compared to jazz-era firms). While the underlying prediction is causal, my measure is too crude to definitively show causal effects. So care should be taken to state findings as consistent with predictions but not definitive. At the same time, I am not aware of any other proxy that approaches the effectiveness of my *New York Times* indicator. With this key variable, I ran a set of regressions to examine its effects on innovativeness and the subtype of group recorded. The results for the effect of anti-jazz sentiments on experimentation and innovativeness are presented in Figure 4.4 (see Table A.10).

Figure 4.4 demonstrates the best-fitting model, which revealed an interesting nonlinear effect. Overall, the greater the anti-jazz pressure, the less innovative Victorian-era firms were. More specifically, the effect of anti-jazz pressure did not negatively affect Victorian-era firms until the sentiment was greater than two co-mentions in the previous month (the mean is four co-mentions and the median is three).[56] I also attempted to calculate the effect for jazz-era firms, but the effect was not statistically significant no matter how I modeled it. This suggests that jazz-era firms may have been unresponsive to anti-jazz pressure with respect to experimentation and innovativeness, which is consistent with the historical rendering in the first part of this chapter.

Anti-jazz pressure did not affect Victorian-era firms' likelihood of recording a white orchestra. In contrast, jazz-era firms were affected in that the likelihood of recording white orchestras was lowest when anti-jazz pressure was zero, increased as anti-jazz pressure began, until at the highest levels of anti-jazz pressure when the white orchestra production declined. Thus, while Victorian-era firms responded to anti-jazz pressure by decreasing their production of black non-orchestras, jazz-era firms often increased the production of white orchestras.

I also found an interesting interaction effect for the relationship between anti-jazz pressure and the likelihood of recording a black non-orchestral group, an effect that supported the historical evidence. The regression results of this interaction effect suggest that when jazz was portrayed as primitive in the public discourse, Victorian-era firms produced *fewer* black non-orchestra recordings, whereas jazz-era firms did not respond to anti-jazz sentiments.

Finally, it turns out that one control variable, whether the recording was of an original piece or whether it was a re-recording (cover) of a previously recorded piece, suggests that white orchestras more commonly re-recorded music whereas black non-orchestras were more likely to record original music. Put another way,

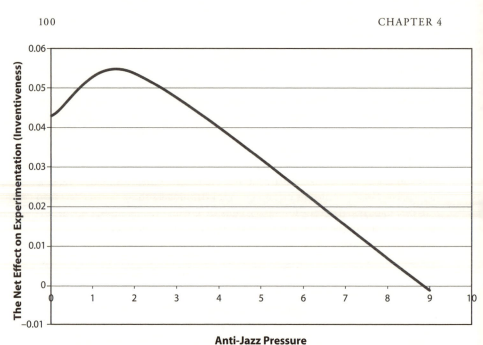

FIGURE 4.4. The effect of anti-jazz pressure (*New York Times* co-mentions of "jazz" and "primitive") for a Victorian-era firm recording's instrumental combinatorial uniqueness (innovativeness).

black non-orchestras were more likely to be originators, while white orchestras tended to be followers. One needs to be careful here as it may appear that white orchestras were following black non-orchestras. A closer look at the actual recordings invalidates that conclusion. A better description is that white orchestras followed one another—recording one another's music. Black non-orchestras, however, more consistently recorded more original music and spent less time re-recording the music of others. This is an important finding (and interpretation) to keep in mind for the discussion in chapter 6 about adoption narratives.

The Results of Studies 1–3

The three studies provide some solutions to the puzzle that was the catalyst for this chapter. The onset of the market for jazz brought potential changes along instrumental, stylistic, and racial dimensions—which were rooted in highbrow-lowbrow class differences. The analyses here provide some evidence that Victorian-era firms did not become more instrumentally exploratory as the market evolved but that this was more a function of the negative jazz pressure in the public discourse than the passage of time. Anti-jazz pressure led Victorian-era firms to be less innovative and less likely to record the black non-orchestral groups that were the center of the market.

At the same time, my earlier work with Owens (2004) suggests that Victorian-era firms' temporal invariance in experimentation and innovation was also driven by the firms' goal of exploiting the resources and market position they had through their experience in recording classical music. When the anti-jazz backlash occurred, it appears that their response was to return to this core competency even though it was not at the center of the market. Jazz-era firms, on the other hand, lacked any internal or external sources of inertia with respect to what type of music to record. Consequently they entered the market very innovatively.

If one observed this market by only looking at the late 1920s, one might see a partitioned market that looked very familiar to Schumpeterians. However, one would miss the evolution of the market from one where the incumbent innovativeness at the market's birth was greater than that of new entrants to one in which experimentation and innovation was largely, albeit decreasingly, occurring through the newer entrants. This is not what happened. All the while, Victorian-era firms fought to have the center of the market remain closer to symphonic music, where their competitive advantage rested. Finally, the findings on group race and style are clear and direct. Victorian-era firms were less likely to record black non-orchestras (Table A.9), and this was at least in part related to the anti-jazz pressure Victorian-era firms faced (Table A.10).

IMPLICATIONS FOR THE SHAPING OF JAZZ

I began this chapter questioning why incumbents would be first movers in the market for recorded jazz—a musical stylistic innovation—then pull away from this innovation that initiated the market for recorded jazz. I offered that the answer to this question can shed light on the role of record companies in the evolution of the recorded jazz canon. I believe that the motivating puzzle can be largely, but incompletely, understood in terms of how the market for recorded jazz evolved. Chapters 5 and 6 will help us understand this even further, but we already know quite a bit.

Instrumental experimentation does seem to have come from the jazz-era firms—but largely in the early 1920s when they first entered the market. They entered the new market more radically but then reduced their innovativeness over time. It appears that Victorian-era firms initiated a market but were not well-positioned to exploit it beyond being first movers. However, with the market opportunity clearer, jazz-era firms entered and reshaped the market by advancing along dimensions that were less viable for Victorian-era firms. In this way, my answer to this chapter's puzzle involves a hybrid of the Schumpeterian explanations presented at the outset.

It appears, then, that in addition to the geographic influences discussed in chapters 1–3, recorded jazz was shaped by at least two additional competing forces in the 1920s: (1) the efforts of Victorian-era firms (and the cultural elite) to officially establish jazz as a hybrid of symphonic music performed by Anglo Americans; and (2) the actions of jazz-era firms that expanded recorded jazz with non-orchestral African American groups and more innovative music. Time would favor the music more associated with jazz-era firms, although this was not at all obvious during the 1920s or 1930s. That is, though on average black non-orchestral recordings had appeal, most of the purchasing white public considered the chief representative of jazz to be Paul Whiteman, the exemplar of symphonic jazz. And although his popularity dramatically waned after the 1930s, one cannot fully understand big band jazz of the 1920s and 1930s without appreciating Whiteman as a reference point. In other words, we will find as we proceed through the rest of *Shaping Jazz* that understanding the 1920s is crucial in understanding how jazz evolved. Victorian-era firms and groups like Paul Whiteman were critical in shaping what became jazz standards, as the decisions they made as to what to record (whether due to anti-jazz pressure or their core competencies) drew more attention to some songs and tunes than others, with real consequences for the canon. In short, the sheer output and marketing of the larger and better-connected Victorian-era firms ensured that their jazz offerings would have a substantial long-term impact on recorded jazz and the songs that came to represent it.

Early jazz threatened the identity of firms that dominated the recording industry during a period in which the definition of high culture was being challenged and transformed.[57] In this chapter I have emphasized two factors that caused tension for the Victorian-era incumbents seeking to commercialize a popular musical form without betraying the elites with whom they were associated. First, although not the first to record jazz, African American musicians were clearly associated with the radical innovation of jazz, which increased the new genre's illegitimacy. Second, the highly improvisational and occasionally extemporaneous nature of the jazz associated with smaller white groups and African Americans (today often labeled as traditional New Orleans jazz) made it stylistically radical for Victorian-era firms and their constituents who were accustomed to operatic or symphonic music. Victorian-era firms experienced anti-jazz sentiment after initially recording jazz—and this pressure affected their recording decisions. The firms responded by recording music that minimized social sanctions.

The next two chapters take this as a point of transition. Chapter 5 extends the reaction by Victorian-era firms to anti-jazz pressure through the lens of pseudonyms. Here I provide an example of organizational deception to make a larger argument on how organizations can shape a market like the one for recorded jazz through deceptive acts. Chapter 6, the final empirical chapter, returns to analyses of individual recordings to show how this early period influenced our definition of jazz as something that met a primitive-to-refined narrative, which ultimately privileged the long-run appeal of some songs and tunes over others.

Chapter 5

THE SOCIOLOGICAL CONGRUENCE OF
RECORD COMPANY DECEPTION[1]

The name [California Ramblers] was chosen in true fashion of the day,
slightly exotic and definitely non-east coast, which seemed to indicate that
their music was totally new and unconventional. (There were also the
Original Memphis Five, Original Indiana Five, and Tennessee Tooters,
Arkansas Travelers and many more, strictly New York based bands.)

—HANS EEKHOFF (LINER NOTES TO *The California
Ramblers 1925–28*, TIMELESS RECORDS

When I was coding data for the analyses that ultimately constituted chapter 4, I
came across a very interesting component of the discographical data. Among the
rich data embedded within the jazz discographies are pseudonyms of various recording groups; that is, there were notes indicating that a recording by a particular
group was also released by that same group under a completely different name.[2]
Initially I found this amusing and left it at that; as the epigraph suggests pseudonyms are not new or even unique to jazz. Musicians and artists use false or multiple names to disguise racial identities, secretly record for competitors, or perform
a style of art that they don't want associated with their current identity.[3] But as I
began to run analyses and consider the role of record companies (often through
their labels) during the 1920s, none of these reasonable rationales was supported
by what I was seeing in the data.

More and more it began to appear as though the record companies were influential in the creation of many recording groups' pseudonyms as acts of deception.
Such influence was unexpected but not altogether surprising, as the intellectual
property rights of most musicians in this period typically lasted only until the recording was made, giving record companies the latitude to market each group as
they saw fit. If we view recording groups' pseudonyms as acts of deception, we
then need to consider psychological models of persuasion in marketing research,[4]
institutional theory emphasis on decoupling and symbolic management,[5] the impression management of stigmatizing actions,[6] and a vast literature on fraud.[7] Indeed an entire field of forensic accounting is devoted to deception in financial
reporting.[8]

In these types of studies the main targets of deception are usually the external
constituents (or audience members like investors and consumers) that affect the
financial success of the focal organization, where deception is used to financially
benefit the organization at the expense of these constituents. For example, in

product markets deception may involve a firm's attempt to mislead consumers by inflating its products' consumption value. Deception would be successful if demand increased or consumers purchased the products in response to the inflated value.

Continuing the theme from chapter 4 on organizational identities and the trajectory of jazz, this chapter examines deception through the lens of organizational role identities,[9] where role identities are a function of when an organization was founded.[10] This chapter also complements the work of a broader set of scholars who have examined organizational identities and their relationship with the organization's outputs and external constituencies.[11] At the same time, the stance here is unique and important for grappling with this particular puzzle. To better understand pseudonyms one should consider the fact that organizations that strongly value their role identity may deceive to preserve that identity—even when the deception does not increase consumer demand and profits of the particular set of products involved.

Understanding the role of pseudonyms returns us to Victorian-era firms—the firms founded before the commercialization of recorded jazz—and the anti-jazz pressure they faced. Drawing on over a year of research with Young-Kyu Kim, I provide evidence that these firms used deception to overcome two types of identity threats: (1) their association with profitable but illegitimate types of jazz; and (2) the actions of newer entrants that blurred the incumbent firms' identity. I will show that for Victorian-era firms, preserving an incumbent role identity required publicly distancing themselves from illegitimate jazz that not only was less costly to produce but also exhibited greater market demand. While we know from chapter 4 that Victorian-era firms produced both "lowbrow" and "highbrow" products, they used pseudonyms to present themselves as primarily producers of highbrow products.

PSEUDONYMS AND THE MARKET FOR EARLY JAZZ

I am studying pseudonyms as deceptive acts used by firms to preserve and heighten their role identities in the early jazz market. Many of the recordings released by the key firms were actually re-released songs by artists the same firms had previously recorded. Table 5.1 provides examples of seven randomly selected groups of musicians in my sample who recorded songs that were re-released by their record companies and existed in that company's catalogues (sometimes under that company's different labels). For each pair, a recording was initially released under the original name and then re-released under the pseudonym. The name pairs are representative in that the pseudonym typically bore no resemblance to the name of the group that actually recorded the song. The exception is the recording by Charlie Davenport, which was re-released as Cowcow Davenport. While pseudonyms generally appear in song discographies and catalogues, they were otherwise rarely

TABLE 5.1. Recording Groups' Original Names and Their Pseudonyms

Original name	Pseudonym
Wisconsin Roof Orchestra	Miami Society Orchestra
Louis Armstrong and His Savoy Ballroom Five	Eddie Gordon's Band
Charlie Straight and His Orchestra	Manhattan Imperial Orchestra
Chuck Nelson and His Boys	Eddie Walker and His Band
Ezra Buzzington (Ezra Buzzington's Rustic Revelers)	Joseph Simpkins and His Rube Band
Charlie Davenport	Cowcow Davenport
King Oliver and his Dixie Syncopators	Aurora Aristocrats

advertised to the public. This absence of marketing for pseudonyms reinforces the contention that key constituencies were unaware of the prevalence of pseudonyms, an important point I will return to later in this chapter.[12]

It is also important to note that although 13% of the recordings in my data were those of groups with pseudonyms, only a small fraction (1% of all recordings, or 7.7% of all recordings made under pseudonyms) were made by a firm's competitors. The majority (92.3%) of the recordings made under pseudonyms were produced by the company that initially recorded the artists (often on different labels owned by the same company). This set of pseudonyms is the focus of the investigation. The remaining 86% of the recordings were not re-released under pseudonyms. Record company information is missing for the remaining 1% of the recordings made under pseudonyms.

Chapter 4's findings imply that there are two general propositions about the use of pseudonyms for identity preservation. First, recordings were more likely to be re-released under pseudonyms when the producing firm had an identity associated with the cultural elite and Victorian values. Second, the use of pseudonyms by these firms was strategic. In particular, pseudonyms were more likely to be used on "illegitimate" (lowbrow) products and less likely to be used on the most "legitimate" (highbrow) products. This was especially true for firms associated with the cultural elite and Victorian values. Once created, the pseudonyms were used to inflate catalogues with fictitious but legitimacy-enhancing products. This use of pseudonyms was driven by the diverging tastes of the mass market (which drove profits) and the cultural elite (which conferred legitimacy). The mass market preferred lowbrow jazz over highbrow jazz, where lowbrow jazz was typified by African American and Creole musicians in smaller improvisational groups and highbrow jazz was music characterized by larger groups of classically trained white (Anglo) musicians who played more symphonic arrangements.[13] Music closer to the lowbrow form of jazz had greater market success than music closer to the more highbrow jazz.[14] On the other hand, the cultural elite vigorously advocated for the more classically influenced symphonic jazz and attempted to confer legitimacy and sanctions through their influence as cultural arbiters (e.g., critics) and policy-makers (see chapter 4).[15]

Pseudonyms were used to preserve a firm's identity while selling the profitable but identity-threatening products to the mass market. That is, rather than over-produce less profitable highbrow products, Victorian-era firms used pseudonyms to deceive observers into believing that their production of cultural products was consistent with their Victorian-era identity. As a result, these firms had some success in decoupling their position in identity space from their position in product space.

The remainder of this chapter provides richness to the context and tests this theory on pseudonyms using data on 1920s Midwest jazz recordings. I present two studies in which deception is a key decoupling response to market and institutional pressure: rather than just produce more recordings to bolster their legitimate product categories (which these firms did as well), Victorian-era firms used pseudonyms to artificially inflate their inventory of legitimate products. Moreover, as further evidence that this was due to strategic actions, I show that Victorian-era firms used pseudonyms to sharpen their identities when the actions of their less legitimate competitors made the Victorian-era firm identities more difficult to distinguish.

TESTING VICTORIAN-ERA FIRMS' PROPENSITY TO USE PSEUDONYMS

For evidence of this relationship between Victorian-era firm identities and pseud-onyms I use three sets of multivariate analyses using the recordings. First I test whether recordings were more likely to be re-released under a pseudonym when the producing record company was a Victorian-era firm. That is, Victorian-era firms did not employ pseudonyms randomly, just as they did not randomly record particular types of groups. Rather, these firms were more likely to use pseudonyms and to do so strategically for certain types of recording groups. Testing this propo-sition will shed light on whether Victorian-era firms were not only sensitive to preserving their role identities but also more willing to use this particular decep-tive strategy as a means of reinforcing their identity as highbrow producers.

Second, I test whether Victorian-era firms were strategic in their selection of songs to be re-recorded under pseudonyms by examining whether Victorian-era firm recordings of less legitimate groups were re-released under pseudonyms more frequently than were the recordings of more legitimate groups (versus a null of using pseudonyms indiscriminately). If the proposed relationship between Victorian-era identity and pseudonyms is correct, Victorian-era firms would have used pseudonyms to decouple what they actually produced (their position in product space) from what they were publicly understood as producing (their posi-tion in identity space). Drawing from the race and style typology in chapter 4, I

expected that these firms would have been less likely to re-release the recordings of
white orchestras (the type most acceptable to the elite) under pseudonyms but
more likely to re-release the recordings of black non-orchestras (the least acceptable type to the elite). Doing so would be an act of presenting themselves as congruent with their organizational identity as Victorian-era firms. Moreover, as I will
discuss at the end of this chapter, these same acts affected the evolution and shape
of jazz over the long run.

My third test also builds upon chapter 4 by testing whether pseudonym activity of Victorian-era firms was influenced by the competitive actions of the new
entrant jazz-era firms. Here I build off of the rationale that other threats to
Victorian-era identity would lead to pseudonym use. Pseudonyms could have
been used to heighten Victorian-era firms' identity as highbrow producers when
the actions of their jazz-era competitors made it more difficult for constituents to
discern the identity of the highbrow producers. This suggests that pseudonym
activity among Victorian-era firms would have increased during periods when
their identity as highbrow producers was challenged. To capture this challenge, we
will look at the period in which jazz-era firms began to expand their offerings and
the market matured. It turns out that one reason why the innovativeness of jazz-
era firms diminished during the late 1920s (see Figure 4.3) was that they began to
record all forms of jazz, including the music of white jazz orchestras. Recall from
chapter 4 that, especially in the early 1920s, the market was more segmented:
highbrow jazz was primarily associated with Victorian-era firms (white musicians
performing symphonic jazz) and jazz-era firms were associated with a lowbrow
form of jazz (African American musicians closer to the "hot" rather than the symphonic style). The actions by jazz-era firms would complicate matters, however,
making it more difficult for a Victorian-era firm to be distinctly highbrow. Pseudonyms could have helped make it appear that Victorian-era firms continued to be
associated with highbrow jazz even in the face of increasing confusion over the
distinctiveness of their identities.

Turning to the discographical data, I used two indicators, shown in Figures
5.1a and 5.1b as a proxy for the actions of the jazz-era competitors that threatened
the distinctive identity of Victorian-era firms. The first can be used to test whether
recordings were more likely to be re-released under pseudonyms by Victorian-era
firms when jazz-era firms infiltrated the market identity space for highbrow music.
The greater the proportion of white orchestra recordings that jazz-era firms recorded, the less distinct was the identity of the Victorian-era firms. As Figure 5.1a
shows, this proportion generally increased over the 1920s, with an average of 44%
of white orchestra recordings produced by jazz-era firms in the latter half of the
1920s (1925–29). Under these conditions, Victorian-era firms should have responded by using pseudonyms to bolster their identity as a means of competition
within a niche in the market identity space (cf. Ruef 2000).

The second indicator allows us to test whether Victorian-era firms used pseudonyms during periods in which a higher proportion of the jazz market was com-

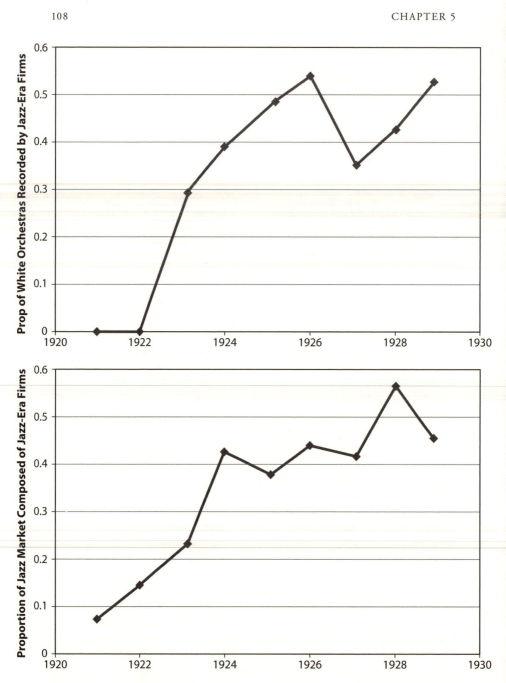

FIGURE 5.1. (a) The proportion of white orchestras recorded by jazz-era firms. (b) The proportion of the jazz market composed of jazz-era firms.

posed of new (jazz-era) entrants. We can see in Figure 5.1b that this proportion rose over the 1920s, although it was stable during the mid-1920s after the initial rush of new entrants between 1921 and 1924. The higher the proportion of new entrants in the jazz market, the more critics of the overall jazz recording market may have characterized it as producing less legitimate music. Here again, Victorian-era firms would have used pseudonyms to more clearly differentiate themselves when the actions of competitors blurred the identity of Victorian-era firms.

WHY DECEIVE?: FIRM IDENTITIES AND THE COSTS AND SUCCESS OF HIGHBROW VERSUS LOWBROW RECORDINGS

As in chapter 4, I used Midwest data on recordings from 1920 to 1929 to track recording groups' pseudonyms. Using the discographical component of the Midwest data, a dummy variable was assigned the value of 1 each time a recording was re-released under a pseudonym. This dependent variable restricts the variable to equal 1 only when the pseudonym used for the re-recording is that of the record company under which the recording was originally issued.

To verify the assertion on the relationship between the type of record company, subgenre of jazz, cost of production, and success of recordings, two sets of variables from the data on jazz recordings were employed. First, using Phillips and Owens's (2004) coding scheme, I extracted the number of takes for jazz recordings in our sample from catalogue numbers. Multiple takes during the 1920s were very costly, resulting in musician and equipment fatigue. As with any cost, companies sought to minimize the number of takes. Second, also drawing from Phillips and Owens's study, I counted the number of times a song was re-released by multiple labels as an indicator of recording success. Re-releases by multiple labels indicated increases in that original recording's popularity with respect to consumers. The more popular a song, the more companies and labels re-released the song. Thus, the number of re-releases is a supply-side indicator of recording success. Tables 5.2 and 5.3 show how these two indicators of cost and success vary by type of record company and type of group recorded.[16]

Overall, Victorian-era firms had greater production costs (1.91 vs. 1.54, $p < .01$) and lower market success (3.04 vs. 3.24, $p < .05$) in the market for early jazz than did jazz-era firms. With respect to the type of group recorded, there are important similarities and differences between the patterns seen in the tables. In both, the music of white orchestras was more costly to record than that of the other types of jazz groups (2.42 for Victorian-era, 1.89 for jazz-era, $p < .01$). At the same time, songs by white orchestras were the least successful of the four types for both Victorian- and jazz-era firms. Black non-orchestras were among the most successful for each type of firm, although for Victorian-era firms black orchestras had the lowest costs per recording. However, these differences should not distract from the main implication of the tables: recordings of highbrow groups (white orchestras)

TABLE 5.2. Victorian-Era Firms' Recording Costs and Market Success of Recordings by Type of Group

	Cost of recording: # of takes	Success of recording: # of reissues
All recordings	1.91	3.04
White orchestras only	2.42	2.63
White non-orchestras only	1.95	2.84
Black orchestras only	1.69	3.09
Black non-orchestras only	1.79	3.26

cost more and were less successful than those of lowbrow groups (black non-orchestras) independent of the type of firm.[17] By these indicators, there would seem to be little justification in being more closely aligned with white orchestras.

These tables illuminate a critical point that drives the mechanism underlying the motivation for the use of pseudonyms: Victorian-era firms used pseudonyms to preserve their identity without bearing the economic costs of producing more costly highbrow records that were also less appealing to the mass consumer. In chapter 4 I showed that Victorian-era firms were—all else equal—more likely to record white orchestras and less likely to record black non-orchestras (Table A.9). Moreover, the effect for black non-orchestras was largely driven by anti-jazz sentiments in the public discourse (Table A.10). This was not sufficient to preserve their identity, however. Victorian-era firms, while tending more toward highbrow versus lowbrow recordings, could pursue that strategy only so far because in the long run this was a losing proposition. Black non-orchestras were less costly to produce and more successful in the marketplace. Although 50% of Victorian-era firms' offerings were those of black non-orchestras (Table 4.3), they used deception through pseudonyms to minimize what the elite would observe when looking at an inventory of these firms' offerings. Although the cultural elite may have monitored what types of jazz a firm produced, Victorian-era firms' strategy could suc-

TABLE 5.3. Jazz-Era Firms' Recording Costs and Market Success of Recordings by Type of Group

	Cost of recording: # of takes	Success of recording: # of reissues
All recordings	1.54	3.24
White orchestras only	1.89	2.28
White non-orchestras only	1.90	3.36
Black orchestras only	1.48	2.73
Black non-orchestras only	1.43	3.46
N = 244 recordings		

ceed because elites rarely purchased records or attended performances.[18] Even upper-middle-class consumers, the segment of active consumers most likely to reflect the cultural elite's tastes, enjoyed forms of jazz considered lowbrow. Victorian-era firms, already having produced more highbrow forms of jazz than their jazz-era competitors, needed a way to continue sending a strong signal of their identity without sacrificing their position in the market for jazz. Pseudonyms helped serve that purpose.

QUANTITATIVE EVIDENCE OF THE PROPENSITY TO USE PSEUDONYMS

The analysis for my first proposition—that recordings were more likely to be re-released under a pseudonym when the producing record company was a Victorian-era firm—used logistic regressions where the full results for all of my statistical tests (Figures 5.2, 5.3, and 5.4) are provided in Phillips and Kim (2009). In addition, I first conducted a t-test showing that the proportion of recordings under pseudonyms re-released by Victorian-era firms was greater than that for jazz-era firms (13% vs. 9%, $p < .01$). An inspection of the data revealed that every firm in my sample (whether Victorian-era or jazz-era) used pseudonyms at least once. The key difference was that the rate of use was significantly greater among Victorian-era firms. Further examination revealed that the difference was greatest for recordings by black non-orchestras, where 19% of black non-orchestral recordings produced by Victorian-era firms were re-released under pseudonyms (versus only 12% of black non-orchestral recordings produced by jazz-era firms). These simpler but more intuitive mean comparisons suggest that recordings by Victorian-era firms were more likely to be re-released under pseudonyms and more likely to be re-released strategically.[19]

Figure 5.2 shows the (net) log odds of a recording being re-released under a pseudonym as a function of whether the group was a black non-orchestral group and the firm was Victorian-era or jazz-era. The first bar indicates that, as expected, Victorian-era firms were much more likely to rename black non-orchestras with pseudonyms than any other type of group ($p < .01$). These firms also had the lowest likelihood of renaming a white orchestra ($p < .05$; the second bar in Figure 5.2). There were no statistically significant differences for black orchestras or white non-orchestras (all labeled as "All Other Groups"). The only effects occur for the types of groups most clearly associated with highbrow (white orchestra) and lowbrow (black non-orchestra) forms of jazz.

The evidence suggested that Victorian-era firms were more likely to act deceptively through the use of pseudonyms. When I first saw this result, I suspected that Victorian-era firms were targeting black non-orchestras that had been associated with appealing or commercially successful recordings. This would mean, for example, that a group led by someone like Louis Armstrong would have been a more

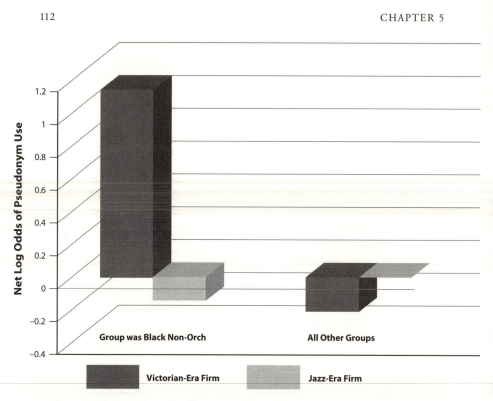

FIGURE 5.2. The net log odds of a recording being reissued under a pseudonym as a function of whether the group was a black non-orchestra group and the firm was Victorian era or jazz era. Only the first bar is statistically significant.

attractive target than a much lesser-known group. This would be a compelling alternative to what I have been suggesting. However, I found no evidence that more successful groups or recordings were being re-released under pseudonyms. While recordings that were re-released under pseudonyms have an average market success of 3.01, songs that were not re-released under pseudonyms have an average success of 3.15 (the difference is not statistically significant). Even among the subset of recordings by Louis Armstrong (the most prominent representative of the black non-orchestra category), firms were not more likely to select his more popular recordings to re-release under pseudonyms.[20] As someone who has spent his academic career in business schools, I would have been quite happy to show that Victorian-era firms were selecting songs to re-release under pseudonyms that were commercially "better." However, I never found any evidence that commercial success had anything to do with the logic used by Victorian-era firms. If anything, the full models seem to point more toward the fact that firms selected groups that were *unknown* to the market. Picking lesser-known groups is more supportive of an explanation involving deception, especially when the effects are most associated with Victorian-era firms.

QUANTITATIVE EVIDENCE OF
THE ROLE OF JAZZ-ERA FIRMS

It also turns out that, with respect to my second test, Victorian-era firms increased their use of pseudonyms when the actions of jazz-era firms clouded the identity of Victorian-era firms. When jazz-era firms recorded songs by white orchestras (the first of the two proxies), thus making it less clear that Victorian-era firms occupied the role of highbrow cultural producer, Victorian-era firms used pseudonyms in an attempt to bolster their identity ($p < .01$). Victorian-era firms' use of pseudonyms was greater when there was competition over highbrow products from jazz-era firms; I used the proportion of jazz orchestras produced by jazz-era firms as an indicator. The regressions also show that Victorian-era firms used pseudonyms more during periods in which the market was proportionally dominated by jazz-era firms. Here I used the proportion of jazz in the market produced by jazz-era firms as the second proxy. Figure 5.3 shows the (net) log odds of a Victorian-era firm using pseudonyms as a function of the proportion of the market share held by jazz-era firms across the range of the data (mean = .43, max = .56). It suggests that the greater the market share held by jazz-era firms, the less distinct the identities of the Victorian-era firms, and thus the more likely Victorian-era firms used pseudonyms, with black non-orchestras as the key targets ($p < .05$).

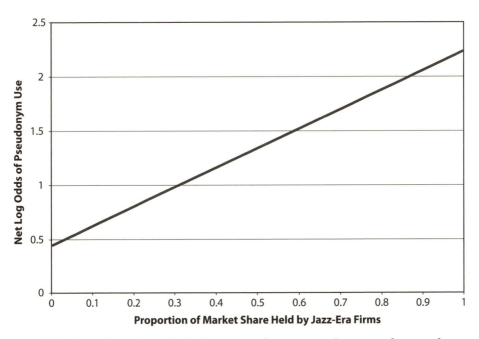

FIGURE 5.3. The net log odds of a Victorian-era firm using pseudonyms as a function of the proportion of the market share held by jazz-era firms.

QUANTITATIVE EVIDENCE OF THE USE OF PSEUDONYMS
TO RECONFIGURE LOWBROW MUSIC AS HIGHBROW MUSIC

As interesting as this evidence is, it is insufficient to simply say that Victorian-era firms used pseudonyms more often than jazz-era firms or to only demonstrate the conditions under which they used them. In order to verify that the strategic use of pseudonyms by Victorian-era firms was a means to appear more highbrow, it is necessary to test whether the fictitious names selected by Victorian-era firms, especially for black non-orchestras, suggested a more legitimate group. In other words, what was needed was a test of whether pseudonyms of lowbrow groups produced by Victorian-era firms were relabeled with highbrow names that were more consistent with elite values. The purpose of this final test, then, was to determine whether black non-orchestras would be renamed as "orchestras" by Victorian-era firms at a greater rate than would other types of groups. It was also important to verify that this effect applies only to black non-orchestras.

A Heckman probit regression was used for this test, where the probit captures whether the fictitious new name of the group contains the word "orchestra" (the dependent variable). For example, if the original name of the group was Damon Phillips and His Hot Five, the model would estimate whether the fictitious renaming was something like the Beale Street Orchestra, where the variable would equal 1 since the term "orchestra" was present in the new name. If the identity-based explanation about pseudonyms is correct, Victorian-era firms would be more likely to alter the names of black non-orchestral groups to include the term "orchestra"—enhancing their highbrow identity.

Figure 5.4 shows the results of the test. Each bar represents one of two regression results. Each model was similar in its specification but differed in the subset of recordings that they operate on. The first bar represents the likelihood of renaming black non-orchestras as "orchestras" ($p < .05$). The second bar of represents an alternative explanation: that Victorian-era firms converted *any* non-orchestra to an orchestra at a greater rate than jazz-era firms did, independent of the race of the group. However, here there was no effect for Victorian-era firms (it was negative but statistically insignificant). In other words, the only groups that Victorian-era firms renamed as "orchestras" were black non-orchestras.

WHY DID THIS DECEPTION GO UNDISCOVERED?

A unique aspect of this chapter is that it examines deception where there is no evidence that constituencies learned of the deceptive acts. How could this have occurred? One possibility is that pseudonyms existed in the catalogues of record company offerings that were not available for mass consumption. However, the pseudonyms listed in the discographies from which we drew our data were ex-

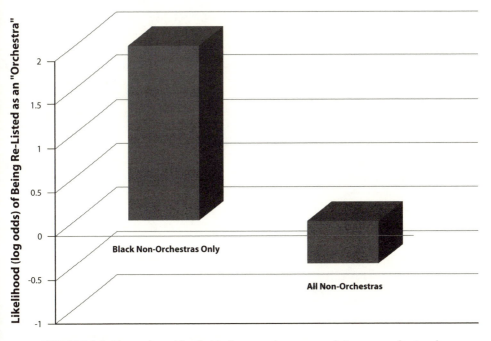

FIGURE 5.4. The net log odds of a black non-orchestra group being renamed using the term "orchestra." Midwest jazz recordings, 1920–29.

tracted by jazz collectors and aficionados from records that physically existed. If this is the case, then why didn't the two key constituents, cultural elites and mass market consumers, uncover the deception like jazz collectors did?

The answer for each constituency is different, but both hinge on the fact that the record companies actively marketed recordings under the actual names but much less actively marketed re-releases under any pseudonyms. As verification, Kim and I conducted a supplementary analysis in which we searched for actual group names and pseudonyms in the display advertisements of five newspapers: the *Chicago Defender, Chicago Tribune, New York Times, Wall Street Journal,* and *Washington Post.* We reasoned that one indicator of whether firms were marketing records under pseudonyms would be through advertisements of such recordings. We thus compared their rate of advertising to the rate of advertising of recordings of actual groups. We found that 19% of the groups recorded by Victorian-era firms were advertised under their actual names and no instances of a Victorian-era firm advertisement mentioning the name of a pseudonym. Thus, although Victorian-era firms listed pseudonyms in their catalogues, and physical copies existed (or they would not have appeared in our data set), they were not advertised to the public. This is consistent with the evidence that no recordings listed under pseudonyms had any substantial market success.

The lack of advertising of groups with pseudonyms is important because it suggests how these deceptive practices were not noticed. The cultural elite, while actively sanctioning lowbrow jazz in general, rarely purchased the music. Their critiques of it were rarely about specific recordings. To the extent that they were familiar with the music, it would have been via live performances, if at all (the jazz of black non-orchestras was rarely played on the radio during the 1920s). The fact that Victorian-era firms did not market their pseudonymous groups in ads would have been sufficient to close the circle on deception with respect to the cultural elite constituency. The only public representation of the pseudonyms would have been the firms' catalogues, which typically listed group names with no information to verify authenticity.

Consumers would have not been likely to uncover the deception either. They would have purchased recordings of relatively few groups with highbrow-oriented names, especially those that were unknown to the public and not marketed through advertisements. Thus, once again the deception would have been able to persist given the fact that the firms avoided advertisements of pseudonymous groups.

The particularly rich product- and firm-level data allowed an opportunity to control for many alternative explanations as to why Victorian-era firms engaged in such deception. For example, the statistical analyses controlled for a firm's size and scope, advertising behavior, and founder experience, as well as the characteristics of the groups and recordings and time trends I identified in earlier chapters. There are, however, other alternative explanations that control variables cannot directly address. One possibility is that Victorian-era firms used pseudonyms to bolster their identity with respect to the market for classical music. Here one might argue that because the primary market for Victorian-era firms was the more prestigious market for classical music, actions in less successful markets, such as jazz, would be used to ultimately serve the market for classical music. The lack of data makes this alternative difficult to dismiss outright. However, it seems implausible primarily because after 1917 classical music underperformed compared to more popular (jazz) music, just as highbrow jazz recordings underperformed with respect to lowbrow jazz. According to Walsh (1942), Eldridge Johnson (the president and founder of Victor Records) was thankful for the popular records they sold under their label because these records helped compensate for losses from classical records. Jazz had become the center of the market for recorded music. It is unlikely that Victorian-era firms were purposely underperforming at the market center to gain advantage in a more peripheral segment.

Indeed, this reality of the market prevented Victorian-era firms from exclusively recording highbrow jazz or even calling all of its groups "orchestras" even if the underlying music was not legitimate. Less legitimate lowbrow jazz records had to be released under their original names because these records best captured consumer demand. Victorian-era firms would have lost even greater market share if they had disguised all of their recordings as highbrow jazz.

Another alternative is that pseudonyms were used so that white (Anglo) consumers could purchase the more lowbrow jazz without bearing any stigma associated with it. However, there was no evidence that the pseudonyms were advertised in newspapers or magazines, making it unlikely that white consumers would be aware of which pseudonyms matched lowbrow records or whether pseudonyms existed in the first place. Moreover, one would suspect that such a strategy would have involved Victorian-era firms choosing groups with successful lowbrow recordings to rename as pseudonyms. However, the opposite appears to be true: not only is the average appeal of a tune or song selected to be re-released under a pseudonym less than that of other recordings (3.15 vs. 3.01), the difference is more striking when considering the subset of black non-orchestras that Victorian-era firms targeted for pseudonymous re-releases. The black non-orchestras that Victorian-era firms targeted for pseudonymous re-releases performed more poorly than the black non-orchestras they did not target (2.65 vs. 3.30, $p < 0.01$). This suggests that when choosing black non-orchestras as candidates for pseudonyms, Victorian-era firms focused on those that were less popular in order to maximize deception.

IMPLICATIONS FOR THE SHAPING OF JAZZ

Victorian-era firms deceived, and they did so with a purpose. They used pseudonyms to preserve their organizational identities, which were under threat whenever the firm was associated with music deemed illegitimate by the cultural elite. This meant renaming black non-orchestral groups, as an association with these groups would call into question the purity of Victorian-era firms. The renaming itself was strategic, often using new names that signaled a higher-brow form of jazz (e.g., including the word "orchestra" in the new name). Victorian-era firms also used pseudonyms when their position in the market was made ambiguous through the actions of jazz-era firms. The more difficult it was to distinguish the position of Victorian-era firms, the more likely they were to deceive through pseudonyms.

It is important to emphasize that the use of pseudonyms arose from a tension, or incongruence, between the "right" position in identity space and the most profitable position in product space. Recordings by black non-orchestras were more commercially appealing than those by white orchestras, which were also more costly to record. If an early jazz record company cared only about maximizing profits, the mix of products would lean more heavily toward black non-orchestras and less toward white orchestras. Victorian-era firms faced a dilemma, however, given that their organizational identity was associated with records that were more costly and less appealing in the marketplace. One of their solutions was to produce the music of black non-orchestras but use pseudonyms to understate their association with these groups.

Especially when viewed in conjunction with the findings in chapter 4, this chapter points to an interesting picture, one in which Victorian-era firms' recording decisions were motivated by a need for identity preservation. Not only were Victorian-era firms more likely to minimize their association with black non-orchestral groups in the face of anti-jazz sentiments, but the use of pseudonyms allowed these firms to participate more fully in the center of the market for jazz while preserving their identity as highbrow producers. These deceptive acts also allowed Victorian-era firms to more sharply signal their identity when the actions of competing jazz-era firms made it less clear that Victorian-era firms were distinctly associated with highbrow music.

What we remember as early jazz—and the mix of recordings that seeded the discographical canon—requires better understanding how and under what conditions recordings as musical artifacts were generated. This mix of early jazz recordings was influenced by the race and style of the group, the social and market positions of the record companies, and their audiences' reactions to these positions and offerings.

Victorian-era firms produced more than half (53%) of the original recordings in my Midwest sample of the 1920s. Their actions are no trivial matter to the evolution of the market for jazz recordings. Moreover, it is important to understand not only which songs and tunes the Victorian-era firms seeded the canon with but also the factors that led to *which* seeds they offered to the market. Victorian-era firms followed two tracks, one based on what they were publicly associated with (e.g., what they marketed) and one based on what they actually produced. In terms of the composition of the discographical canon, what was actually produced takes precedence, but how we perceive that production has to also be viewed from the lens of the organizational identity of record companies and labels.

For example, if jazz-era firms had maintained identities distinct from those of Victorian-era firms (instead of recording a broader range of jazz in the late 1920s), the acts of deception documented here would have diminished and thus the race and style of groups recorded by Victorian-era firms would have been more transparent. This is not a trivial matter, as observers would have immediately seen recorded jazz as more dominated by black non-orchestras than was actually the case, and this in and of itself would have influenced the discourse around jazz, as well as the social recourses allocated with respect to jazz, in ways we can only partially contemplate. However, jazz-era firms did not maintain distinct identities, and Victorian-era firms gave more attention to white orchestras and less to black non-orchestras than the evidence of actual recordings suggests.

One implication is that recordings by black non-orchestras were disadvantaged by the actions of Victorian-era firms that minimized their involvement with them, whereas the role of white orchestras has been overemphasized. Under this logic, the actions of Victorian-era firms made white orchestras and their recordings more legitimate than they would have been otherwise. They also made recordings by

black non-orchestras less legitimate in ways that affect our contemporary understanding of jazz's evolution. However, I don't believe that this is the case, or at least
that one can make this case in straightforward terms. On the one hand, the persistence of Victorian-era firms may have given greater long-run legitimacy to jazz
recordings by groups that had some symphonic elements, such as Duke Ellington.
It has been noted that Ellington directly incorporated elements of symphonic jazz
into his music, and indeed at one point he was advertised to white audiences as
the "colored Paul Whiteman."[21] The symphonic influence also preceded the big
band swing era of the 1930s, which often consisted of musicians who were alumni
of more symphonic-sounding jazz orchestras from the 1920s. For example, Benny
Goodman, among others, performed in Ben Pollack and His Park Central Orchestra, a group with two violins and a cello as a part of its arrangement.[22] It is
certainly plausible that the attractiveness of Ellington, Goodman, and other big
bands in the 1930s and 1940s was bolstered by the actions of Victorian-era firms
during the 1920s.

I will use chapter 6 to show that while Victorian-era firms suppressed the impact of some black non-orchestras, their desire to avoid an association with these
groups would contribute to their long-run appeal. That is, since audience members did not typically associate Victorian-era firms with certain types of groups,
when Victorian-era firms did, those incongruent recordings meant that audience
members evaluated those recordings differently. I will suggest that music by a
black group did not fare well over time if it was first recorded by a Victorian-era
record company. This was in part because Victorian-era firms' association with
lowbrow jazz seemed stranger than was actually the case but also because lowbrow
recordings by Victorian-era firms were incongruent with a narrative of authenticity, leading them to become less appealing over time.

Chapter 6 incorporates previous chapters and reorients our discussion to the
question of which recordings were more likely to enter the discographical canon
by continuing to consider the longer-run implications of the actions of firms.
Chapter 6 also reincorporates ideas about the reception of cultural products by
asking whether a recording by black musicians or by a jazz orchestra was received
differently when we know that it was originally produced by a Victorian-era firm.

Chapter 6

THE SOCIOLOGICAL CONGRUENCE OF IDENTITY SEQUENCES AND ADOPTION NARRATIVES[1]

———————————————————————

Jazz is an art form that depends on its antecedents. There
must be respect for the people that have gone before.

—JON HENDRICKS, MUSICIAN AND COMPOSER

Defining jazz is a notoriously difficult proposition, but the task is
easier if one bypasses the usual inventory of musical qualities or
techniques, like improvisation or swing . . . ethnicity provides a
core, a center or gravity for the narrative of jazz, and its one element
that unites the several kinds of narratives in use today.

—DEVEAUX, "CONSTRUCTING THE JAZZ TRADITION"

This chapter uses an interesting question to reincorporate the discussion of reception and authenticity from chapters 1–3 with the research in chapters 4 and 5 on the role of firm identities. We will look at the effect of the adoption pattern of a song's originators and its early adopters on the long-run appeal of that song. With the two epigraphs of this chapter in mind, consider four adoption patterns by musician race presented in Figure 6.1. It portrays a recording's adoption trajectory according to the races of the originator and early adopter—something my Midwest data capture.[2] For example, the first row reflects that the initial group to record a tune or song was black (African American), and the early adopter of that musical piece (through recording the tune or song) was white. The last row presents a scenario in which the identities of groups associated with the original recording and the early adoption were both white. The question motivating this chapter is, "Which sequence in early jazz most positively influenced a tune or song's long-run appeal?"

By this point in *Shaping Jazz*, your answer to this question probably is, "it depends," in that we need additional information, namely on the location and record company associated with the initial production. Furthermore, when we evaluate a cultural product such as a recording, we incorporate two important pieces of information. First, we incorporate the narrative of origination and adoption. Second, we pay attention to the identities that have starring roles in that adoption. Thus my evaluation of a song is affected by whether I know the human and organizational actors who created it, where it was created, and who then ad-

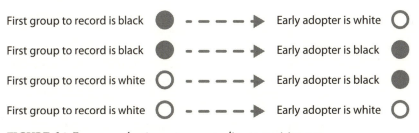

First group to record is black ● ‒ ‒ ‒ ‒ ➤ Early adopter is white ○

First group to record is black ● ‒ ‒ ‒ ‒ ➤ Early adopter is black ●

First group to record is white ○ ‒ ‒ ‒ ‒ ➤ Early adopter is black ●

First group to record is white ○ ‒ ‒ ‒ ‒ ➤ Early adopter is white ○

FIGURE 6.1. Four song adoption patterns according to musician race.

opted it. For members of a particular audience, some adoption narratives are more authentic than others and are thus evaluated more positively. In *Shaping Jazz*, the principal audience is dominated by post–World War II musicians (whom I will call "post–World War II adopters") who selected songs to record.

To answer this chapter's puzzle, I analyzed how these musicians formed the jazz canon of songs through the music they (re-)recorded—thus becoming part of their collective memory.[3] One key issue that underlies the puzzle is whether the long-run success of cultural products is affected by the identities of the product's originators and early adopters. A second issue is whether there is a particular sequence of these identities—and an accompanying narrative—that future musicians privileged in selecting one piece of music to record versus another. Addressing the puzzle thus requires a consideration of the four sequences in Figure 6.1 that post–World War II adopters found to be most congruent with the narrative of jazz's development and diffusion.

It is therefore important to understand the social context of production and consumption in determining the process of categorization, and then link that understanding to the role of identity sequences. In addition, work on the ecology of musical systems,[4] the organizations within art worlds,[5] and studies of the recording industry[6] have highlighted the role of the production system in which art is produced and distributed. Sociology of music scholars have also pointed to factors that affect the formation and reproduction of the musical repertoire.[7] According to this view, genres such as jazz are created and diffused through a network of adopters. This diffusion often has a salient history or pattern. For example, one's evaluation and decision to record a tune or song may be driven by who adopted that cultural object in the past (independent of whether the previous adopter was personally connected to the new potential adopter).

This type of genre formation need not require musicians to intently focus on enacting and maintaining a musical canon. Rather, the key mechanisms are social structural processes where meaning and value evolve with the social structural position of the adopters.[8] Especially when the adoption of a tune has implications for the musician's identity, the identities of previous musicians become important as a categorization tool. For example, Jonah Berger and Chip Heath (2008) found that university students were initially attracted to a particular wristband but then sought to distance themselves from it when they discovered that "geeky" students were also attracted to the same wristband. These processes are common aspects of social behavior in markets and often have underappreciated effects on category formation and meaning, such as with the context of jazz.[9]

THE ROLE OF ADOPTION NARRATIVES IN UNDERSTANDING LONG-TERM APPEAL

The key, then, is to consider how the order of adoption constitutes a narrative in which a song or tune is evaluated as authentic, which thereby enhances its likelihood of being seen as an element of the jazz canon. Making this claim conceptually draws upon the newly reinvigorated scholarship on the evolution of forms and identities in markets,[10] synthesizing this work with models that connect sequences of events to categorization processes, as well as the scholarship on authenticity at the intersection of art and commerce.[11] From these perspectives I consider authenticity as involving the social construction of value, including what narratives are used to evaluate an object.[12]

Within the processes of production and consumption, certain patterns can emerge in terms of the identities of who creates instances of the category as well as who consumes this category.[13] As this process unfolds, a narrative emerges that reifies this pattern of identities as part of the authentic representation of the category. Authenticity is thus represented by a narrative that explains or symbolizes the category's origin and ontology,[14] where my emphasis is not so much on the "accuracy" of the narrative but on the narrative's salience and robustness to the relevant audience (in my case, post–World War II musicians). Take, for example, the case of early German jazz from chapter 3. The dominant narrative for people outside Germany is one that considered the jazz opera as an authentic German jazz output despite the fact that it was infrequently produced compared to Germany's symphonic jazz.

Using an analogy from the world of technological innovations, consider the contrast between (A) a hypothetical 1990s product invented in Silicon Valley (California) by two engineers in a garage that is then adopted by two engineers in an old established firm; and (B) the very same product now invented by the engineers in the established firm and then adopted by the two engineers in a garage. Each pattern of adoption (both A and B) corresponds to a different narrative that influences the categorical meaning attached to that invention. All else equal, when members of the high-tech community in the 1990s who were deciding on which products and technologies to build upon, my claim is that they would have evaluated Sequence A more favorably than Sequence B. If this preference is sufficiently robust, the understanding of the technological category becomes understood—at least in part—with respect to Sequence A. I believe that this would be the case even if in actuality Sequence B occurred more frequently. That is, a powerful narrative could trump the relative frequencies of each sequence.

More specifically, the focus here once again is on why some early jazz tunes and songs (originally recorded from 1920 to 1929) were adopted or re-recorded by post–World War II musicians while others remain far outside the present-day discographical canon. This chapter builds on earlier chapters and engages the discographical jazz canon as a socially constructed categorization process that emphasizes the sequenced identities of two actors: (a) those who originally recorded the music, and (b) those who became the early adopters of the music. Particular combinations and sequences of these two types of actors influenced long-run appeal. The key to the puzzle represented by Figure 6.1 is whether one of the patterns is more associated with the rise of jazz because it conforms to a narrative in which the originators of songs were black and the early adopters were white. However, it is not that black musicians were better sources of jazz standards per se; indeed I discovered that music originated by black musicians had no greater statistical likelihood of influencing the discographical canon than music originated by white musicians. Rather, it was a narrative emphasizing the sequence of black originators, as legitimate representatives of jazz's ("lowbrow") origins, and white early adopters, as legitimate representatives of jazz's ("highbrow") refinement, that improved a jazz song's overall authenticity and thus its long-term appeal. Statistical support for this argument remains after holding constant a host of factors that I have discussed in previous chapters and presented by Kahl, Kim, and Phillips (2010), including other characteristics of the song such as its early success, characteristics of the recording group, and industry dynamics.

And while the puzzle is presented and analyzed here as one of race, I also want to draw attention to a more general process. For example, if I replace race in Figure 6.1 with the geographic social network position discussed in the first two chapters, the opening puzzle of this chapter could be now asked with respect to the position of the originating city. Using the four scenarios in Figure 6.2, we would predict that recordings with trajectories following the first sequence are more associated with long-run appeal compared to the other sequences, in part because the adoption narrative is more authentic (lower-status and exotic origins followed by re-recordings from musicians in the more influential and legitimate, but less exotic, central city).

One can even ask this question by replacing race with firm identities (see Figure 6.3). Again using the four sequences, we would predict that music that was first produced by a jazz-era firm but then early adopted by musicians affiliated with a Victorian-era firm would have the greatest long-run appeal. The advantage of focusing on race is that it is not only salient to fans of the music or as social scientists but also because the intimate relationship between race and jazz can be studied at the recording level of analysis where I can better address some of the

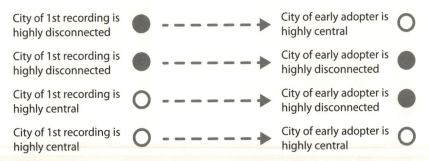

FIGURE 6.2. Four song adoption patterns according to geographical social networks of cities.

alternative explanations to my expectation that the first sequence in Figure 6.1 is associated with the greatest long-term appeal.

This leads to the following general statement: *in many markets the sequence or pattern of identities inherent in the production and adoption of products forms the basis for evaluation and meaning.* The goal here will be to show that future musicians made evaluations in terms of what to (re)record based not only on a song's attributes but also on who sequentially produced and reproduced these products. In the case with jazz where rules around a tune's attributes are ill-defined, the identities of the previous adopters become important social cues.

This chapter proceeds by developing the conceptual relationship between identity patterns, authenticity, and canon formation. I then revisit the historical context of early jazz, building off of work in previous chapters, to clarify why a particular racial narrative was important in the emergence of the discographical jazz canon. This discussion yields the central prediction in two parts: (a) songs/tunes with black originators and white early adopters were more likely to enter the jazz canon as they were congruent with the dominant narrative; and (b) this narrative was strongest for music with additional indicators of a song's authentic origins,

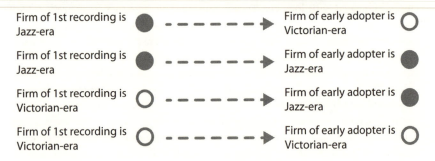

FIGURE 6.3. Four song adoption patterns according to organizational identity.

such as the venue and organizational (recording firm's) association of the recording. While the first part of this prediction establishes the pattern, the second part argues that this effect is not due to race per se.

PATTERNS OF ADOPTION AND AUTHENTICITY IN CULTURAL MARKETS

Sociologists have long argued that the meanings of categories are socially constructed.[15] Economic and organizational sociologists have focused on the expectations, norms, and codes that come to define the categorical membership.[16] While cultural sociology has advanced and continues to advance thinking on genres as classifications,[17] cultural sociologists have also emphasized authenticity as a means to conceptualize the dynamics of groupings and boundaries between groupings.[18] Authenticity can arise in many different ways, but in the context of categories of cultural markets, Richard Peterson notes that authenticity often is claimed through association with "ethnic/cultural identities."[19]

With respect to authenticity and the identities of members of musical communities and art worlds, some members are seen as more authentic in the sense that their identities are deemed as more closely tied to the history and production of the category.[20] This perspective implies that actors often use the identities of these more authentic past producers as a means to evaluate new offerings. For example, let us assume (as Peterson [1997, 151–52] notes) that Loretta Lynn is an authentic producer of country music. This view suggests that insofar as a new artist replicates Loretta Lynn's music (e.g., "Coal Miner's Daughter") and insofar as audiences are familiar with Loretta Lynn, then the new artist is seen as an authentic country musician. This should especially be the case during periods when the boundaries of country music are porous or the musical category is otherwise ill-defined. Thus the general characteristics that come to define this type of category include audience-specific comparisons with past actors and objects that are authentic to that audience.[21] This historical identity–based view emphasizes past identities and experiences. Certain historical patterns of an instance (here captured by the identity of past musicians) become more authentic to an audience than do other patterns.

How, then, do certain identities become authentic? Why is Loretta Lynn and not Elvis Presley a source of authentic country musician legitimacy? In this case, stories that develop about the (difficult) life histories of an artist help authenticate that artist just as for some observers reports of mental illness positively affected the authenticity of Thelonious Monk as an exemplar within jazz.[22] That is, Loretta Lynn is associated with a compelling narrative. Often consumers, artists, critics, or scholars are not selecting the art for its physical and aural characteristics as much as they are for the corresponding narrative and the implications of that narrative for the audience's own identity. Now, I believe that physical and aural characteristics matter a great deal—especially if they are unusual in a way that is congruent with the narrative. Those who are familiar with Monk's unique harmonies and improvisational approach will likely agree. But the more narrow point here is how a narrative can valorize a particular kind of identity as the exemplar of the category. Accordingly, we expect that Loretta Lynn's song "Coal Miner's Daughter," with its direct and defiant autobiographical references to economic poverty alongside the riches of life, enriches her authenticity as well as the authenticity of those within country music who reference her.[23]

In an organizational context, there is evidence that large-scale breweries that produced microbrews under a different label often suffered because audience members thought of them as less authentic and inconsistent with the microbrew narrative of authenticity.[24] Here, the narrative of the brewery matters in determining its beer's authenticity. Similarly, it is not unusual for wineries to showcase the biography of its winemaker, which typically provides a narrative of authenticity rather than a formal résumé of credentials and accomplishments.[25] This is generally consistent with a vast literature that links the evaluation of a cultural good to the identity of the producer.[26]

Audience members may be similarly influenced by other social factors, such as the members' social position, their interactions with past adopters, and the original producer's status.[27] Indeed, a long line of diffusion research suggests that the narrative about an object's previous adopters, rather than just that of the original producer, may be critical information in understanding that object's meaning and value. Because the identities of both the originator and the adopter influence the meaning of what is adopted, it is important to consider both identities in the narrative that authenticates certain exemplars. To return to the example of Loretta Lynn, it is not just her story but also the story about who performs her music (e.g., Tammy Wynette and Emmylou Harris) that help establish Loretta Lynn as an authentic representative of country music. Here again, it is not the characteristics of the music per se but the identity of the music's previous adopters (and the narratives that correspond to that identity) that influence its appeal to future audiences.

Methodologically, it is important to consider the temporal pattern of these relationships as it relates to the narrative that develops.[28] With respect to identities and categories, this suggests the need to examine not just the combinations but also the ordering of original producer and adopting identities when evaluating and categorizing an object. Thus the focus on the temporal order of identities of the actors involved in the origination and early adoption of jazz relates to a developing narrative—an adoption narrative—about jazz. I draw attention the patterns of the identities of the originator and the early adopters (from 1920 to 1929) and then take the perspective of late adopters (post–World War II) who authenticate particular identity patterns as they selected songs to record in creating a discographical jazz canon.[29]

JAZZ AS AN ADOPTION NARRATIVE

Jazz music—even compared to other genres—is characterized as among the most difficult to categorize especially without deep regard to its historical roots.[30] While some argue that the canonization of jazz received increased attention after World War II (when it became more regularly part of university curricula), the makeup and boundaries of jazz continue to be under debate even today.[31] Nevertheless, it is important to note that the post–World War II period was one in which a more collective and corporate effort was under way to construct and solidify the market for recorded jazz.[32]

The ongoing debate on the proper definition of jazz can be traced in key newspaper and musical trade magazines in the 1920s.[33] The focus of these definitions varied widely: the choice of instruments and arrangements of the music, the presence of a particular rhythm, the type of dancing, the presence of vaudeville-like humor and animal noises, innuendo, improvisation, the presence or absence of a melody, and so forth. Jazz was even defined with respect to sexual abnormalities and drunkenness.[34] Indeed, during this period there were several competing definitions of jazz.[35] Consistent across many of these debates, however, was the issue of musician race, which allows us to define identities along racial dimensions as well as identify the developing racial narrative around the authenticity of jazz and the order-of-adoption approach I advocate here.

Key to the racial narrative is no other than Paul Whiteman, who has often emerged during my research of the various puzzles presented in *Shaping Jazz*. Recall (from chapter 3), for example, the 1930 film *The King of Jazz*.[36] The film, a musical starring Whiteman (as the King of Jazz) and his orchestra, was a showcase for the elite's representation of how jazz *should* be performed. In addition, the film shows how jazz was "created" by Whiteman to entertain wild animals and natives (the film's representation of the music's actual originators) as he traveled to "darkest Africa" to go big-game hunting.[37] The racism in the film is obvious but not unusual for this period.[38] The point I want to emphasize is the extent to which the film promotes the narrative of an evolving music, one that began as pure but "primitive" (lowbrow) and emerged as "civilized" (highbrow) and thus broadened its appeal through the involvement of those (in this case, white musicians) who are explicitly distinct from the originators. This film was a key component of the effort to establish Whiteman as the primary representative of jazz to the upper and middle classes.

Although the data later in this chapter show that the "lowbrow-to-highbrow" sequence was not the most common one (we will soon see that the most common sequence was black musicians covering songs originated by other black musicians), it was the most salient and distinct sequence and certainly the key race sequence narrative captured on film and in print. Moreover, these attempts to "refine" jazz have become embedded in our implicit understanding of jazz, such that the refinement motif in early jazz discourse would ultimately make salient the tunes and songs that featured a lowbrow-to-highbrow early adoption pattern.[39]

CAPTURING THE REFINEMENT ADOPTION NARRATIVE

I distinguish dimensions along which the adoption narrative of early jazz was arrayed using data on jazz recordings to speak directly to the puzzle motivating this chapter: the racial sequence of the originators and the early adopters. In addition, other elements of the originator's authenticity are brought into focus with these data to tackle this chapter's puzzle, such as the record company of the initial recording and the venue that the originating musicians were associated with.

Important to the setting is the fact that jazz's origins have always been linked to Africans and their descendants in the United States—whether that depiction was positive or negative. Although jazz's racial origins have from time to time been up for debate, Africans and African Americans have typically been viewed as jazz's authentic originators.[40] In contrast, white musicians in early jazz were more often seen as adopters who broadened and "morally uplifted" jazz music. A pattern of black originators and white early adopters (BO-WA) helped establish the legitimacy of songs and tunes through this lowbrow-to-highbrow narrative.[41] This BO-WA pattern of identities positively influenced appeal, but there are alternative explanations that needed to be addressed with the research design and control variables. For example, white musicians may have had greater economic resources and power, which would have affected both the commercialization of the music as well as its narrative. Moreover, white jazz musicians may be understood more as generalists to the extent that they were more often associated with multiple genres outside of jazz, which potentially made jazz more appealing to a broader and diverse audience group. However, supplemental analyses showed that alternative explanations such as these are not well supported by the results. This gives me greater confidence that the main claim is true: all else equal, songs originated by black musicians and adopted early by white musicians (the BO-WA pattern) were more likely to enter the jazz canon than were songs that resulted from other racial combinations of originators and early adopters.[42]

To the extent that the lowbrow-to-highbrow narrative encompassed more than just race, the BO-WA pattern should be associated with long-run appeal only under certain conditions—such as when other signals of a song's authenticity (consistent with the narrative) are present. Here we consider two indicators that should affect the authenticity of a song's lowbrow-to-highbrow narrative: (1) whether the company that originally recorded the song was affiliated more with lowbrow music than with highbrow music; and (2) whether the group that originally recorded the song was associated with locations and venues that played lowbrow forms of jazz more than highbrow forms of jazz. To be clear, the key argument is that recordings did not benefit from the race-based (BO-WA) pattern if the black originators recorded at record companies known for being more high-brow oriented (Victorian-era firms) or that were associated with highbrow venues (hotels). In these cases, the recordings would be seen as violating the lowbrow-to-highbrow narrative. This leads to a second prediction: the BO-WA pattern was weaker for songs with additional inauthentic indicators (type of record company, group's association with a venue).

A NOTE ON THE DATA

In order to estimate the effect of sequences, the sample of original recordings was restricted to those that had at least one adoption after the original recording but before 1943.[43] This restriction leads to 244 sequences with complete data.[44] Each sequence was then coded for the early pattern of adoption by examining the race of every originator and adopter before 1943. An originator is defined in terms of recording, that is, the identity of the musician or group that first recorded a tune. This captures the actual seeding of the discographical canon and is consistent with the notion that jazz identities and reputations are driven more by (recorded) performances than by composer credits.[45]

Fifty-seven percent of the sequences were racially homogeneous, and the remaining 43% were mixed. Beginning with this mixed-race subset, we initially examined each sequence individually. After an extensive investigation and much misplaced excitement around coding every possible racial sequence combination,[46] it turned out that modeling more detailed sequences produced no greater model fit than simply modeling whether a piece of music originally recorded by one race was ultimately recorded by groups of another race. This resulted in a simpler typology of four possible sequences: black originators with white early adopters (BO-WA); black originators with black early adopters (BO-BA); white originators with white early adopters (WO-WA); and white originators with black early adopters (WO-BA).

In addition to examining the role of Victorian-era versus jazz-era firms, I also looked at the venue musicians were associated with. I posited that audiences incorporated information on a recording's origins when assessing its value. However, cities do not easily separate into highbrow and lowbrow with respect to jazz, in part because cities, especially U.S. cities, typically were locales of both highbrow and lowbrow music. However, within this point of within-city variance lies a key insight. One way that a group would signal an association with more highbrow clientele in any city would be by being affiliated with a hotel.[47] Groups such as Jack Chapman and His Drake Hotel Orchestra were seen as catering to more middle- and upper-class clientele, playing a symphonic form of jazz that had relatively less improvisation and a level of syncopation that was otherwise associated with jazz. Scholars have debated whether a hotel band should actually be considered a jazz group (even when the members of the group were separately seen as jazz musicians), as the emphasis was often more on the ability to read music than on other aspects such as improvisation.[48] Moreover, groups that played in hotels often did not include instruments that were thought to be too aurally dynamic, typically avoiding brass instruments (trumpets and trombones were key instruments in the form of jazz popularized by Louis Armstrong, the Original Dixieland Jazz Band, etc.), and were more likely to have a symphonic jazz sound. Indeed, t-tests revealed that groups publicly affiliated with a hotel were less likely to have trumpets or trombones ($p < .01$). Thus the BO-WA pattern should weaken substantially when the original group was associated with a hotel, making it less attractive for future adoption because it would have violated the lowbrow-to-highbrow narrative. This variable was constructed by examining the name of the group for each recording for the term "hotel." The statistical models also take into account any effect of being associated with a hotel that is independent of the race of the originating group.

RESULTS

Table 6.1 presents the proportions of the four types of originator and early adopter sequences. One key observation is that the BO-WA pattern is not the most frequent pattern. In fact, the BO-WA pattern is the *least* common pattern (16% of cases). This would be puzzling if one were predicting that the most frequent pattern from the early period had the greatest long-run impact. But this is not a story of future musicians seeking to re-record the most prevalent adoption sequences of early jazz. In fact, if we were to simply look at the prevalence of patterns before World War II, we would conclude that the prototypical sequence would be BO-BA (all black), which resulted in 40% of all of the pre–World War II patterns in the sample. However, the narrative surrounding the BO-BA sequence was not as salient in the discourse in newspapers and other publications as the BO-WA sequence despite the respective difference in the frequency of recordings.

The regression results showing that the BO-WA pattern had the greatest long-run appeal are displayed in Figure 6.4 (see Kahl, Kim, and Phillips 2010 for the full models). The figure illustrates the relative impact of the four patterns (with

TABLE 6.1. Proportions of the Four Types of Originator and Early Adopter Sequences

Pattern of originators and early adopters	Proportion
All black	.40
White originators, black early adopters	.27
All white	.17
Black originators, white early adopters	.16

N = 244 recordings

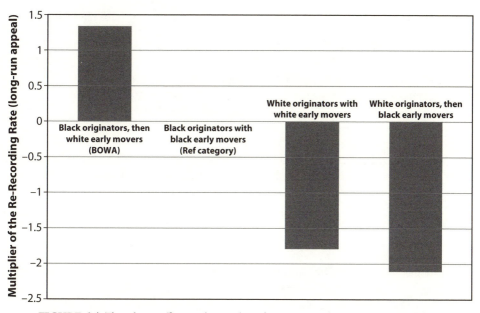

FIGURE 6.4. The relative effect on the number of times a recording was re-recorded from 1943 to 2004.

black originators and black early adopters as the reference category). The results show that BO-WA songs had the greatest likelihood of entering the jazz canon through greater long-run appeal ($p < .001$). *That is, despite the fact that the BO-WA pattern is the least common pattern in early jazz, it is the pattern with the greatest long-run appeal.*[49] Though only the BO-WA variable is statistically significant, the pattern of results is interesting in its own right. In particular, the WO-BA pattern (white originators with black early adopters) is associated with the lowest long-run appeal, as this pattern represents the clearest violation of the lowbrow-to-highbrow narrative. In addition, the WO-WA pattern has a reduced long-run impact (it is statistically less than the BO-WA pattern but not statistically different from the BO-BA pattern). White early adopters of songs originated by whites were less appealing to post–World War II musicians.

The long-run effect of the BO-WA sequence is positive net of a host of control variables that I have used throughout the book. For example, the short-run commercial success and appeal to musicians are included in the model so that the long-run effect is net of any short-run differences that can be caused by fads, unobserved marketing efforts on behalf of the firms, and so forth. These models also controlled for characteristics of the original recording group such as its productivity and experience in order to capture the possibility that the adoption narrative mechanism is not confounded by differences in the skills of each group. Each group's size, instrumental combinatorial uniqueness, proportion of female members, and use of vocals were also coded. The models also included variables to capture the stylistic identities of originators and early adopters (whether or not they were "orchestras") to ensure that we properly identified the effect for race independent of the style of music the group was associated with. The controls for the groups were complemented by controls for the marketing efforts and geographical location of the firms. All of the models also included fixed effects for individual record companies, the city of recording, and year.

Even with these controls, one might wonder if songs that were restricted to the community of black musicians (the reference category) were somehow deficient in their access to resources that led to interest from wider audiences. However, if this were an outcome that associated race with available economic resources, then we would expect the white originator-white early adopter (WO-WA) pattern to be positive and statistically significant as well. However, this is not the case. In robustness checks where the BO-WA variable was simultaneously entered with a covariate for whether there was a white early adopter (independent of the race of the original group), the BO-WA remained statistically significant. In these same models, the independent effect for white early adopter was positive but not statistically significant, reinforcing my contention that the BO-WA effect is robust. Given this, the results suggest that equally successful songs in the short run had very different long-run outcomes when we examine the identity sequence by race.

The test of the second part of the prediction—that the effect for the BO-WA pattern would be erased when other aspects of the initial recording violated the authenticity of the lowbrow-to-highbrow narrative—used interaction effects with the same control variables as in the previous analyses. This narrative should suffer when the original recording was with a Victorian-era firm or when the original group was affiliated with a highbrow venue. Figure 6.5 illustrates the interaction effects across the models, showing that a positive BO-WA effect *required* that originators had other authentic characteristics ($p < .01$). Figure 6.5 highlights the fact that the positive BO-WA pattern drops substantially when the initial recording was done by a Victorian-era firm or when the original group was associated with a hotel. These were violations of the lowbrow-to-highbrow narrative and led to lower long-run appeal. The figure reveals the fact that the findings are about more than the straightforward role of race. Every BO-WA pattern was not associated with long-run appeal; only those that truly signaled authentic origins (from a jazz-era firm, not associated with a hotel) were successful.[50]

ALTERNATIVE EXPLANATIONS

This chapter advances the understanding of how jazz was shaped in a couple of key ways. First, a recording's evaluation was shaped by the identity-oriented combination and sequence of that recording's originators and early adopters. Specifically, this research suggests that when a sequential pattern of identities is consistent with

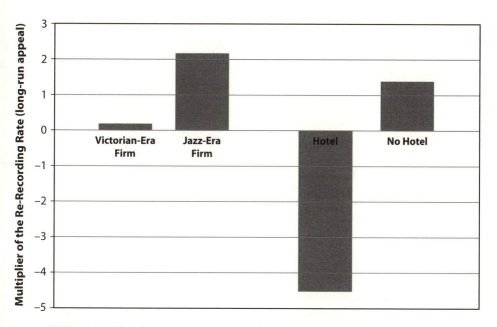

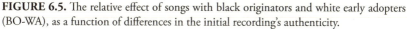

FIGURE 6.5. The relative effect of songs with black originators and white early adopters (BO-WA), as a function of differences in the initial recording's authenticity.

a narrative, the pattern is more authentic (and salient) to later adopters and thereby influences category formation. This emphasizes a new mechanism and unit of analysis: the pattern of adopters and their identities rather than just the identity of the originators or the most recent adopter (a common approach in network diffusion studies).[51]

Second, this chapter suggests a potentially fruitful means of capturing the standards, practices, and conventions that provide the building blocks of genres as categories in cultural markets. The identity of originators and early adopters helped shape the content of the jazz canon, where jazz recordings with fully authentic narratives were more likely to be widely accepted.

In exploring the pattern of early adoption in 1920s jazz, the evidence suggests that a BO-WA adoption pattern became more relevant than other patterns in defining a category because it best matched a dominant narrative. Other patterns, even when represented more frequently, were not reified in our discourse and collective memory. For example, the WO-WA sequence, suggesting a highbrow-to-highbrow pattern, fared poorly in comparison, as it lacked a supporting narrative.

As I did in other chapters, in this chapter I sought to address several alternative explanations during this study. For example, one may argue that the BO-WA pattern may indeed represent two distinct economic characteristics of long-run appeal: quality and market size. Patterns that combine races (WO-BA and BO-WA) increase market reach across segments, so the quality of songs is the only factor that affects long-run appeal. This account suggests that in the short run, status and quality may be less correlated; thus short-run appeal, measured by the total number of adopters and early commercial success, may result from the status of early adopters at the time. However, over time, the discrepancy between status and quality may lessen (due to reduced racism, greater black power, etc.). Thus long-run appeal is more likely to reveal a recording's intrinsic quality.

This explanation is problematic for three reasons. First, the empirical evidence does not support this alternative since there was no supporting evidence that the race of the originator by itself predicted long-run appeal. So if the original songs of black artists were somehow better but suppressed in the short run, we should still see an independent effect of music by black originators after World War II. However, there was no such effect. Second, if we assumed that the songs by black musicians were inherently of higher quality (independent of whether they were originators or early adopters), then the patterns featuring black musicians as both originators *and* early adopters might have strong effects. Again, there was no such effect.[52] Finally, despite the fact that there are several control variables to proxy quality differences between groups and songs (early success, group recording experience, etc.), the results emerge nonetheless.

Another explanation for the long-run appeal of the BO-WA sequence is that this pattern may capture a directional effect of endorsement. A white musician's endorsement of a black musician's song might have been perceived as status enhancing by audience members (e.g., future musicians as well as customers), whereas a black musician's adoption of a white musician's song might have been viewed as status degrading. This explanation provides a complementary mechanism to understand how such role identities came into place. Because they were less often associated with 1920s mainstream white culture, low-status black musicians could have been viewed as unique and original with respect to jazz whereas high-status white musicians could have been perceived as providing a status-enhancing endorsement because they were perceived as (more legitimate) members of the mainstream. Thus two different role identities stem from the different social positions of the two racial groups. More generally, white musicians may have been better positioned to interpret or increase the coverage of black music than black musicians were. If white musicians were deemed more highbrow, they could overcome the typical lack of trust for boundary spanners.[53] In addition, white musicians' re-recordings of black musicians' songs may have had more favorable media coverage because of critics' preference and/or personal connections to them, which could have had a positive imprinting effect on long-run success.

The problem with this explanation is that it privileges white early adopters over the overall BO-WA pattern and interaction effects. For example, this alternative theory of white early adopters as endorsers does not take into account the pattern of interaction effects in Figure 6.5. That is, this alternative explanation does not clearly predict why the BO-WA pattern is *negative* when the originating group is associated with a Victorian-era firm or a hotel. In other words, the findings suggest a penalty when white adopters follow black originators associated with a hotel, a finding that does damage to a "white adopter as endorser" explanation.

At the same time, this points to a limitation of this chapter's analysis. Ideally, one would have finer-grained data on the identities of the late (post–World War II) adopters. That is, I am implicitly assuming that white late adopters and black late adopters are similarly attracted to the BO-WA pattern independent of the late adopter's race, though I doubt that is truly the case. My worry here is tempered, however, by the fact that I am indeed picking up the songs that became part of the discographical canon, which suggests that I am picking up the behavior of the post–World War II musicians of both races who were actively recording; music can only achieve great long-run appeal by being re-recorded by a diversity of musicians.

IMPLICATIONS FOR THE SHAPING OF JAZZ

This final empirical chapter combines the focus on organizations from chapters 4 and 5 with the emphasis on locale and reception in the first three chapters using the concept of the adoption narrative. Jazz was shaped by differences not only in what firms produced but also in how that production informed a "primitive-to-refined" narrative. In many ways this narrative was self-reinforcing. Not only were there real constraints on Victorian-era firms to record and market recordings by black musicians (especially black non-orchestras), but this also would work against the narrative of authenticity as a form of incongruence. Jazz was shaped by a narrative consistent with a particular ordering of identities at the recording group and record company level. The discographical canon should be disproportionately filled with songs that align with this narrative, independent of their "quality."

This chapter also allows an added interpretation of the role of Paul Whiteman. We have seen that Whiteman and other white musicians greatly affected the discographical canon. However, their effect was not necessarily in terms of the recordings they pioneered but in terms of the original recordings of black musicians they re-recorded. Those they did not re-record fell to the wayside, as did the music of white musicians who re-recorded music by white originators. It was the rarest combination (16%) of white musicians adopting songs originally recorded by black groups that won the day. For someone like Whiteman, it was his inauthenticity as an originator that helped qualify him for the role of early adopter.

The irony is that songs and tunes can have long-run appeal even if the identities of the adopters do not. In this way Whiteman and his peers shaped the discographical canon even though they themselves came to be seen by many as outside the canon. The disparaging views they articulated about refining "primitive" music from the African jungle had the unintended long-run consequence of not only making the original recordings more salient but making the refinement advocates increasingly less legitimate as representatives of jazz.

More generally, if the reasoning of this chapter is correct, the exact subtype of a song is (partially) inferred by who replicates that song. When a white musician re-recorded a black jazz originator, audiences altered their interpretation of that recording as well as that of the originator and adopter. When the Rolling Stones covered the songs of blues musicians (e.g., Bo Diddley, Muddy Waters), audiences' evaluations of the blues tunes were altered. I would also argue that many audiences modified their evaluation of the blues musicians that the Rolling Stones and others covered. Today, when jazz musicians cover the music of someone like Kurt Cobain (of Nirvana), audiences alter their understanding of the quality of Cobain's music and the genre in which he and the jazz musician should be placed.

This chapter's findings also suggest that even adoption sequences of geographic markers may affect long-run appeal, a point consistent with my findings in chapter 2. Indeed, after completing this chapter I returned to the data on geography used in the first half of this book. From that, two interesting results arose. First, it turns out that the greater a city's disconnectedness, the more likely its music was re-recorded in a city high in centrality. Second, a disconnected-to-central intercity adoption pattern led to higher appeal compared to all other patterns, followed by a central-to-central intercity adoption pattern. The other possible adoption patterns were not statistically significant. And although those findings on geography were consistent with this chapter's findings on race, the statistical models for geography often did not converge, leading me to not lift these results to the level of those in this book's main analyses. Still, the pattern is consistent with the lowbrow-to-highbrow findings, and I hope that it helps fuel future research on adoption patterns.

Chapter 7

PULLING IT TOGETHER AND STRETCHING IT BEYOND

There are a million good tunes.

—MARIAN MCPARTLAND (MUSICIAN, COMPOSER)

"Star Dust" [considered by most to be a jazz standard]
rambles and roams like a truant schoolboy in a
meadow. Its structure is loose, its pattern complex. Yet
it has attained the kind of long-lived popularity that
few songs can claim. What has it got? I'm not certain. I
know only that it is beautiful and I like to hear it.

—OSCAR HAMMERSTEIN II (1985)

Many consumers, performers, and students of jazz would agree with McPartland that there are a "million good tunes." Of course only a small fraction of the "million" represents the market for jazz music as jazz standards, as tunes that are somehow disproportionately appealing. Moreover, as the second epigraph suggests, defining and understanding why a particular tune is worthy of being a standard (having the highest appeal), simply based on the tractable or observable features of that tune, has led many gifted scholars down intellectual rat holes. This book is about understanding which tunes had disproportionate long-run appeal based on the congruence of social cues, which gave a dynamic structure to jazz as a market category. In particular, *Shaping Jazz* is about the role of geography and organizations in determining which of those "million" have shaped jazz through their ascension into the discographical canon of recordings.

Throughout this book I have used the end of each chapter to summarize my insights on how geography and organizations shaped jazz. I culminate that exercise here. I begin with a general discussion based on the findings of my empirical work and then use this discussion to draw out generalizations and scope conditions of my overall findings. This will help me discuss contexts outside cultural markets where my ideas should be informative, such as the markets for nanotechnology, green energy, and software—all of which are the types of markets that will figure prominently in the foreseeable future of the U.S. economy. As a final matter, I will consider the example of bottled water that set the stage for this book.

PULLING THE EMPIRICS TOGETHER TO UNDERSTAND
THE MARKET FOR JAZZ AS A TRAJECTORY

When I was in the middle of writing this book, trying to grapple with the best way of communicating my research project, I was fortunate to have a transformative discussion with a luminary in sociology (who also happened to be a jazz musician). As I "sat at his feet," we had a rich discussion on the evolution of jazz over the twentieth century. I remember it as a wonderful romance of jazz and the various styles through which it has evolved.

Well, at least up to a point. Our intellectual love-fest with jazz stopped short when we got to jazz fusion—the electronic-influenced form of music that emerged in the 1960s but achieved broader attention when Miles Davis released "Bitches' Brew" in 1970. It was immediately clear that my colleague found jazz fusion very unappealing, and truth be told, it is not particularly appealing to me either. However, before we could bond over our mutual distaste for jazz fusion, I decided to try an explanation motivated by my research. I asked him whether he thought jazz fusion was bad *because* it was labeled as jazz or was jazz fusion something he inherently disliked. This led him to pause and, I believe, realize that what he had coded as inherently bad was actually something he saw as a misclassification of jazz.[1]

I'm not a fan of jazz fusion, but what I truly dislike is the genealogical derivative of jazz fusion: "smooth jazz." Many of the pioneers of smooth jazz (e.g., Kenny G) emerged from jazz fusion groups.[2] Although there are various types of smooth jazz, it is a form of music that is often characterized as instrumental versions of popular songs of the day, with improvised solos after a chorus or two of the tune is played. Often the accompanying instrumentation is programmed, although is this is not always the case. Of course, I can't claim that smooth jazz is inherently bad, and some smooth jazz musicians can play as well as (or better than) traditional jazz musicians. The problem for me as a fan (but not an academic) is that it is called "jazz" in the first place. Indeed, *Shaping Jazz* suggests that we will remember smooth jazz as jazz to the extent that (1) it is marketed and sold as jazz by commercial interests; (2) the mass consumer comes to view it and purchase it as legitimate jazz; (3) tunes or styles originated by smooth jazz musicians are re-recorded over time by musicians who are themselves classified as jazz musicians (similar to the way that Miles Davis helped legitimate jazz fusion); and (4) social cues such as smooth jazz's organizational or geographic sources serve a larger narrative that bolsters its legitimacy. To the extent that these things happen, not only will smooth jazz be considered as legitimate jazz, but our understanding of jazz will be reshaped.

I hope this does not happen, but this book project has taught me that not only is such an outcome well within the realm of possibility, but there is already evidence of the four criteria I just outlined. Here is one way that we will know for sure: anthologies of jazz in the year 2100 would include people like Kenny G alongside Armstrong, Goodman, Parker, Davis, Coltrane, and Marsalis—as painful as it sounds to present-day ears. It is also possible that Kenny G will fall outside most academics' definition of jazz—similar to Paul Whiteman—but still be a pivotal figure in jazz evolution.[3] Indeed, as ethnomusicologist Chris Washburne notes, Kenny G already "assumes significant definitorial role in popular conceptions of what jazz is."[4] Years from now Kenny G may very well be understood as a key figure in understanding the evolution of jazz. I, on the other hand, as a detractor, might then be included in the long and unflattering list of naysayers across the decades who clung to the past too long, hoping for the non-inclusion of new forms of jazz.

When a consumer or musician evaluates a piece of music, there are a range of factors that are taken into account, one of which is how the work is framed or categorized. In *Shaping Jazz* I argue and provide evidence that information about the origin and history of a product is often very important in the evaluation process. Evaluating products using ahistorical and myopic theories or perspectives, or that only take into account information in a snapshot of time, will often lead one astray when attempting to categorize or otherwise evaluate that product. This is why when looking at the long history of the market for jazz music, Kenny G's relevance must be taken seriously in discussions of the canon.

In *Shaping Jazz*, I have emphasized the initial geographic and organizational sources of music, as well as the role identities of its adopters. This is not because I think key individual innovators are irrelevant but because we already know a lot about them. The greater gaps in our understanding include the locales where music emerged and the commercial interests that produced the music and ensured its position in the collective identity of our market-oriented society. Moreover, the intellectual gaps in our understanding of cultural markets are not just on the production side (Did different locales or firms produce different music?) but often lie on the perception and reception side (Do we hear and experience the same music differently depending on the locale or firm associated with it?). What I offer is a way to think about geography and organizations in markets like the one for jazz recordings.

PULLING TOGETHER THE ROLE OF GEOGRAPHY

The first three chapters of *Shaping Jazz* focus on the role of geographical origins in the long-run appeal of recorded jazz. While there is substantial work on music "scenes," this work has often emphasized the unique outputs of particular locales and then examined the evolution of the genre from that perspective. Many of those studies are rich and informative. However, the first half of *Shaping Jazz* draws attention to the reception of cultural products and how this reception is a function of the geographical origin independent of the production or supply-side characteristics. If you recall my obsession with water in the introductory chapter, I suggested that the same water might taste different if I thought that its source was upstate New York or New Zealand. The first three chapters suggest that the same jazz tune or song is heard differently depending on its origin and that this difference in reception depends on congruence: whether there is something strange or difficult to classify about the music. So, strange-tasting water from an unusual place tastes better than the same strange-tasting water from a traditional source. A strange sound is more appealing if I know that the source is a disconnected place. A jazz opera sounded better and more authentic when it was associated with Austria and Germany than an earlier French work by Ravel that could have been just as easily classified as a combination of jazz and opera.[5] In this way, the first half of the book shows how this congruence with respect to geography can affect the reception of music independent of its actual production.

In chapter 1 I showed that the appeal associated with geographic origins (captured by the location's disconnectedness) had important implications for the shaping of jazz. Disconnectedness (rather than centrality or isolation per se) mattered because of the congruence of social cues around the context of production and could only be properly understood by focusing on difficult-to-categorize music. For example, given the value of novelty often attributed to jazz, one might guess that using rare instruments would be advantageous in terms of the success of the recording. Indeed, jazz has been often associated with contesting its own boundaries with music featuring difficult-to-categorize innovations. However, I found that the appeal of this type of recording was largely contingent on the identity of its source. A recording with rare instruments, for example, had a greater long-run appeal but *only* when the source was also unusual (i.e., highly disconnected). Otherwise, that same tune was left on the sidelines of history. Particularly important is the fact that all of the evidence points to a stronger reception- (or demand-) side story rather than a production- (or supply-) side story. Cities high in disconnectedness were *less* likely to produce difficult-to-categorize music; most of the recordings in these cities were devoted to replicating the style and music of more connected cities. However, whenever difficult-to-categorize music happened to be produced in highly disconnected cities, only then did that music have an amplified long-run appeal to those outside that city. Members of the jazz community disregarded recordings that were unoriginal or were already stylistically legitimate when they were from a disconnected source. My findings suggest that we may be overstating the inherent uniqueness of particular scenes. Often special musical scenes are products of perception, not production.

What became clear during the research for *Shaping Jazz* is that for congruence to be a useful construct one needs to understand the perspective of the receiver, including the schema and scripts they employ. I believe that disconnectedness was important because cultural markets are the type of context where the social information of nonexistent relationships is as valuable to members of a social system as the relationships that do exist. Moreover, when relationships capture social distance, disconnectedness influences notions of distinctiveness and exoticism. This concept of disconnectedness is quite helpful in understanding the emergence of the discographical canon, but it also provides a link from a social structure of production to a social structure of reception and reorients attention toward normative versus non-normative actions and characteristics.

Chapter 2 emphasized that mobility-based centrality was associated with objects and elements that were original but within the accepted category system. Within the emergence of the discographical jazz canon, the primary role of cities high in centrality—such as New York—was as places where music was arbitrated, legitimated, and constructed as jazz. Much of this had to do with the relatively high concentration of musicians and their audiences that resided in the highly central locations. However, the role of highly central cities was also influenced by the fact that they were the chief locations of the recording infrastructure (especially the music recording studios). I found that successful music from disconnected sources seemed to follow a three-stage diffusion pattern: (a) emergence from a disconnected source; (b) early adoption by musicians in central cities; (c) a geographically broad diffusion.

Chapter 2 also drew attention to the role of geographical mentions, whether in the title of the music or the name of the group. Either type of mention enhanced that music's appeal, especially when the source was high in disconnectedness. Music from disconnected sources had greater appeal when there was a geographic mention, although the type of geographic mention (e.g., how localized the mention was) did not seem to matter. The evidence suggests that geographic mentions made the actual geographic origin of the music more salient. When that origin was high in disconnectedness, the added salience of the original location increased the music's appeal.

Early German jazz (chapter 3) provided a unique opportunity to explore a case that did not seem to fit my model to better refine my thinking. We saw how the identity of a location affects how music is perceived, integrated, (re-)produced, and interpreted as an export. Germans experienced early jazz through the rich classical lens of German musical culture, but the music was also performed by musicians steeped in Germany's musical tradition and recorded within an industrial infrastructure that was second only to that of the United States.[6] The result was the production of jazz that was exceptional in volume and narrow in terms of style (but not lower in quality). Simply put, Germany produced a lot of symphonic jazz. And although New York City was also an active source of symphonic jazz, it was more fundamentally the source of multiple and diverse styles of jazz. In contrast, the recordings from Berlin rarely deviated from the symphonic form. Today we discount this music because it has moved from the center to the periphery of the market for jazz. Or, to be more exact, jazz was reshaped in a way that placed symphonic jazz at its periphery. Among the implications is that there is a positive association between the diversity of the subtypes of jazz a locale sustained and the likelihood that the city was prominent as jazz evolved.

PULLING TOGETHER THE ROLE OF ORGANIZATIONS

The remaining empirical studies (chapters 4–6) focused on sociological congruence and how firm actions influenced the canon of recorded jazz. Chief among my insights is that Victorian-era firms' recording decisions were motivated by a need for identity preservation and that this need drove decisions on the type of music that was made available in the marketplace as jazz. That is, individual firms chose recordings that aligned with their identities. When one considers that the long-run appeal of a product is a function of a firm's imputed identity, the result was music that was shaped by record companies' attempts to negotiate the constraints of their position in identity space with its opportunities in product space. In other words, jazz music from record companies that were perceived as legitimate was more appealing but only when the characteristics of the music were congruent with the record company's identity.

For example, chapter 4 demonstrated that recorded jazz was shaped by the efforts of Victorian-era firms (and the cultural elite) to officially establish jazz as a hybrid of symphonic music ideally performed by white (Anglo) Americans, as well as by the actions of jazz-era firms that expanded recorded jazz with non-orchestral African American groups and more innovative music. While on average black non-orchestral recordings had appeal, the chief representative of jazz to most of the (white) purchasing public was Paul Whiteman, the exemplar of symphonic jazz. My research suggests that Victorian-era firms and groups like that of Whiteman were critical for understanding which tunes became jazz standards, as the decisions they made as to what to record drew more attention to some songs and tunes than others, with real consequences for the canon. In short, the sheer output and marketing of the larger and better-connected Victorian-era firms ensured that their actions (such as re-recording the music of other firms) would have a substantial long-term impact on recorded jazz and the songs that came to represent that canon.

Chapter 5 continues the discussion of Victorian-era firms, demonstrating how they used pseudonyms as a means of deception to preserve their organizational identity. Victorian-era firms faced a dilemma, given that their organizational identity was associated with records that were more costly and less appealing in the marketplace. One of their solutions was to produce the music of black non-orchestras that were more appealing to the consumer but use pseudonyms for these groups and thus understate their association with them, as Victorian-era firms' association with black non-orchestral groups would have called into question the moral high ground of such firms. The renaming itself was strategic, as it often involved creating new names that signaled a more highbrow form of jazz (e.g., "orchestra"). Victorian-era firms also used pseudonyms when their position in the market was made ambiguous through the actions of jazz-era firms. The more difficult it was to distinguish the position of Victorian-era firms, the more likely they were to deceive through pseudonyms.

Chapter 6 uses the idea of adoption narratives—an explanation or symbol of jazz's origin and its ontology—to link the idea of congruence to that of shaping jazz. The point of adoption narratives is not so much about the "accuracy" of the narrative but on the narrative's salience to the relevant audience. Thus, although the "lowbrow-to-highbrow" narrative was not the most common adoption sequence, it was associated with the greatest appeal, just as the appeal of the jazz opera from Germany was not the type of jazz most frequently produced in Germany (in fact, jazz operas were rare). The key lesson is that adoption narratives that produced the greatest appeal may not have reflected the most common sequence.

Chapter 6 also returned to the role of locale that was the focus in the first three chapters, but the locale was couched within the concept of the adoption narrative. Adoption narratives help explain or symbolize a category's origin and its ontology as authentic. Parallel to the pattern of disconnected-to-central city diffusion uncovered in chapters 1 and 2, chapter 6 also draws attention to the lowbrow-to-highbrow pattern of BO-WA. Here the role of central cities is similar to that of white early adopters in that their influence on the canon was not necessarily in terms of the recordings they pioneered but which original recordings they rerecorded. For someone like Whiteman, it was his inauthenticity as an originator that helped qualify him for the role of early adopter—albeit with no intention of creating a canon that musicians, consumers, and critics today use to organize jazz. This is why I believe that whether a tune ultimately "belongs" in the canon is partially inferred by who replicates it, as well as by the manner in which they replicate it. It is also how I see jazz as shaped through an iterative process of production and reception.

STRETCHING IT BEYOND TO UNDERSTAND AMBIGUOUS MARKET CATEGORIES AND MARKET IDENTITIES

I see the market for jazz as having similarities with other markets where novelty is rewarded. To the extent that value is driven by novelty and quality is difficult to objectively determine, social cues around the context of production become critical in assessing meaning (*What is it?*) and value (*How much do I like it?*). Constructing the meaning and value of jazz is impossible without social cues, and congruence is one way in which social cues are organized and represented. But this is not unique to jazz. Take, for example, three market categories: nanotechnology, green technology, and software.[7]

One characteristic of these ambiguous market categories is that they are ones in which typicality is not very meaningful and boundaries are porous. The criteria for categorical membership are not only dynamic but can be driven by endogenous processes where the actions of current members or new entrants shape firm, product, and labor market identities. What is also obvious about these types of categories is that they are technologically oriented settings where innovativeness tends to be sought after and rewarded, which affects the ambiguity around categorical membership.

You would be hard-pressed to find a common or consistent indicator of a firm or product's membership in these market categories. Answering the question "What is nanotechnology?" for example, presents some of the same challenges as answering "What is jazz?" Explaining the categories of software or green technology is not any easier. For example, the *Financial Times*, a publication that engages investors and other market participants, defines green technology as "an umbrella term encompassing the investment asset class, technology and business sectors which include clean energy and environmental, sustainable or green products/ services. . . . The term should be differentiated from cleantech, although often used interchangeably, since cleantech generally refers to the emerging financial industry."[8] Nanotechnology is a similarly ambiguous market category, as Granqvist, Grodal, and Woolley note:

> The most widely adopted definition of nanotechnology refers to the control of matter between approximately one and 100 nanometers. . . . This definition is, however, contested and unclear, which has resulted in a wide spectrum of existing research and development activities being bundled together under the same label . . . incumbents from industries ranging from sporting equipment and textiles to drug delivery, semiconductors and photovoltaic devices, have become labeled as nanotechnology even though many have only a marginal or even tenuous link. (2012)

This broad definition makes it very difficult for categorical membership to be determined and runs the risk of the rendering the category meaningless. Often the political process of accounting for diverse constituencies provides little opportunity to coalesce around particular organizational forms and product characteristics. From a market category perspective, one problem with these kinds of markets is that they constitute multiple technologies, products, and services similar to the way that jazz encompasses multiple styles and instruments. As a result, we are left with a diverse array of products and organizational subtypes that are a source of ambiguity to audience members.

At the same time, categorically ambiguous markets can be fertile sources of technological and conceptual creativity where innovations and labels more easily arise, including instances where new categories can be invented without immediate backlash in part because there are fewer normative constraints.[9] Take, for example, "green nanotechnology," a hybrid created by the U.S. Environmental Protection Agency (EPA) when they concluded that they needed to better understand the human and environmental effects of the growing but ambiguous field of nanotechnology, which led to establishing a project with the National Nanotechnology

Institute around 2005. The goals of green nanotechnology tend to be expressed with respect to the production of solutions, such as to "produce nanomaterials and products without harming the environment or human health" and to "produce nanoproducts that provide solutions to environmental challenges."[10] One of its early goals was to "identify what is and what is not 'green' in nanotechnology."[11]

While this hybridization may appear to be an opportunity for cynics and parody (consider "nano jazz" or "green jazz" as new combinations of ambiguous categories),[12] I believe that this is better seen as an instance of two innovation-oriented categories having sufficient ambiguity that their combination can spark entrepreneurial opportunities with the potential for great appeal. Here is how Barbara Karn, an EPA scientist and early advocate for green nanotechnology, opened a talk to material scientists in 2006:

> [I]magine yourself just being a material scientist when somebody asks, "Well, what about this material? Is it toxic?" "Are you protecting yourself in the laboratory just in case it is?" "What if it gets out?" "Is it going to kill the fish?" "Is it going to bioaccumulate, so that in the end we get some harmful effect, because we've eaten that fish?" It's a little bit different way of thinking. But we need each other. We need people who are very good at making and characterizing materials and also people who can say, "Maybe we should look at whether these are dangerous or not?" And in making the materials, there may be better ways—this is where the "Greenness" comes in—that you can make them. You have the expertise in materials, and then you can make them in a way that they would not be harmful, if we design them right in the first place. (Karn 2006)

Moreover, whereas it is difficult to find consistent definitions of what it means to be "green" or what nanotechnology means, their combination need not share that same level of ambiguity. For example, I was struck by three things when reviewing several reports, scientific and popular articles, documents from university labs, new venture announcement of product releases, and a new journal called the *International Journal on Green Nanotechnology*: (a) there is a consistent—albeit broad—definition of green technology; (b) the definition was controlled by a limited number of influential actors—such as the U.S. government, American Chemical Society, and the Pew Charitable Trust; and (c) green technology is often framed as a solution to the frustratingly slow and uneven emergence of nanotechnology, in that orienting nanotechnology around "greenness" unites the technological, financial, and political forces in ways that larger, more ambiguous categories have been unable to.[13] A larger lesson for me, however, was that the combination of ambiguous categories need not share the ambiguous nature of the "parent" categories while retaining many of the opportunities embedded in each category.

This is important because it points to one way that convergence and solidification of category meaning can occur. Otherwise, it is not at all clear that markets like nanotechnology or green technology can survive under increasing ambiguity that continuously erodes category boundaries.[14] It is not unusual for emerging markets to have ambiguity, as many scholars have pointed out in markets such as those for automobiles, telephones, computers, and hedge funds.[15] But usually the ambiguity around the typical representation of the category diminishes. In fact, there are strong reasons to believe that this reduction in ambiguity is consistent with the stability and success of these markets.[16] So far nanotechnology and green technology do not appear to have trajectories toward categorical clarity, leaving one to ask whether market categories such as these have long-run viability. Will they collapse under the weight of ambiguity and go the way of other short-lived markets that collapsed, such as the ones for artificial intelligence or disk arrays?[17] The worry then is that given the empirical evidence from organizational scholars, nanotechnology and green technology would have a more difficult chance of survival.

And yet jazz has persisted for decades as an ambiguous, dynamic, and porous market category. And it is not alone. The software industry has persisted as an ambiguous category as well.[18] How is it that the criteria for categorization are ambiguous but at the same time persist? How do some market categories avoid collapsing under the weight of ambiguity? In considering the market for jazz recordings alongside other markets categories I have noted here, some commonalities do appear and suggest an avenue for better understanding the persistence of these types of markets.

Instead of typicality (the most common or average representation in a market), the market for jazz (and, to a lesser extent, software) has often coalesced around a changing set of exemplars or luminaries. I believe that most consumers of jazz music orient their understanding of the genre around a set of famous tunes, musicians, or record labels. Tunes that were big hits or flops became points of reference, as did very (un)successful musicians, especially when they were not "typical." In chapter 1 we learned that even though disconnected cities were more conformist on average, we disproportionately rewarded the relatively few unique and difficult-to-categorize recordings that emerged. Consider Figure 3.5, which maps cities and exemplars by the instrumentation used on 1929 recordings. Although we might think of someone like Duke Ellington or Paul Whiteman as representing music from New York, it turns out that they are atypical. Louis Armstrong, for example, is not typically Chicago, where all of his early recordings were made. Chapter 3 also pointed out that although the jazz opera represented German jazz, the music most often produced in Germany was symphonic jazz. In chapter 6 I demonstrated that although music consistent with the primitive-to-refined narrative had the highest appeal, these were not the most frequent adoption patterns. These are all examples of rare types that became exemplars. In some cases other market participants followed and conformed to the exemplars, but at the time of their initial market success they were not typical. They may appear typical retrospectively if our biased recollection leads us to conjure groups that sounded like them. But this is often a result of acts of post-rationalization.

More generally, I believe that markets like jazz persist when the market is continuously reshaped by successes that become the exemplars that the market can organize around. In this way a successful IPO can (re)define or (re)shape a market, where our evolving understanding of the market may rise and fall with the fate of the exemplar. That said, the unfinished work here is to better understand the factors that lead to these successes in ambiguous market categories. One reason why exemplars are so important to my formulation is because of my emphasis on *what sells for jazz*, rather than the universe of jazz in all of its manifestations. I would even go further to say that I privilege the role of commercialized jazz in affecting our understanding of the genre, even though it omits important performances that were not captured through recordings and elevates those market participants with social, political, and economic resources.[19] Beyond jazz, I am suggesting that at the end of the day, the market categories for nano or green technologies may not be understood in technological terms, as least as first-order effects. Rather, these technologies (or their combination) might instead be understood in terms of their early big commercial successes or failures. Then these successes, as exemplars, will be used to reinterpret and rationalize these market categories more coherently around a sociologically congruent narrative.

Jazz, software, bottled water, wine, restaurants, and many other settings involve categories for which social cues are important (e.g., "Silicon Valley startup"); the salient cues for nano or green technology may differ, but I expect that they will eventually arise if these categories are to persist. Moreover, sociologically congruent narratives are critical to understanding the longevity of the ambiguous categories, even if the narrative is completely retrospective. It is similar to Duncan Watts's conclusion about how we understand the value of the *Mona Lisa*, which he reaches using arguments and evidence from historians that it was a piece of art that was much less regarded until a compelling narrative involving national identity emerged.[20] However, once it achieved its stature as great art, reinterpretations of its quality became partially decoupled from its history, leading Watts to conclude: "It sounds as if we're assessing the quality of a work of art in terms of its attributes, but in fact we're doing the opposite—deciding first which painting is the best and only then inferring from its attributes the metrics of quality" (2011, 58–59).

Work on software as a market category has also identified that some markets persist despite being difficult to define.[21] In software, for example, there are constant influxes of new entrants (often pursuing high risk–high reward ventures). This can happen in emerging markets, of course, but persistence requires that new entrants continue to flood the market even past the early stage of emergence,[22] where ambiguity is associated with relatively low barriers of entry. For example, in software, nanotechnology, and green technology markets, a wide variety of technologies compete and combine to obtain social and economic resources. Moreover, the ambiguity of the market category is attractive for new entrants to the extent that the identity and the meaning of its products are malleable. Again, software is a useful example. Here venture capitalists are attracted to new ventures since they have latitude in framing the purpose and actions of the new ventures without the same constraints and sanctions that accompany more rigid and rule-bound categories.[23] Thus, not only might the initial barrier to entry in ambiguous categories be low, but as the market shifts the ambiguity allows a new entrant more freedom to modify its identity and in some cases influence the identities of its competitors.

STATUS AND MARKET IDENTITIES

Much of *Shaping Jazz*, especially the latter half of the book, focuses on the market identities of firms, how audiences influence firm actions, and the dimensions along which organizational and artistic innovation could take place. And although there is substantial published work on the role of status in markets,[24] I have been cautious in anchoring my theory around the role of status. Much of the work on status and market behavior theorizes and tests in markets that are in equilibrium (mature markets) or where status is derived from actors with stable identities. This is well reasoned since a setting typically requires an articulated status order.[25] In addition, the tastes and behavioral norms are often fixed such that audiences have a set of stable criteria to evaluate firm offerings. Neither of these characteristics—a robust status order or fixed tastes—exists in an emerging cultural market.

This does not mean that the many insights from scholarship on status in markets cannot find resonance within *Shaping Jazz*, but it does mean that the status dynamics are often more nuanced. For example, chapters 4 and 5 suggest a form of high-status conformity where Victorian-era firms publicly avoided associations with lowbrow jazz to the point of producing symphonic jazz and deceiving through the use of pseudonyms. In these cases higher-status firms were seeking to demonstrate their commitment to their core audience: the cultural elite.[26] At the same time, there were aspects of the early jazz market that do not find easy parallels in previous work on status in markets. One big difference is that the entire market was in a dynamic state, where its very structure was endogenously driven and constantly reshaped by the actions of the market participants. In other words, the actions of firms were altering the entire category of jazz during and after the 1920s in powerful but often unforeseen ways. Audiences and their tastes were equally unstable, and this, too, added to the dynamic character of the market. So while past work on status in markets applies to the market for early jazz, its applications are limited, but limited in a way that can fuel deeper theorizing.

The challenge for more expansive work is to understand what a theory of status and conformity in markets—or more generally what a theory of market identity—looks like in emerging or dynamic markets where many of the sociological or economic tools available are underconceptualized.[27] I believe that a key component to more developed thought is recognizing that market identities, just like the categories, typically have strong path dependence and that status orders and the positions within them are among the emergent properties that coalesce as social organization occurs. In these settings, audiences dominate to the extent that they are in agreement and firm actions are easy to observe. Either way, the decisions by audiences are among the factors that shape the category in ways that are rarely anticipated in nascent markets. As a result, future research should proceed on two fronts. First, we would be well served by focusing on the construction of status orders and market identities in emerging and transitioning markets as processes rather than on the consequences of status orders and market identities in stable markets. This is no easy task, but it is already happening. Indeed, the goal of understanding market and categorical emergence is at the forefront of the work of many organizational and economic sociologists, such as Howard Aldrich, Patrik Aspers, Glen Carroll, Lis Clemens, Neil Fligstein, Mary Ann Glynn, Mark Granovetter, Michael Hannan, Kieran Healy, Donald MacKenzie, Doug McAdam, Victor Nee, John Padgett, Laslo Polos, Woody Powell, Wes Sine, and David Stark. Second, I believe that we need to have more room for exploratory empirical and inductive work so that we can also ask, "What do the data say?" rather than only ask, "How well do the data support our arguments?" While I like both of these questions, I favor the more exploratory approach when dealing with the subject of emerging markets. In *Shaping Jazz* I have attempted to place a stronger emphasis on the former over the latter, or at least to balance the two, and to leave a greater focus on deep theorizing for grander theorists.

ASSIGNING PRODUCTS TO CATEGORIES

I believe much of the work in *Shaping Jazz* can shed new light on markets in general, bolstering the work of scholars who have come to understand that markets cannot be understood without modeling audiences as active participants.[28] Too often audiences are seen as passive recipients or actively monolithic evaluators that receive a producer's offerings and evaluate whether the offerings apply to the category. But my findings combined with other work on the role of market intermediaries suggest that in markets like jazz at least two other factors matter. First, the audience itself is not simply admitting offerings into a focal category but *actively assigning* offerings among categories. When I see a penguin I not only say that a penguin is not a fish but actively assign it to the category of bird. Second, assignments by audiences shape the boundaries of categories. When I say that a penguin is not a fish but a bird, my assignment can simultaneously alter the coherence and boundaries of the categories for fish as well as those for birds. This process of assignment not only shapes markets but ultimately affects whether that market will ultimately survive. And while one person assigning penguins is one thing, a set of diverse (and sometimes disparate) audiences assigning cultural objects or cutting-edge technologies can lead to complex and ambiguous categories. Moreover, the active assignment in markets like jazz can create instances where the producer's intentions can be decoupled from the categorization and evaluation process—such as when artists are labeled as jazz artists against their wishes.

Recall that this process of active assignment occurred with the labeling of *Jonny Spielt Auf* as a "jazz opera" in chapter 3 even though Ernst Krenek, the opera's composer, opposed that categorization. Also consider a more recent example: trumpeter Olu Dara's response to a question in 2000 by *Jazz Weekly*'s editor-in-chief, Fred Jung.[29]

> FRED JUNG: Did you ever consider yourself as being a jazz musician?
>
> OLU DARA: No, I never called myself that. I never considered myself that. . . . That name was put on me. I used to laugh when they called me that. I said, "My God, I'm not a jazz musician at all." . . . I felt that the other stuff I was playing was much more important than the jazz I was playing.
>
> FRED JUNG: So who is Olu Dara?
>
> OLU DARA: A musician/songwriter.

Indeed, even musicians now regarded as jazz greats, such as Sarah Vaughan feel that this categorization has been assigned to them against their wishes. As she noted in a May 1982 *Down Beat* magazine interview, "I don't know why people call me a jazz singer, though I guess people associate me with jazz because I was raised in it, from way back. I'm not putting jazz down, but I'm not a jazz singer. . . . I've recorded all kinds of music, but (to them) I'm either a jazz singer or a blues singer." To her point, in the introduction I discussed listening to Sarah Vaughan as something that was instrumental in my understanding the jazz canon. The song that so moved me was a recording in the 1973 *Smithsonian Collection of Classic Jazz* of "It Ain't No Use," a tune known and recorded much more often as a blues song. But I initially only knew it as a classical jazz tune because the collection assigned it as such.

The active assignment of Dara and Vaughan parallels the findings by nanotechnology scholars Granqvist, Grodal, and Woolley. These scholars find that some entrepreneurs have been labeled as nanotechnology firms despite their wishes. According to one entrepreneur they interviewed: "I remember the first time we got invited to this [nanotechnology] conference . . . and I said to our VP of marketing at that time, 'I really don't know that we want to be associated with this stuff, honestly' . . . and they gave awards out to the five firms most likely to succeed, and [my firm] was one of them."[30] My argument here is that this active assignment, though it can occur in a number of settings, will be a much more central process in markets characterized by ambiguity. A growing number of organizational and economic sociologists believe that ambiguous markets arise and thrive if their ambiguity lowers the barriers of entry in such a way that a diverse array of forms can classify themselves—or be classified by others—as members of the respective category. Not knowing what a typical member of a category is gives entrants and audiences a great deal of leeway, which creates an endogenous process whereby increasingly diverse entrants shape the meaning of the category.

STRETCHING IT TOO FAR: SOME LIMITATIONS AND WHERE THE CONTEXT OF PRODUCTION MATTERED LEAST

There are some facets of jazz that do not easily extend to other markets. For example, jazz is oriented around exemplars as well as the discographical canon in a way that serves as a point of coordination between actors. That is, while the nanotechnology and software industries may rely on exemplars to evaluate organizations and products, these settings do not (yet) have a direct equivalent of a canon that allows entities to coordinate. Thus jazz as a market category uniquely benefits from path-dependent references to past tunes and styles. This gives jazz a dimension along which social organization occurs, one often not seen elsewhere. One can certainly imagine a similar parallel in the use of patents in many settings, but software, nano, and green technologies are sufficiently ambiguous as categories that a unifying technical compass appears to be more elusive.

Another point to keep in mind is that my study is on the market for jazz *recordings*, not on jazz in its entirety. Although I believe that the market for jazz is a substantial force in understanding the structure and meaning of jazz overall, it is unwise to try to extend my findings to the performances of jazz that were never recorded. Unrecorded jazz likely represents a much more diverse set of performances than I can contemplate with my data on actual recordings. To give the most salient example of how the study of recorded jazz is different from the study of jazz in its entirety, consider the fact that jazz began in New Orleans but that none of these early performances was recorded. Instead, Chicago and New York City are the birthplaces of recorded jazz. Thus, although the discographical data on recordings are the most comprehensive documentation of recorded jazz, capturing jazz in sixty-seven cities on five continents through 1933, I captured music where there was an infrastructure and demand sufficient enough to facilitate recordings. This is, of course, a common curse of archive-based research, but it is potentially dangerous in a study of cultural markets when there is substantial evidence that underground (noncommercialized) cultural scenes are often authenticated on the basis of how their music is distinguished from commercialized music.[31]

Finally, there is a more extended limitation that also points to some new insights. As I alluded to in chapter 2, one of my discoveries is that most of my models that explain the long-run appeal of jazz recordings have greater explanatory power before the 1960s than after the 1960s. This is not shocking for at least two reasons. First, it is intuitive that models predicting the success of music from the 1920s and early 1930s would have less predictive power the further one went into the future. Second, it is well-known that the 1960s was a period of social and

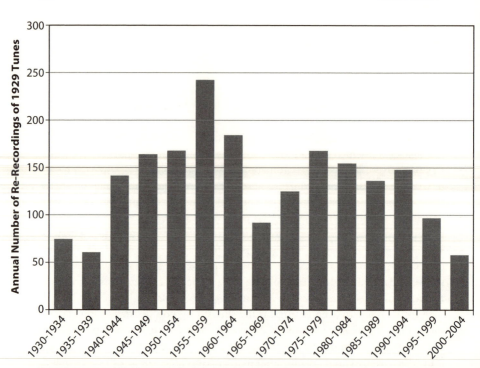

FIGURE 7.1. Annual number of re-recordings (appeal) of all songs/tunes originally re-corded in 1929 ($N = 189$).

cultural transformation in the United States that altered both the production and the reception of many cultural forms.[32] In particular, the 1960s was a period in which jazz was associated with countercultural and antitraditionalist movements and in which many musicians were pursuing "jazz beyond jazz,"[33] suggesting that much of the music of early jazz might have been set aside as too backward looking or might even have been viewed as contentious. Indeed, this transformational period in U.S. history meshes in interesting ways with my data and findings. Consider Figure 7.1, which shows how often, over time, jazz music originally recorded in 1929 was re-recorded by other artists—what I have used as my measure of appeal throughout this book. For example, from 1990 to 1994, jazz songs and tunes originally recorded in 1929 were re-recorded about 150 times. I selected 1929 because it was a peak year of production, but a look at other years in the 1920s and early 1930s produced patterns similar to those shown in Figure 7.1. The figure shows that 1929 jazz recordings were re-recorded at an increasing rate until mid-century (with big jumps in the early 1940s and late 1950s) until they dropped substantially in the 1960s. Then after a rise in the 1970s the re-recordings decreased again. It's a bimodal distribution.

It turns out that my statistical models do a much better job of predicting re-recordings before the 1960s (the first "hump") than after the 1960s. It is not that people were not re-recording 1929 jazz after the 1960s; they clearly were. Rather, the reasons why they re-recorded after the 1960s less often had to do with the concepts and mechanisms I have discussed in *Shaping Jazz*. To be clear, my model estimates are statistically significant for my post-1960s data but to a diminished enough degree (and with a poorer model fit) that I find it more accurate to state that *Shaping Jazz* is much more a story of the early period (the first "hump").[34]

In some ways this is gratifying, as it matches my intuition that the further one gets from 1929 the less likely factors in the 1920s and 1930s drive results, although I would have expected a gradual decline if that was all that was going on. The bimodal distribution is different, and I have at least three explanations for it. First, jazz took a major turn stylistically in the 1960s, mirroring a transformation of American culture, with the rise of free jazz and experimental music by artists trained as jazz musicians. For my purposes, a relevant component of this change was a cultural rejection of the past. It was less legitimate for a musician to re-record a 1920s tune instead of recording an original one. For example, the Association for the Advancement of Creative Musicians (AACM), the musical component of a larger social movement in the 1960s, notes that its members were very thoughtful about creating "original" music that was a clear break from tradition.[35] Here "original" meant not necessarily rejecting the tradition of jazz outright but combining it with other genres and styles of music, which substantially decreased the value of tunes and songs from the 1920s and early 1930s.

My data suggest that earlier movements and musical "revolutions" in jazz (e.g., bebop), though thoughtful about creating new music, emerged using the music that preceded it as a reference point to a greater degree than did musicians in the 1960s. One way in which this was done was by taking familiar music—such as jazz first recorded in 1929—and playing it in new ways. As musicologist Scott De-Veaux argues, "Charlie Parker and Dizzy Gillespie . . . were not trying to disengage from the 'commercial' music world so much as to find a new point of engagement with it" (1997, 17). As DeVeaux notes, the avenue for the point of engagement was largely rooted in instrumental virtuosity and improvisation, and was less about abandoning the tunes themselves. The 1960s, by comparison, were more about playing new music in new ways. It was quite consistent for a bebop-era musician to record a jazz tune from the 1920s like "I Got Rhythm," but this would have been much less normative during the 1960s.

Second, demographically, the number of key musicians of the late 1920s and early 1930s and their audiences would have been much smaller by the 1960s. The Jazz Age community was getting older by this time, and some of the appeal of their music likely diminished as musicians and their fans passed away. Table 7.1 gives a sense of this timing. The first column in the table lists some of the most well-known artists of the 1920s (listed alphabetically by first name), a group I selected based on my knowledge of the history. Then I located each artist's date of

TABLE 7.1. Birth and Death Dates of Early Jazz Luminaries

Artist	Birth	Death
Bennie Moten	1894	1935
Duke Ellington	1899	1974
Earl Hines	1903	1983
Fats Waller	1904	1943
Fletcher Henderson	1897	1952
Francis "Muggsy" Spanier	1906	1967
Frank Trumbauer	1901	1956
Isham Jones	1894	1956
Jean Goldkette	1893	1962
Jelly Roll Morton	1885	1941
Johnny Dodds	1892	1940
Leon Roppolo (NORK)	1902	1943
Louis Armstrong	1901	1971
Merritt Brunies	1895	1973
Nick LaRocca (ODJB)	1889	1961
Paul Whiteman	1890	1967
Ted Lewis	1892	1971
William McKinney	1885	1969
Average (median), rounded to nearest year	1896 (1895)	1959 (1962)
Average (median) of 192 musicians on www. redhotjazz.com	1905 (1905)	1955 (1960)

birth and death. The most important aspect of the table is the fact that the average date of death for all the artists is 1959 (the median date is 1962). To help ensure that my selection was not biased, I consulted the most comprehensive online source of early jazz that I am aware of: the Red Hot Jazz Archive (www.redhotjazz .com). Their listing of individual jazz artists includes 192 musicians. The last row in Table 7.1 shows the average and median birth and death dates of all 192 artists. The numbers are slightly different than those I calculated (average date of death is 1955, the median is 1960), but the conclusion is not. Most of the artists were deceased by the 1960s. The musicians who were transforming jazz by the mid-1960s did so after the death of many of the early jazz pioneers.

The point here is only to suggest that the reason behind the bimodal distribution in Figure 7.1 was partially demographic, in that the passing away of the Jazz Age generation would have also affected the rate of re-recording the music of that period. The other side of this demographic point, also made by scholars like Faulkner and Becker,[36] is that the 1960s musicians were children who came of age during and after World War II, where their musical reference point would have been dominated by bebop and the explosion of recordings during the mid- to late 1940s. For these musicians (e.g., Eric Dolphy, born in 1928; Ornette

Coleman, born in 1930; Albert Alyer, born in 1936; Charlie Haden, born in 1937; and Freddie Hubbard, born in 1938), a recording from the Jazz Age would have been much less salient. Many of these musicians instead developed their skills by sitting in with bebop bands as teens. Their exposure to and interactions with the early jazz artists would have been less frequent and intimate, and accordingly their connection to that music would have been qualitatively different than that of earlier musicians. The connection to my model is straightforward: my key dependent variable was often the appeal of a recording captured by re-recordings made by fellow and future musicians. The data in Table 7.1 give rise to the possibility that the shift of the social and demographic organization of musicians altered the appeal either directly or indirectly by invalidating some of the underlying assumptions (e.g., that artists would have been familiar with the original context of production, the salience of geographic references, the impact of symphonic jazz, etc.).

The findings and implications of my work in *Shaping Jazz* are thus novel but limited. They seem to apply best to emerging markets and markets otherwise characterized by ambiguity around the meaning of categories and identities. My work matters less to markets where expected behavior is stable and captured coherently among audience members. Methodologically, my focus on the role of initial conditions has been effective, but I have been able to verify my conceptual model consistently only within a generation. I am elated by the fact that I can understand the appeal of a song for thirty years of dynamic sociopolitical activity (e.g., from 1925 to 1955), but even the strong factors that my models capture begin to falter with the generational turnover that accompanied the societal transformation of the 1960s.

One of the most significant points of *Shaping Jazz* is that perception and reception are often more powerful than we recognize and can powerfully relate to geographic and organizational identities, as well as other aspects of the context of production. The process of researching this book has shaken my confidence in production- (or supply-) side models of market behavior. The production side obviously matters and is the best approach in many markets. But in many more markets that are increasingly common in Western societies, modeling the audience side as actors that construct meaning and value is something that will become increasingly important. Moreover, this is not just a matter of asking whether particular social cues signal meaning or value; cues should be considered in conjunction with the context of production (the producer, location, etc.), as well as whether they fit into narratives. To put it simply, I believe that more markets have features of the market for jazz than we realize in our world in which the structure, strategy, and operations of the industrial age still dominate (and potentially cloud) our thinking. I believe instead that we should be attempting to understand other newer markets—like that for bottled water—where determining quality is elusive when the focus is on production-side attributes.

AN EPILOGUE: BACK TO BOTTLES OF WATER

I began this book with my unusual fascination with water, but one more piece of personal history will enable us to come full circle. My interest in bottled water is rooted in a conversation I had over two decades ago when a prescient friend told me that the U.S. market for bottled water would someday be large and profit-able—where people would pay a dollar for a bottle of water. I was incredulous. But now, if you stop by my office you may be subject to an informal taste test. In one of my desk drawers, hidden from view, I have a stash of different bottled wa-ters with labels that claim to represent several countries and refer to a number of sources: mountains, volcanoes, glaciers, underground, vapor, and so forth. I have a much better appreciation for how this market works, but over two decades ago I could not understand why someone would spend a dollar on something that was "free." After all—and here comes the mistake I made—isn't the water all the same?

By now I hope you see that the response to this question could (and, in a sense, did) take an entire book to write. However, the question would have to be asked in a more specific way. For example, from the production side one can ask whether types of bottled water are chemically different across brands or when compared to a generic tap water. The answer is often, but not always, yes. Several of the ten or so bottles of water in my drawer taste a little different from one another. It is a separate question altogether about assigning values to those differences in terms of "taste" or appeal. "Taste" is a function of perception and familiarity as much as differences on the exact composition of the water. In fact, I see it as matching my use of the word "appeal" when I talk about successful jazz recordings. I do not know if differences in composition make a drink of water any more or less inher-ently better than whether differences in instrumentation, country of origin, or the race of the musicians make a jazz recording any better or worse.

The Internet is awash with water taste tests, nearly all of which are unscientific, and most individually are unconvincing as they are constructed more for enter-tainment than academic advancement. That said, the aggregate evidence is com-pelling as nearly every taste test or study supports the idea that not only are taste differences hard to perceive but perceptions of tastes are easily manipulated. It is as if we are all in on the joke—except that not only do many of us drink bottled water daily but we have our favorites, those for which, for us, define what good water should taste like.

Take, for example, a water-testing prank conducted by comedians Penn and Teller on their television series for Showtime:

> The hosts began with a blind comparison in which 75 percent of New Yorkers preferred city tap to bottled waters. They then went to the Left Coast and set up a hidden camera at a trendy southern California restaurant that featured a water sommelier who dis-pensed elegant water menus to the patrons. All bottles were filled out of the same hose

in the back of the restaurant; nevertheless, Angelenos were willing to plunk down nearly $7 a bottle for L'eau Du Robinet (French for "faucet water"), Agua de Culo (Spanish for "ass water") and Amazone ("filtered through the Brazilian rain forest's natural filtration system"), declaring them all to be far superior to tap water. There's no accounting for taste.[37]

Here is what happened when the waiter offered the "Amazone" water:

> WAITER: "Amazone is *filtered* by the Brazilian rainforest's natural filtration system . . . [and] has one of the oldest creatures from the Amazonian Rainforest placed in the bottom of the bottle, the Brazilian spotted arachnid [a big black spider is located on the bottom of a bottle of tap water] . . . it actually adds to the medicinal qualities of the water."
> [AFTER tasting the water, the customers gave their assessment.]
> CUSTOMER A: "I just thought it was fresher . . . it felt purer."
> CUSTOMER B: "Ok, I can taste the difference on this one."
> CUSTOMER C: "Definitely taste the minerals, it is a harder water."

Of course the point of the prank is that all of the water tasted by the customers came from the same source: a water hose in the back of the restaurant. But to me, the more interesting issue is not how people fall for the gag but that I and everyone who watched the gag can also have clear preferences for one type of water over another. Moreover, my interest as an academic is not so much whether one particular water tastes better than another but rather what the forces are that might shape our understanding of what good and typical water is. For me, the compositional differences are a concern only when they serve a congruent narrative. Even if I can detect differences in the taste of various bottles of water, narratives and congruent social cues help order those differences.

Shaping Jazz suggests that the marketing and packaging of different bottled waters influence our notion of what is good (or appealing). One of the things that draws us in is the congruence of the product's narrative. For example, if I can alter a water to taste "cooler," it will sell better if I tell you it is from a glacier. I am interested in which narrative will be more compelling ("healthy," "natural," "local," "green," or some combination) and whether that narrative becomes dominant enough that it ultimately shapes how we think of water. I'm not interested in which water will "win" but in the process that leads to the win.

This book is more about how jazz was shaped than about the particular songs that constitute the shape. I have focused on the forces that organized an ambiguous market and provided structure to it despite the fact that it is defined by improvisation, experimentation, perpetual originality, and paradigm-destroying innovation. It is a genre that celebrates iconoclasts as models to emulate. And yet it has organizing conventions that prevent it from dissolving. I have focused on these conventions (jazz standards or the discographical canon) that organize the market for jazz. I am not so much interested in which recordings became standards, even when the appeal of the recording was my dependent variable. Instead I have sought to examine the how and the why rather than the what.

I believe my discoveries are largely right. But time will reveal where I came up short, and years from now I might look back and see misinterpretations. My hope, however, is that I have been successful in my effort to produce a compelling work that is methodologically and conceptually solid enough to build upon by refining what I have found or (even better) taking my insights to places well beyond what I am currently able to envision. There would be no greater reward for a kid who decades ago opened up his parents' jazz collection and found out that the liner notes and credits were as fascinating as the music itself.

Appendix

TABLE A.1. Descriptive Statistics for Data

	Mean	S.D.	Min	Max
Worldwide[a]				
City-level long-term appeal of songs	89.74	266.08	1	2892
City effective size centrality	1.07	2.16	0	14.93
City structural disconnectedness	1.59	0.58	1	2.885
City is network isolate	0.60	0.49	0	1
Number of recording sessions in city (divided by 1,000)	1.09	3.70	0	44.21
Number of recording groups that never left city	9.96	29.64	0	213
Log (# songs city was first mover on)	1.33	1.11	0	4.77
Log (songs produced worldwide)	5.48	1.57	0	6.63
Entering city	0.01	0.11	0	1
Exited city	0.01	0.08	0	1
Midwest[b]				
Long-term appeal of the recording	30.66	102.1	1	1561
City effective size centrality	3.4	2.27	0	7.14
City structural disconnectedness	1.2	0.2	1	2.25
City is network isolate	0.16	0.36	0	1
Rare instruments used on the recording	0.13	0.34	0	1
Group name signals clear music style	0.39	0.49	0	1
Sexual reference signaled ("jelly" in the title)	0.01	0.08	0	1
Short-term appeal of the recording (# of pre–World War I re-recordings)	1.21	0.7	1	11
Pre–World War I commercial success of the recording (# of reissues)	3.06	2.2	1	24
Produced by a Victorian-era firm	0.53	0.5	0	1
Firm-level annual count of *New York Times* ads	6.28	11.07	0	181
Firm was one of largest four	0.35	0.48	0	1
Recording in record company headquarters	0.06	0.24	0	1
Size of recording group	6.65	3.82	6.75	3.82

TABLE A.1. (*continued*)

	Mean	S.D.	Min	Max
Midwest[b] (*cont.*)				
Instrument combinatorial uniqueness	195.4	26.57	157.2	291
Group's first recording	0.42	0.49	0	1
Group records in multiple cities	0.21	0.41	0	1
Total number of recordings to date by the group	10.15	13.22	1	87
Recordings per date by the group	3.15	2.64	0.2	24
Group has female members	0.31	0.46	0	1
Group members are white	0.29	0.45	0	1
Group has a designated leader	0.2	0.4	0	1
Group has a designated arranger	0.05	0.21	0	1
Group was only assembled for recording (does not perform as a group)	0.01	0.11	0	1
Group labeled as a "band"	0.05	0.23	0	1
Group name has a geographical reference	0.15	0.36	0	1
Recording has vocals	0.51	0.5	0	1
Average degree of centrality of group's musicians	148.9	65.68	0	220
All members recording for first time	0.01	0.7	0	1
Recording was first take	0.68	0.47	0	1
Group name features person's (leader's) name	0.85	0.35	0	1
Recording title has one word	0.05	0.21	0	1

[a]$N = 331$
[b]$N = 1,752$

TABLE A.2. Random and Fixed-Effects Regression Using Worldwide Data on a City's Recordings to Predict Long-Term Citation Count (Appeal) of Original Songs Produced in That City

	City random effects	City fixed effects	Fixed effects, without isolates
City effective size centrality	.01 (.03)	−.003 (.03)	−.01 (.04)
City structural disconnectedness	.38 (.21)*	.48 (.23)*	.82 (.32)**
City is network isolate	.34 (.14)**	.41 (.15)**	
Number of recording sessions in initial city (divided by 1,000)	.02 (.01)*	.03 (.01)*	.03 (.01)*
Number of recording groups that never left city	−.00 (.002)	.00 (.002)	−.003 (.003)
Log (number of songs city was first mover on)	.83 (.07)**	.80 (.08)**	.95 (.14)**
Entering city: no production in prior three years	.47 (.68)	.66 (.71)	
Exited city: no production in three years post	−.54 (.72)	−.69 (.73)	
Log (total songs produced world-wide)	.37 (.16)*	.36 (.17)*	−.19 (.21)
City and regional fixed effects	No	Yes	Yes
Year dummies	Yes	Yes	Yes
Constant	−2.48 (.49)**	−2.71 (.51)**	−.80 (1.15)
Log likelihood (df)	−1363.12 (37)	−1048.10 (37)	−461.70 (19)
N of cases	331	306	125
N of cities	67	42	20

Note: One-sided t-tests.

$*p < .05$

$**p < .01$

TABLE A.3. Results from Midwest Data on Recordings (1920–29): Negative Binomial Regression Predicting a Song's Long-Run Appeal from Date of Recording till 2005

	Model of main effects
City effective size centrality	.01 (.12)
City structural disconnectedness	1.07 (.58)*
City is network isolate	1.08 (.38)**
Rare instruments used	−.03 (.18)
Group's name signals clear music style	.70 (.16)**
Sexual reference signaled ("jelly")	1.10 (.49)*
Number of pre –World War II re-recordings	.74 (.10)**
Early commercial success	.21 (.03)**
Victorian-era firm	−.59 (.27)*
Firm-level annual count of *New York Times* ads	−.00 (.01)
Firm was one of largest four	−.06 (.34)
Recording in city of record company headquarters	.12 (.27)
Size of recording group	−.04 (.03)
Instrument combo uniqueness (logged)	−.00 (.00)
Group's first recording	.16 (.16)
Group records in multiple cities ("mover")	−.27 (.23)
Group's total number of recordings to date	−.01 (.01)
Group's recordings per date	−.01 (.02)
Group has female members	.43 (.20)*
Group members are white	1.18 (.20)**
Group has a designated leader	.53 (.28)+
Group has a designated arranger	.16 (.39)
Group assembled for focal recording ("accompanied by") only	−1.62 (0.69)*
Group labeled as a "band"	.25 (.28)
Group name has a geographical reference	−.42 (.18)*
Recording has vocals	−.09 (.15)
Average degree of centrality of group's musicians/1,000	3.41 (1.43)*
All members recording for first time	1.25 (.69)+
Recording was first take	.61 (.20)**
Recording title has one word	1.03 (.30)**
City dummies	Yes
Record company and label dummies	Yes
Year dummies	Yes
Constant	−5.42 (1.26)**
Log pseudolikelihood (df)	−5621.01 (50)

Note: One-sided t-tests; N = 1,752 recordings; robust standard errors (by 355 recording groups).
*$p < .05$
**$p < .01$

TABLE A.4. Interaction Effects for Figures 1.5a, 1.5b, and 1.5c from Midwest Data on Recordings (1920–29): Negative Binomial Regression Predicting a Song's Long-Run Success (Count from Date of Recording till 2005)

	Model for Figure 1.5a	Model for Figure 1.5b	Model for Figure 1.5c
City effective Size centrality	.03 (.12)	–.02 (.09)	.01 (.12)
City structural disconnectedness	.74 (.63)	1.69 (.54)**	1.08 (.58)+
City is network isolate	1.11 (.36)**	1.09 (.37)**	1.08 (.38)**
Rare instruments used	–3.22 (1.44)*	.03 (.18)	–.03 (.18)
Victorian-era firm	–.50 (.27)+	–.61 (.27)*	–.59 (.27)**
Group's name signals clear music style	.69 (.16)**	3.27 (.88)**	.70 (.16)**
Song title has "jelly"	1.10 (.49)*	1.07 (.49)*	7.25 (1.43)**
(Disconnectedness) × (rare instrument)	2.26 (1.20)*		
(Disconnectedness) × (group has clear style)		–2.21 (.73)**	
(Disconnectedness) × ("jelly")			–5.28 (.95)**
Controls from main model (Table A.3)	Yes	Yes	Yes
City controls	Yes	Yes	Yes
Record company and label controls	Yes	Yes	Yes
Year controls	Yes	Yes	Yes
Constant	–5.10 (1.30)**	–6.45 (1.20)**	–5.47 (1.26)**
Log pseudolikelihood (df)	–5618.09 (51)	–5615.79 (51)	–5620.41 (51)

Note: One-sided *t*-tests; N = 1,752 recordings; robust standard errors (by 355 recording groups)
*$p < .05$
**$p < .01$

TABLE A.5. Results from Worldwide Data on 1929 and 1933 Recordings: Negative Binomial Regression with Robust Standard Errors Predicting a Song's Geographical Spread till 2005

	Main effects for 1929	Main effects for 1933
Annually updated number of re-recordings (cumulative appeal)	.01 (.005)**	.02 (.005)**
City's effective size centrality	.18 (.23)	4.69 (3.83)
City's structural disconnectedness	43.55 (15.27)**	16.01 (12.75)
City is network isolate	1.03 (.41)*	2.94 (2.65)
Proportion of initial city's recordings that were original	−.73 (.38)*	−.25 (.60)*
City controls	Yes	Yes
Record company and label controls	Yes	Yes
Year and time trend controls	Yes	Yes
Constant	−57.38 (20.43)**	−47.26 (38.03)
Observations	14,362	8,208
Recording groups	189	114
Log pseudolikelihood (df)	−21,869.33 (43)	−11,479.85 (37)

Note: One-sided t-tests.
*$p < .05$
**$p < .01$

TABLE A.6. Results from Worldwide Data on 1929 and 1933 Recordings: Negative Binomial Regression (Zero-Inflated) with Robust Standard Errors Predicting a Song's Annual Appeal till 2005

	Model for Figure 2.3
The number of re-recordings of the tune in previous year	.09 (.02)**
Cumulative count of re-recordings to date	.002 (.001)*
Number of times song was recorded in cohort's initial year	.78 (.22)**
City's effective size centrality	−.19 (.04)**
City's structural disconnectedness	1.23 (.37)**
City is network isolate	−.42 (.21)*
Song title is not in English	.39 (.18)*
Song title has geographic reference	−.97 (.43)*
(Disconnectedness) × (title has geographic reference)	.58 (.33)*
Recording was part of 1933 cohort	−1.98 (.34)**
City controls	Yes
Record label controls	Yes
Year and time trend controls	Yes
Constant	−.92 (.54)*
Log likelihood (df)	−3041.26 (47)

Note: One-sided t-tests; $N = 22,661$ for 303 recording groups.
*$p < .05$
**$p < .01$

TABLE A.7. Results from Worldwide Data on 1929 and 1933 Recordings: Negative Binomial Regression (Zero-Inflated) with Robust Standard Errors Predicting a Song's Annual Appeal from Berlin and the Legitimacy of Paul Whiteman, Duke Ellington, and Louis Armstrong as Jazz Exemplars

	Whiteman	Ellington	Armstrong
Number of re-recordings of the tune in previous year	.09 (.02)**	.09 (.02)**	.09 (.02)**
Cumulative count of re-recordings to date	.002 (.001)*	.002 (.001)*	.002 (.001)*
Number of times song was recorded in cohort's initial year	.31 (.30)	.33 (.31)	.35 (.31)
City's effective size centrality	−.28 (.07)**	−.22 (.06)**	−.22 (.06)**
City's structural disconnectedness	.91 (.43)*	1.24 (.38)**	1.24 (.38)**
City is network isolate	−.43 (.21)*	−.44 (.21)*	−.44 (.21)*
Song title is not in English	.37 (.19)*	.38 (.18)*	.38 (.18)*
Song title has geographic reference	−.11 (.12)	−.10 (.12)	−.11 (.12)
"Paul Whiteman" with "Jazz" in *New York Times*	−11.74 (6.28)*	−10.28 (6.26)*	−10.41 (6.26)*
"Duke Ellington" with "Jazz" in *New York Times*	−8.63 (4.02)*	−8.23 (4.01)*	−8.68 (4.01)*
"Louis Armstrong" with "Jazz" in *New York Times*	17.66 (5.76)**	18.15 (5.76)**	18.39 (5.77)**
Original recording in Berlin	−1.40 (.79)*	.02 (.55)	−.11 (.55)
(Berlin) × ("Paul Whiteman" with "Jazz")	37.06 (17.82)*		
(Berlin) × ("Duke Ellington" with "Jazz")		−33.08 (13.18)*	
(Berlin) × ("Louis Armstrong" with "Jazz")			−26.40 (12.57)*
City controls	Yes	Yes	Yes
Record label controls	Yes	Yes	Yes
Year and time trend controls	Yes	Yes	Yes
Constant	−.45 (.59)	−.85 (.54)	−.86 (.54)
Log likelihood (df)	−2965.42 (48)	−2964.44 (48)	−2965.42 (48)

Note: One-sided *t*-tests; $N = 21,964$ for 303 recording groups.
*$p < .05$
**$p < .01$

TABLE A.8. Interaction Effects for Figure 4.3 from Midwest Data on Recordings (1920–29): OLS Regression Predicting a Recording's Innovativeness (Log of Instrumental Combination Uniqueness)

	Model for Figure 4.3
Victorian-era firm	.06 (.08)
Recording group is black non-orchestra	−.03 (.01)*
Recording group is white orchestra	.04 (.02)*
Recording made from 1920 to 1925	.12 (.04)**
Recording made from 1925 to 1927	.04 (.02)*
Recording made from 1927 to 1929	Reference
(Victorian-era firm) × (1920–25)	−.11 (.04)**
(Victorian-era firm) × (1925–27)	−.05 (.02)**
Song or tune was an original recording	−.002 (.007)
Proportion of market is jazz-era new entrants	−.13 (.07)*
New York Times mentions of "jazz" and "primitive" in previous month	.000 (.004)
No *New York Times* mentions of "jazz" and "primitive" in previous month	.05 (.07)
Individual instrument controls (piano, trumpet, drums, violin, etc.)	Yes
Other controls from Table A.3	Yes
City controls	Yes
Record company and label controls	Yes
Constant	20.07 (12.33)
R^2	.29

Note: One-sided *t*-tests; N = 2,343 recordings; robust standard errors (by 389 recording groups).
*$p < .05$
**$p < .01$

TABLE A.9. Logistic Regressions from Midwest Data on Recordings (1920–29): Predicting the Likelihood of Recording White Orchestras and Black Non-Orchestras

	DV = white orchestra (0,1)	DV = black non- orchestra (0,1)
Victorian-era firm	.85 (.28)**	–.67 (.27)**
Log (instrumental combinatorial uniqueness)	1.42 (2.32)	–3.47 (1.11)**
Song or tune was an original recording	–.76 (.23)**	.34 (.16)*
Proportion of market is jazz-era new entrants	3.05 (1.41)*	.79 (1.13)
New York Times mentions of "jazz" and "primitive" in previous Month	–.02 (.22)	.09 (.11)
No *New York Times* mentions of "jazz" and "primitive" in previous Month	.17 (1.57)	–.83 (1.04)
Other controls from Table A.3	Yes	Yes
City controls	Yes	Yes
Record company and label controls	Yes	Yes
Year controls	Yes	Yes
Constant	–40.58 (14.55)**	33.85 (10.05)**
Log likelihood (df)	–492.34 (44)	–1106.25 (44)

Note: One-sided t-tests; N = 2,343 recordings; robust standard errors (by 389 recording groups).

*$p < .05$

**$p < .01$

TABLE A.10. Interaction Effects for Figure 4.4 from Midwest Data on Recordings (1920–29): OLS and Logit Regressions Predicting (1) a Recording's Innovativeness (Log of Instrumental Combination Uniqueness); (2) Recording White Orchestras; and (3) Recording Black Non-Orchestras

	Instrument combination uniqueness (Figure 4.4)	Recording white orchestras	Recording black non-orchestras
MODEL	OLS	Logistic	Logistic
Victorian-era firm	.07 (.09)	.97 (3.92)	-2.04 (3.75)
Song or tune was an original recording	.01 (.01)	–.74 (.22)**	.38 (.16)*
Proportion of market is jazz-era new entrants	–.13 (.17)	19.95 (12.44)	3.59 (3.66)
Number *of New York Times* mentions of "jazz" and "primitive" in previous month	.002 (.008)	–.58 (.33)*	.15 (.13)
No *New York Times* mentions of "jazz" and "primitive" in previous month	.07 (.09)	–13.70 (5.92)*	–1.06 (1.74)
(Victorian-era firm) × (number of *New York Times* mentions of "jazz" and "primitive" in previous month)	–.01 (.005)*	–.11 (.10)	–.19 (.08)*
(Victorian-Era Firm) × (no *New York Times* mentions of "jazz" and "primitive" in previous month)	–.09 (.05)*	–.34 (1.49)	–.75 (.95)
Other controls from Table A.3	Yes	Yes	Yes
City controls	Yes	Yes	Yes
Record company and label controls	Yes	Yes	Yes
Year controls	Yes	Yes	Yes
Constant	4.83 (.36)**	–16.26 (22.52)	4.60 (21.04)
R^2	.24	—	—
Log likelihood (df)		–468.18 (56)	-1095.08 (52)

Note: One-sided *t*-tests; N = 2,343 recordings; robust standard errors (by 389 recording groups).
*$p < .05$
**$p < .01$

Notes

INTRODUCTION: SOCIOLOGICAL CONGRUENCE AND THE SHAPING OF RECORDED JAZZ

1. See the Lord Jazz Discography, which advertises 1,192,200 tune entries in its CD_ROM 11.0 version.

2. See Babon 2006; Cheyne and Binder 2010.

3. Bourdieu (1984) 2000; Lamont and Molar 2002, 168.

4. My emphasis is different from but partially inspired by a simultaneous reading of Zerubavel 2003 and Moretti 2005. See also Lena 2012 on creative narratives in rap music.

5. The notion of congruence is pervasive in the social science even if the idea is not specifically called "congruence"; e.g., see Homans 1961; Sampson 1963; Griswold 1987; Swidler 1986; Fine 2003; Fiske and Taylor 1991; Phillips 2003; Dowling 1994; Bridges, Keller, and Sood 2000; and Connell and Gibson 2003.

6. Giddens and DeVeaux 2009, 306–20, 332–35.

7. Berrett 2005, 150.

8. See also Koenig 2002, a labor of love in which the author captures the discourse that mentions jazz music in the popular and musical trade press.

CHAPTER 1: THE PUZZLE OF GEOGRAPHICAL DISCONNECTEDNESS

1. Consistent with work within ethnomusicology, I will be focusing on the *discographical* jazz canon: the set of songs that come to be associated with the genre as indicated by how frequently they are recorded over time (Pond 2003, 17). These songs are regarded as jazz standards or songs that "a professional musician may be expected to know" (Witmer 1994, 1155). Although the musicians and styles properly associated with a jazz canon are under active debate by jazz musicians, critics, and scholars (DeVeaux 1991; Brown 2004), there is greater agreement on which songs might be included (see also Faulkner and Becker 2009 on the role of the jazz repertoire). As of May 6, 2012, the website for the House of Tarab is http://www.houseoftarab.com/. Two of the six members are of Arab descent.

2. I use the term "re-recorded" instead of "cover" to discuss the act of future musicians recording a song that was previously recorded. The two terms are not the same. A "cover" is a term more accurately applied to other popular genres such as rock and roll, where the musicians more strictly follow the tune and lyrics of the original recording (as aptly put by Howard Becker in a 2011 personal communication). It is more typical in jazz that the original recording is reinterpreted rather than strictly followed, even though during the 1920s many of the initial re-recordings were closer to strict replications than reinterpretations, making both terms ("re-recording" and "cover") applicable. That said, throughout *Shaping Jazz* I emphasize the term "re-recording" as it more easily encompasses both exact replications and reinterpretations of original recordings.

3. I would like to thank Beth Bechky, Candace Jones, Jesper Strandgaard Pedersen, Silviya Svejenova, and the other members of the European Group for Organizational Studies (EGOS) track on cultural industries in 2008. Many of the ideas of this chapter were nourished from these EGOS cultural industry discussions.

4. Merton (1957) 1968, 1968; Podolny 1993.

5. Becker 1951; Hebdige 1979; Griswold 1987; Babon 2006; Johnston and Baumann 2007; Cheyne and Binder 2010; Price 1989; Fine 2004; Grazian 2003.

6. Fine 2003.

7. Simmel (1908) 1950, 143; Burt 1982, 1992.

8. Padgett and Ansell 1993; Fernandez and Gould 1994.

9. Griswold 1987. I would also encourage my organization and economic sociology colleagues to also read Alexander 2003, as it is an excellent survey.

10. See Johnston and Baumann 2007 on exoticism; see Cheyne and Binder 2010 for the value of foreignness in hip-hop.

11. Peterson (1997) is key among those who offer parallel arguments within their work on authenticity, and Becker (1982) provides insights on understanding reputation in art worlds. However, Fine (2003) is particularly explicit in linking the authenticity and appeal of a producer's outputs to the social structural position of the cultural producer.

12. E.g., Becker's (1997) concept of the outsider.

13. Simmel (1908) 1950; Kanter and Khurana 2009.

14. Coleman 1988; Burt 2005.

15. Martin 1995; Connell and Gibson 2003; Fine 2004; Cheyne and Binder 2010.

16. Crawford and Magee 1992; Block 1997; see also "Jazz Has Got Copyright Law" 2005 on the jazz canon and copyright law.

17. Menon and Pfeffer 2003; Phillips 2003.

18. DeVeaux 1991; Berliner 1994; Block 1997.

19. Faulkner and Becker 2009; see Lena 2012 on the evolution of genres.

20. This is a generalization, as there are wonderfully rich counterexamples that make the qualifier "without any other information" critical. Many, for example, would vigorously debate whether a hypothetical recording of "Take the 'A' Train" by Kenny G would be a legitimate jazz performance as Kenny G's association with traditional jazz may threaten one's understanding of jazz as a genre, a topic covered by Chris Washburne (2004) and one that I examine in the final chapter.

21. Witmer 1994, 1155; Pond 1993; Block 1997.

22. Block 1997. For a more in-depth treatment of free jazz that embeds the music in its social and political context, see Jost 1994.

23. Bryson 1996. The terms "song" and "tune" typically refer to an emphasis on the verbal lyrics (song) or melody (tune) of a musical piece. Given that jazz standards often have lyrics associated with them and were often sung during early jazz, I often use the term "song" generally to refer to either definition (see also Stanfield's similar usage in his study of "St. Louis Blues" [2002]). That said, many re-recordings of a piece over time, even if lyrics were initially central, evolved to an emphasis on the melody or "tune."

24. Johnston and Baumann 2007.

25. Peretti 1998; Kenney 1999; Gioia 1997.

26. See http://www.lordisco.com; Kernfeld and Rye 1994, 1995.

27. DeVeaux 1997.

28. In Phillips 2012 I conduct a more explicit analysis of the effect of the Depression on the long-run appeal of jazz, where I focus on the products of startup record companies and labels founded in 1929 and 1933.

29. Also see musicological studies of jazz's core repertory from 1900 to 1942 (Crawford and Magee 1992; Kernfeld and Rye 1994, 1995). I follow these studies by modifying Rust 1969 using the Tom Lord discography (2005, 2010).

30. To ensure that these bandleader mobility networks were not simply a proxy for some other more consequential network, I examined several alternative networks that were geographically structured: patterns of opera conductor mobility, Vaudeville circuits, record label ownership patterns, and the co-occurrence of cities in periodicals and journals on art using online article searches (Rich 1976; Smith 2003; Wertheim 2006; Tschmuck 2006). None of these efforts produced a network similar to the network of jazz musician mobility.

31. Throughout this book's analyses, I control for both the record label and the overarching record company that may own one or more labels (like Victorian-era firms), although in this period for many firms these were one and the same.

32. I statistically verified that a city's disconnectedness was distinct from its centrality, isolation, and other local market conditions (Phillips 2011).

33. Sutton 1994.

34. Austin 1925; Laubenstein 1929; Ogren 1989; Peretti 1992; Gioia 1997.

35. Among the most informative were autobiographies by Paul Whiteman, Michael Danzi, Gavin Bushell, and Baby Dodds (Whiteman and Whiteman 1926; Danzi 1986; Bushell 1998; Gara 2002).

36. See also Koenig 2002.

37. Satterfield 1956, 86.

38. Burt 1991; Baraka 1995; Whiteoak 1994; Nakienė 2003.

39. The Red Hot Jazz Archive website provides sound clips of music from the period under study. To compare recordings in close temporal proximity, listen to "Ain't Misbehavin'" (http://www.redhotjazz.com/lao.html) recorded by the Armstrong's orchestra in

July 1929 and "A Monday Date" recorded in December 1928 by his Hot Five (http://www
.redhotjazz.com/hot5.html).

40. Leonard 1962; Levine 1989; Peretti 1998; Lopes 2002.

41. Wolfe 1929; Hurston 1942; Gold 1957; Maurer 1976; Allen 1984; McCrum, Mac-
Neil, and Cran 1992, 237.

42. It is often lost on contemporary observers that "Jelly Roll" Morton's name was
much more likely to refer to his sexual prowess than to a pastry or dessert.

43. Nelson 2003; Zeitz 2006.

44. Light 1977, 473.

45. In Phillips 2011 I demonstrated how city-by-city mobility networks were created by
coding the movement of bandleaders across cities as they recorded music and elaborate on
how I calculated centrality and disconnectedness using three-year moving windows. We
will not discuss the technical aspects of that work here in order to keep focused on the task
of answering this chapter's key questions.

46. While difficult to observe with available data, the touring of "sidemen" that worked
for the bandleaders created a secondary network of musicians worldwide (Danzi 1986;
Bushell 1998; Miller 2005). Through letters and the exchange of recordings, knowledge of
jazz's development and reception was facilitated by these sidemen as well as the group's
leader. Jazz also spread through consumers who traveled with recordings across cities. My
main interest, however, is in the emergence of jazz standards, for which the network of
bandleaders was primary.

47. Bushell 1998; Miller 2005, 142–46.

48. Bushell 1998. See also Danzi's 1986 autobiography as an American-born, Berlin-
based, touring jazz musician in the 1920s.

49. I have truncated my full description of how I constructed disconnectedness to instead focus more directly on the jazz setting, but it is discussed more thoroughly in Phillips
2011. The key to my operationalization of disconnectedness is to first take the complement
of the normalized asymmetric city-by-city mobility matrix and then calculate the effective
size of each city in the complement. This is used to calculate disconnectedness for the panel
data for every city in each three-year moving window. In my data, disconnectedness is not
highly correlated with centrality, a fact that I elaborate on in Phillips 2011, 445–46.

50. Ogren 1989; Kenney 1993; Peretti 1992; Gioia 1997.

51. Hurston 1942; Gold 1957; Maurer 1976; Allen 1984.

52. Grazian 2003. See also Connell and Gibson's examination of other genres such as
world music (2003).

53. Robustness checks with Heckman models (selecting on whether a city records jazz
in the first place) as well as supplemental analysis for song or city outlier effects yielded results similar to those reported.

54. As I coded the data for this study I noticed a difficult-to-observe measurement
error. That is, a few recordings have the same title but are not the same songs. In many cases
one can easily discern the difference by listening to the music; however, not all recordings
are available for audio comparison. To proxy the effect on measurement, I entered a variable

for the 4.4% of the cases in which the *title has one word*, as this measurement error was most commonly associated with one-word titles (e.g., "Sugar").

55. About 70% of all of the recordings have a long-run appeal that is less than that of "Harlem Flat Blues." A 70th percentile quantile regression of long-run appeal on city disconnectedness specifies the changes in the 70th percentile appeal as a function of city disconnectedness. See Koenker and Hallock 2001 as well as Phillips 2011, 474–76, for an explanation that relates to the appeal of early jazz recordings.

56. In contrast to focusing on instruments that are unusual or rare in early jazz, one might instead ask how disconnectedness fared with recordings that used instruments intimately linked with early jazz, such as the banjo (Austin 1925; Parsonage 2003) and saxophone (Birchard 1925; Laubenstein 1929; Adorno 1941, 46; Schuller 1986; Murray 1996, 11–12; Segell 2005). For robustness, I used this logic in supplemental analysis. As expected, songs with these representative instruments from cities high in disconnectedness were less appealing (statistically significant).

57. I also conducted several robustness checks to verify these findings, including analyses that excluded the outliers, added additional control variables, and tested model specifications that treat the highly skewed dependent variable differently (OLS, logistic regression, GEE, Heckman two-stage, etc.).

58. Danzi 1986, 23–24. See also Miller (2005) on overseas jazz tours for the importance of keeping abreast of the popular trends and tunes.

59. Fitzgerald (1922) 2003; Jackson 2003.

60. See also Titon 1995; Kenney 1999; Berliner 1994.

61. Gara 2002.

62. Students of popular culture may note that my notion of appeal is based on the attention from fellow and future musicians, and is not consumer appeal (Zukin and Maguire 2004). That said, an examination of my data reveals that the top re-recorded tunes (above the 75th percentile) are those that also had high consumer appeal. In other words, the top re-recorded songs and tunes also appear to have had the greatest consumer appeal.

CHAPTER 2: FURTHER EXPLORING
THE SALIENCE OF GEOGRAPHY

1. Danzi 1986; Bushell 1998; Miller 2005.

2. My assumption is that the location of a record's manufacture is the same as the location of the actual recording—at least at the country level. This assumption appears to be the most valid in places high in disconnectedness since their record company representation was smaller and recording studios were often co-located with other production facilities. The larger the record company, the weaker this assumption was. Occasionally a record label noted when the location of the recording differed from the location of production (manufacture), which I took into account during my survey. In addition, through consulting several sources (such as Sutton 1994, Gronow and Saunio 1998, Sutton and Nauck

2000, and Tschmuck 2006) and my discography data, I separated additional labels that were sold under a local label but recorded and manufactured elsewhere as this would distort the effectiveness of a label's geographic information.

3. First accounts of musicians during this period (e.g., Danzi 1986) point to the use of imported records to keep abreast of new music. Learning from recordings has been a principal way jazz musicians have learned how to solo and improvise (Berliner 1994, 64, 95–97; Faulkner and Becker 2009).

4. These cities were the source of 74.9% of the jazz recordings. A vast proportion of these were by local musicians in that they only recorded in the same city. Thus I have concluded that around three-quarters of the community of musicians lived in New York, Chicago, or London.

5. According to historians like Catherine Campanella (2007, 89) the song refers to the vacation place Milneburg at Lake Pontchartrain outside New Orleans. Paul Mares and Leon Roppolo composed that title as "Golden Leaf Strut." During a recording session pianist Jelly Roll Morton added a prelude and the authors decided to name the song "Milenburg Joys." The print version has the name "Milenberg Joys," probably due to a spelling or transmission error; there is no place that's called Milenberg.

6. Kenney 1993.

7. For this calculation I used the recordings on which Jelly Roll Morton was a featured name and that he was the first to record. Thus I did not include the recordings with NORK and many other pieces that he composed but was not the first to record, such as "Wolverine Blues." Also, I used the median, given the skewness of the appeal for Morton's music (a few big hits, many more with little appeal). That said, using the average revealed the same contrast.

8. Phillips 2012.

9. These results were also confirmed with quantile regressions, similar to the results in chapter 1.

10. The endorsement by influential early adopters (in this case, musicians in central cities) is a pattern replicated with musician race in chapter 6, where song and tunes that were originated by African American musicians but then picked up by white musicians had amplified long-run appeal.

11. In Table A.5, where the dependent variable was the annual number of cities a song or tune was re-recorded in (or the geographic spread), each cohort was analyzed separately since I found very distinct effects for each cohort. In the second analysis (Table A.6) the dependent variable is the annual number of re-recordings (annual appeal); here the behavior of recordings between the cohorts was not particularly distinct. In fact, the two cohorts show similar effects, with the main difference being that music from the 1933 cohort had lower average appeal. Thus the models in Table A.6 combine the two cohorts and include a dummy variable for whether the recording was part of the 1933 cohort.

12. This behavior of middle-level musicians has similarities to some results presented in my work on status and conformity (Phillips and Zuckerman 2001), where I noted that middle-status actors with questionable membership are more likely to conform to market norms to signal that membership. However, in this jazz context the middle-level musicians

I studied did not appear to be recording music from disconnected sources to signal membership. Rather it was competition between them that led them to record music to distinguish themselves from one another. High-status musicians may not have needed to re-record these songs and tunes to distinguish themselves from others. So, while I have identified a "middle effect" with these musicians, it is not the same "middle effect" I identified in Phillips and Zuckerman 2001.

CHAPTER 3: SOCIOLOGICAL CONGRUENCE AND THE PUZZLE OF EARLY GERMAN JAZZ

1. Weimar Germany (1918–33) was characterized as a period of exceptionally active creativity and cultural experimentation that ended with the rise of the Nazi Party.

2. I would like to thank Franziska Wilke, who provided invaluable transcriptions and translations of dozens of liner notes from early German jazz anthologies that were originally written in German.

3. Gombrich 2000; Johnson, Dowd, and Ridgeway 2006.

4. Griswold 1987; Baumann 2007; Lena 2012.

5. Griswold 1987, 1081.

6. See Cheyne and Binder 2010.

7. Gombrich 2000, 313.

8. I would like to thank Wolfram Knauer (Jazzinstitut Darmstadt), Guy DeFazio (Center for Jazz Arts), and Rainer Lotz.

9. Cook 1989, 30.

10. Ferm 2008; Cook 1989.

11. Rye 2009, 2010a, 2010b.

12. Nowakowshi (2009) has identified an iteration of the SSO (playing in the more symphonic style) performing in Vienna in 1922 as part of a revue of "30 Negroes."

13. Bergmeier and Lotz 1986.

14. Bushell 1998; Kater 2003.

15. Leonhard and Stoffel 1997.

16. We are most confident in specifying that among white Americans, those most drawn to Whiteman's music would be those represented by newspaper readership from the *New York Times*. We have no direct data on Whiteman's appeal among illiterate citizens or white Americans who would have otherwise been outside this readership.

17. Berrett 2005, 150. A 1926 poll of University of Arkansas students published in the *American Mercury* reported that they considered Paul Whiteman the "greatest musician," with Beethoven coming in second (Mencken 2003, 167).

18. Seldes 1924.

19. As Lopes (2002) notes, the mid- to late 1930s ushered in a period of greater public recognition of black musicians as professionals who represented what was considered highbrow as well as lowbrow art.

20. Kater 2003; Poley 2005; Ferm 2008; see also Steinmetz 2007.

21. In addition, Rye (2010a) notes that sometime during 1924–25 a former pianist from the SSO founded a group in Berlin called the G. Rutherland Neger-Jazz-Orchester. There are no existing recordings of this group, but we surmise from the title and the style of the SSO that the music was more symphonic in nature.

22. Bushell 1998; Miller 2005.

23. Bushell 1998, 57.

24. Kater 1989; Robinson 1994; Saunders 2004.

25. Adorno 1941.

26. See Koenig 2002 and Walser 1999 for a combined reprinting of jazz discourse from over seventy U.S. publications up to 1929. Matthew F. Jordan (2010) has studied the parts of French culture that resisted jazz.

27. "Jazz Bitterly Opposed in Germany," *New York Times*, March 11, 1928.

28. Simon 1992, 44.

29. "Jazz Bitterly Opposed in Germany" 1928, 8.

30. Ibid., 293.

31. Danzi 1986.

32. I would like to thank Julie Seiber Boyd, chair of the Cambridge Szeged Society and Mátyás Seiber Trust, for pointing out that Mátyás Seiber also composed under the pseudonym G. S. Matthis.

33. We could not identify recordings or find additional information for "Chips" or "Cecelia" from 1926 to 1927.

34. The Harry Reser Band played closer to Whiteman's style but with some very good banjo solos; Reser was the banjo player.

35. I wish to thank German jazz historian Hans Pehl, who helped me track down the playbill.

36. Berrett 2005.

37. Other instrument categorizations that we used produced diagrams similar to what is presented here.

38. We distinguished the trumpet from the coronet in our listing of modern symphony instruments. Because Whiteman often substituted a coronet for a trumpet, the recordings from Germany appeared more symphonic than his recordings. If we include the coronet as a modern symphonic instrument, Whiteman's recordings have the highest percentage of symphonic instruments.

39. Robinson (1994, 121).

40. Perle 1993; Robinson 1994.

41. Motherwell 1929; Niles 1928.

42. Heuchemer 2002.

43. "Jazz" 1928.

44. Fleischmann 1928.

45. Hill 1927.

46. *New York Times*, November 18, 1924.

47. See Green's comparison of *Jonny Spielt Auf* to *L'Enfant et les Sortileges* by French composer Ravel (1984).

48. Of course, much of my analysis holds constant the fact that Germany lost World War II, an event so monumental that it is difficult to contemplate the question of how the fate of symphonic jazz and the evolution of jazz in general would have been different if World War II had not happened or if the Axis Powers had won the war.

49. Lewis 2009; Walser 1999.

50. Kater 2003.

51. This resistance was not against all "Negro" music, as it did not apply to Negro spirituals (*New York Times*, July 27, 1926). Spirituals did not carry the same cultural weight as jazz and were not threatening; they were considered authentic music by blacks who incorporated the religion of western Europe for the consumption of other blacks.

52. *New York Times*, May 17, 1933.

53. E.g., Lopes 2002; Kater 2003; DeVeaux 1991.

54. Lang and Lang 1996.

55. Dickos 2002.

56. Gamard 2004.

57. Robinson 1994; see also Adorno 1941, 2002.

58. Berrett 2005; Bushell 1998.

59. Johnson, Dowd, and Ridgeway 2006.

60. One of my clever reviewers pondered whether the opposite might have been true: If Germany had had an increased influence over jazz (let's say by winning World War II), would Paul Whiteman's legitimacy be greater today?

61. DeVeaux 1991; Gioia 1997; Lopes 2002; Kater 2003.

CHAPTER 4: SOCIOLOGICAL CONGRUENCE AND RECORD COMPANY COMPARATIVE ADVANTAGE

1. Arrow 1983; Reinganum 1983, 1985; Scherer and Ross 1990; Farrell and Saloner 1986; Gilbert and Newberry 1982.

2. Hannan and Freeman 1989; Hedberg 1981; Miller and Chen 1994.

3. Christensen 1997; Hendersen 1993; Henderson and Clark 1990; Tushman and Andersen 1986.

4. Part of this explanation was first suggested to me by Lori Rosenkopf.

5. My use of "black" is an overgeneralization referring to both African American and Creole but largely African American. I believe that I have taken sufficient care in my analyses so that this overgeneralization should not alter any of my conclusions. My use of "white" is a more frustrating grouping, as it encompasses those of Anglo-European descent as well as more marginalized Jewish and Irish Americans. This study's vast breadth and level of analysis is not conducive to empirically addressing this finer-level distinction, but that does not mean that I do not believe that such a distinction is not relevant. At the same time, I believe that the greatest impact of this lack of distinction is not the thrust of my conclusions per se but the accuracy of the empirical tests. For example, I would expect that any

results I currently have for white orchestras to be even stronger if I examined the subset of whites who are Anglo.

6. I first developed this typology with David Owens (Phillips and Owens 2004), but over time I continued to explore, understand, recast, and test it in various ways.

7. Leonard 1962; Schuller 1968; Levine 1989; Peretti 1992; Kenney 1993; Dowd 2003.

8. DiMaggio 1992; Kenney 1993; Lopes 2002; Mooney 1972; Peretti 1998.

9. My statistical analysis is at the record company level, controlling for different individual labels in the jazz market. One reason why this is important is that during this period the market was segmented by race (and ethnicity in some cases) such that a company might have a record label that targeted African Americans (called race records) that was different than the label that targeted white consumers. However, from the beginning, jazz was a genre that transcended racial boundaries in that both white and black consumers listened to jazz records, even when the labels were not the same. I also controlled for individual record companies and labels, which allowed me to separate out idiosyncratic strategies particular companies might have, such as selling music marketed as jazz under multiple labels. Separate controls for companies and labels adjust for this and other differences in firm strategy and structure. That said, the most typical reason for multiple labels in my sample was to enable a company to sell different styles or genres of music. It was unusual to find the same company releasing jazz under different labels.

10. Kenney 1999.

11. Fligstein 1987.

12. Negus 1999.

13. Kenney 1999.

14. Feather 1993; Kenney 1999; van der Tuuk 2003.

15. See van der Tuuk's (2003) findings on the role of mail order and department stores. Although department stores were not the main outlet for jazz recordings, for decades after World War II until recently, music stores played a key role in shaping genres through the way store managers grouped and categorized their music for customers (see Holt 2007 on how Tower Records framed and categorized music). Currently firms like Gracenote that place digital music tracks into particular genres (see http://www.gracenote.com/casestudies/itunes/) play a compelling role in shaping genres. In general, the current shift to online purchases of digitized music may align the market for recordings more closely with the market in the 1920s in a number of ways.

16. Gronow and Saunio 1998.

17. Peretti 1992; Schuller 1968.

18. Kenney 1993; Kofsky 1971; Slotkin 1943.

19. Brunn 1960; Kenney 1999; Leonard 1962; Peretti 1992. I say "purportedly" because record sales data for this period are difficult to uncover, and even when they are found they are unreliable.

20. Kenney 1999, 63.

21. Stinchcombe 1965; Landes 2000.

22. Kenney 1999.

23. *Who Was Who in America* 1962; Welch and Burt 1994.

24. Overacker 1933; *Wall Street Journal*, January 9, 1920, p. 9.

25. Aldridge 1983.

26. Leonard 1962; Mooney 1972. My review of *Ladies Home Journal* magazines from the early 1920s found that Victorian-era firms typically had full-page ads on the first page of the magazine (see Figure 4.2a). This is important as *Ladies Home Journal* was a key outlet for anti-jazz rhetoric in the early 1920s, publishing such articles as "Unspeakable Jazz Must Go!" (1921), "Back to Prewar Morals" (1921), and "Does Jazz Put the Sin in Syncopation?"

27. Melosi 1990.

28. *Who Was Who in America* 1962; Welch and Burt 1994.

29. Titon 1995, 218.

30. E.g., Leonard 1962; Walser 1999.

31. Kenney 1999, 51.

32. Titon 1995; see also Bryson 1996; Peterson and Kern 1996.

33. None of the jazz-era firms in my sample was owned by African Americans. At this time there was only one African American firm (Black Swan), which operated briefly but not in the Midwest, where these data are drawn from.

34. I also checked ads in African American newspapers such as the *Chicago Defender* and found (as expected) that for a label like Okeh, orchestras were less often featured.

35. van der Tuuk 2003.

36. Ibid., 91. Paramount was one of the jazz-era firms.

37. Music historian W. H. Kenney has noted that Eldridge Johnson, the founder and president of Victor, considered jazz to be roughly a third of the market during the 1920s (personal correspondence with the author).

38. Kenney 1993; Leonard 1962; Peretti 1992.

39. Berger 1947; Leonard 1962; Peretti 1992; Koenig 2002.

40. Leonard 1962.

41. *New York Times*, December 10, 1922.

42. See "What's the Matter with Jazz?" 1924.

43. See Gusfield 1955, 1963.

44. Leonard 1962.

45. This tension involving anti-jazz sentiments was not something that was restricted to the recording industry as many organizations associated with jazz had to respond to anti-jazz sentiment. For example, piano roll producers who were traditionally associated with classical music had to publicly defend themselves against attacks that they were producing jazz piano rolls. "Respectable" dancing venue proprietors, who could profit from the popular dances that accompanied symphonic jazz or jazz orchestras, shunned any association with jazz. As one dance hall proprietor in Chicago emphatically put it: "sensual stimulation of the abominable jazz orchestra with its voodoo-born minors and its direct appeal to the sensory centers, and if you can believe that youth is the same after this experience as before, then God help your child" (Koenig 2002, 163). See also DiMaggio 1982 on the reaction by the elite to popular culture in the field of art museums.

46. Kenney 1993, 80.

47. According to Kenney, "The 'flapper,' named for the birdlike arm movements involved in dancing 'the Charleston,' carried a reputation for unconventional behavior. Sometimes known as 'Jazz Babies' or 'Gold Diggers,' younger women defiled the world of Victorian domestic propriety" (1999, 103).

48. Kenney 1999; Gracyk 2000.

49. However, as Rick Kennedy (1994) notes in this study of Gennett, it is unclear whether Gennett's management realized that Morton was African American. Kennedy shows that in general, Gennett was quite innovative, experimental, and entrepreneurial in terms of the range of their recordings.

50. Those familiar with Carroll and Swaminathan's research on breweries (2000) may see parallels between their work and my Study 3 as both claim that markets can be divided into identity spaces that prevent larger generalists from directly competing with specialists. I agree, although the studies of brewers emphasize the relationship between the firm identities and the identities of audiences (consumers). Something like that is probably going on here, but I have less information available on consumer identities to substantiate that point. Rather, my key audience is the elite. Another difference is that my context is one of an emerging market, where even incumbents have malleable identities and are able to influence the criteria for legitimacy, as we will see in this chapter as well as chapters 5 and 6.

51. One of the challenges with historical data is that sometimes the variables I wish to employ are missing. None of my supplemental analysis suggests that this adversely affects my results. The main consequence is that often the number of cases varies somewhat from analysis to analysis. Accordingly, analyses in this chapter use not just the 1,752 original recordings of 355 groups (as in chapter 1) but all recordings, bringing the sample that I analyzed to 2,343 recordings by 389 groups. This larger sample included both the original recordings and any re-recordings before 1943.

52. See Phillips and Owens 2004 for the use of "orchestra" in a group's name. For the jazz pictorials we used Driggs and Lewine 1996; Ward and Burns 2000.

53. Here "black" includes Creole, although socially they were a different group (especially in the Louisiana area). "White" is capturing all people of European descent, although my theory should apply most strongly to Anglos. If I had more fine-grained data I would expect to find different results for white musicians who were from Jewish, Irish, Italian, or other southern European communities.

54. As a validity check I also ran similar models for the other two types of groups (black orchestras and white non-orchestras). In particular, I looked at the likelihood that Victorian-era firms recorded groups that were black (similar to that of Sam Wooding). I also looked at groups that were white but did not perform the orchestral style of jazz (e.g., ODJB). However, analyses for these types of groups did not produce consistent or robust statistical results.

55. I suspect that there was substantial innovation outside recorded music at that time. But that only speaks to my contention that what the industry produced and marketed as jazz during the 1920s (rather than innovations that were never recorded) shaped our understanding of the genre—as most of what we currently "know" is drawn from the recordings

by these firms. In this way, the firms are archivists of jazz in ways that production of culture scholars have identified in other musical genres.

56. If one instead models this as a linear effect, the estimate is negative but only marginally significant.

57. DiMaggio 1982; Levine 1988, 1989.

CHAPTER 5: THE SOCIOLOGICAL CONGRUENCE OF RECORD COMPANY DECEPTION

1. A version of this chapter was published as Phillips and Kim 2009.

2. Rust 1969; Lord 2005, 2010.

3. Sutton 1994.

4. Gardner 1975.

5. Pfeffer 1981; Perrow 1985; Westphal and Zajac 1994, 2001.

6. Sutton and Callahan 1987; Elsbach and Sutton 1992; Elsbach, Sutton, and Principe 1998.

7. E.g., Akerlof and Romer 1993; Galbraith 2004.

8. Pope and Ong 2007.

9. White 1981; Zuckerman 1999; Gioia, Schultz, and Corley 2000.

10. Stinchcombe 1965; Hannan et al. 2006.

11. Albert and Whetten 1985; Elsbach and Kramer 1996; Carroll and Swaminathan 2000; Lounsbury and Rao 2004; Hsu and Hannan 2005.

12. Although we lack clear data on the release date of the pseudonyms, a wealth of anecdotal evidence, bolstered by the work of discographers (Sutton 1993), conversations with jazz curators at university libraries, and jazz collectors, indicates that the recording of the original group preceded the release of the recording under the pseudonym.

13. Leonard 1962; Levine 1989; Lopes 2002.

14. Kenney 1999.

15. Leonard 1962; Levine 1989; Ogren 1989; Kenney 1999; Phillips and Owens 2004.

16. None of the recordings made under pseudonyms in our sample was re-recorded. This is one of many findings that led us to conclude that there is no evidence that pseudonyms had any success in the market.

17. Titon 1995; Kenney 1999.

18. Leonard 1962; Kenney 1999.

19. It is important to note that Young-Kyu Kim and I also verified the robustness of the Victorian-era dummy variable by conducting additional analysis that included dummy variables for the largest firms: Victor and Columbia (as well as Brunswick). Indeed, our argument is based on the founding period of the firms in our sample, not their size, scope, or other unobserved characteristics that may be associated with these market leaders. If our measures were simply due to one of the large firms, then these dummy variables may have explained away the Victorian-era variable. However, in each of these models the Victorian-era variable easily retained statistical significance. This was not surprising given that my

models already have a set of firm-level controls that capture size and scope, but it was an important validation.

20. Kim and I examined Louis Armstrong specifically because he is an outlier on almost every dimension available to us (e.g., his recordings are about three times as successful as the average recording and his songs are almost twice as likely to be completed on the first take), and we wanted to ensure that our results were not driven by his inclusion (or exclusion) in the sample.

21. Mooney 1972; Welburn 1986; Berrett 2005.

22. There is a wonderful video (from 1929) of Pollack's jazz orchestra that features Goodman, Jack Teagarden, and others (http://www.youtube.com/watch?v=HrI5oW2ykuU). The video also provides a window into the transition from the Whiteman-influenced symphonic style to the swing style that Goodman would eventually shape.

CHAPTER 6: THE SOCIOLOGICAL CONGRUENCE OF IDENTITY SEQUENCES AND ADOPTION NARRATIVES

1. An earlier version of this chapter was published as Kahl, Kim, and Phillips 2010. Kahl is an expert on categorization in emerging systems and Kim had the initial empirical intuition around modeling sequences.

2. My use of the term "originator" is based on identifying the group associated with seeding the discographical canon. Originators are those who are the first to record and may not be the actual composers of the music. This term is appropriate when studying jazz, when artistic ownership among peers and critics often derives from recorded performances that capture interpretations of compositions over the actual compositions (e.g., Coleman Hawkins's identification with "Body and Soul").

3. Lang and Lang 1988.

4. Becker 1982; Bourdieu and Johnson 1993; Bourdieu 1996.

5. DiMaggio 1987; Lopes 1992.

6. Hirsch 1972; Peterson and Berger 1975.

7. Roy and Dowd 2010; Faulkner and Becker 2009; Kremp 2010.

8. Briscoe and Safford 2008; Coleman, Katz, and Menzel 1966; Veblen 1899.

9. E.g., Veblen 1899.

10. See Hsu, Hannan, and Kocak 2009 for a summary.

11. Brooks 1978; Medin and Schaffer 1978; Abbott 1995; Fine 2003; Grazian 2003; Peterson 2005.

12. Carroll and Wheaton 2009, 2.

13. Cf. Rao, Monin, and Durand 2003.

14. E.g., Fine's (2003) conceptualization of biography and works of art, as well as Carroll, Khessina, and McKendrick's (2010) notion of the social lives of products. In his work on the authenticity of self-taught artists, Fine argues that the work itself does not matter as much as the biography of the artist.

15. Durkheim (1912) 2001.

16. Hannan, Polos, and Carroll 2007; Phillips, Turco, and Zuckerman 2013.

17. DiMaggio 1987; Lena 2012. For links to recent organizational and cultural sociology, see Hannan, Polos, and Carroll 2007, 38; Hsu and Hannan 2005, 479–80.

18. Fine 2003; Peterson 2005.

19. Peterson 2005, 1086–87.

20. Fine 2003.

21. The appeal to identities of members over prototypical characteristics closely resembles a debate in cognitive science about categorical structure. Rosch and Lloyd's view (1978) is that certain members represent the typical traits that come to define a category. Others focus on the individual instances that tend to define the category (see Brooks 1978). The processes are different. In Rosch and Lloyd's view, actors invoke the general rule to evaluate new instances; in Brooks's view, actors compare the new with past experiences of similar objects.

22. See Kelley 2009, in which the debate around Monk's mental condition is analyzed.

23. The first verse is as follows: "Well, I was born a coal miner's daughter; In a cabin on a hill in Butcher Holler [in Kentucky]; We were poor but we had love; That's the one thing my Daddy made sure of; He shoveled coal to make a poor man's dollar."

24. Carroll and Swaminathan 2000.

25. See Heimoff and Harlan 2010. For an academic treatment, see Roberts and Khaire 2009.

26. E.g., Becker 1982; Phillips and Kim 2009.

27. Berger and Heath 2008; Briscoe and Safford 2008; Fleming, Simcoe, and Waguespack 2008; Strang and Tuma 1993.

28. Abbott 1995.

29. Peterson 2005; Faulkner and Becker 2009.

30. Note the wide variety of jazz's definitions in Adorno 1941; Ogren 1989; Gioia 1997; Lopes 2002; and Jackson 2003.

31. Gioia 1997; Thomas 2002.

32. DeVeaux 1997; Gioia 1997.

33. Shaw 1924; Austin 1925; Davidson 1925; Osgood 1926; Stringham 1926; Laubenstein 1929.

34. "Eye Jazz" 1928; Laubenstein 1929; Leonard 1962.

35. Lopes 2002.

36. Anderson 1930.

37. As of September 27, 2012, a clip of the cartoon exists (2:52 in length) on YouTube under the title: "King of Jazz: cartoon section": http://www.youtube.com/watch?v=rFXsfR xOjUM&feature=related.

38. See Kofsky 1998 for a political-economic analysis of race in jazz.

39. The *Jazz Singer* (1927) was another movie featuring jazz, but it did not directly confront the ontology of jazz as *The King of Jazz* did. Magee (2000, 2006) argues that Al Jolson's performance in the *Jazz Singer* of songs such as Irving Berlin's "Blue Skies" made

the song *less* likely to be seen as jazz music, although the song had other "markers" of being a jazz song.

40. This is not to say that some white musicians and critics did not contest the African origins of jazz (Gioia 1997; Sudhalter 1999); our point is that the overwhelming consensus was that jazz's beginning was coupled with black (African and African American) identities.

41. DiMaggio 1982; Levine 1989.

42. The models I will be referring to in this chapter can be found in Kahl, Kim, and Phillips 2010.

43. With this restriction, we calculate the Inverse Mills Ratio to adjust for whether the song was one of the 12.8% re-recorded at least once (Heckman 1976).

44. We made the adjustments using the Inverse Mills Ratio (Heckman 1976).

45. Of course, the financial incentives often conflict with this aspect of jazz culture, where assignment of originality (and thus royalties) is attributed to the composer.

46. For example, a three-recording mixed-race sequence with a black originating group was coded be Black-White-Black, Black-Black-White, and Black-White-White. In supplemental analysis Kim and I looked at sequences of up to seven, with many different sequences of black and white musicians. In the end, however, the only thing that resulted in explanatory power (in both a statistical and historical sense) was the simple originator-early adopter approach we use here.

47. Kenney 1993; Lopes 1992.

48. Smith and Guttridge (1960) 1988; Lopes 2002.

49. Note that when testing for the four different adoption patterns, including a separate dummy variable to independently capture the race of the original group is redundant. That said, I reran this analysis to examine whether only the race of the originating group mattered; however, these effects did not produce significant results. The overall effect of the originators being black was positive but not statistically significant; only the BO-WA sequence yielded statistically significant results.

50. Each of the interaction effects was re-run with the opposite racial pattern—white musician originators with black early adopters—but none of the results was statistically significant.

51. Even in these situations, enthusiasts may influence category-defining processes by favoring a certain pattern of adoption over other patterns (e.g., advocating for a particular narrative).

52. A regression models the mean, so in effect I'm stating that black musicians as originators were on average not associated with music that had greater long-run appeal. This may be surprising to some who have luminaries such as Louis Armstrong or Earl Hines in mind, but this is where it is important to keep in mind that my analyses are dealing with averages. For every Armstrong or Hines there were artists we have never heard of and who were not associated with music that had long-run appeal. These musicians effectively "cancel out" the luminaries.

53. Fleming and Waguespack 2007.

CHAPTER 7: PULLING IT TOGETHER
AND STRETCHING IT BEYOND

1. Kevin Fellezs (2011) has thoughtfully analyzed fusion as a form of music in which its categorical membership was and continues to be contested. That said, its association with jazz emerged discursively and was reinforced by such Miles Davis (an exemplary jazz figure) recordings as "Bitches Brew." If Davis was recording the most commercially successful form of the music, and Davis was one of the key figures of jazz, we would therefore conclude that it must be a type of jazz.

2. Before embarking on his solo career, Kenny G was the saxophone player for the group called the Jeff Lorber Fusion in the late 1970s.

3. As added evidence of his membership in the genre of jazz, Kenny G had a weekend booking to perform at the famous Blue Note jazz club in New York City in November 2012. The other artists with a weekend booking that month included the Chick Corea and Stanley Clarke Band, Ellis Marsalis Quartet, and Manhattan Transfer, all of whom most observers easily categorize as jazz musicians.

4. Washburne 2004, 97. Washburne makes an objective and very compelling argument for Kenny G as a true (albeit controversial) jazz figure, especially if one looks at the modern trajectory of jazz.

5. See Green 1984.

6. Gronow and Saunio 1998.

7. For recent and exemplary work on these respective categories, see Sine and Lee 2009 on green technology; Granqvist, Grodal, and Woolley 2012 on nanotechnology; and Pontikes 2012 on software.

8. See http://lexicon.ft.com/Term?term=green-technology (accessed September 27, 2012).

9. While scholars like Greta Hsu (2006) have noted the conditions under which movies suffer from spanning multiple genres (e.g., a cowboy-horror film), the combination of jazz with other musical genres does not appear to have the same constraints and has indeed been one of the reasons why jazz has persisted.

10. See Schwarz 2008.

11. See Schmidt 2007.

12. Although it is less developed as a market category, "green software" is another example of a hybrid of two ambiguous categories (Shenoy and Eeratta 2011).

13. See Green Chemistry Institute 2011.

14. Granqvist, Grodal, and Woolley 2012.

15. Rao 1994; Barnett 1995; Kahl 2007; McWhinney 2009.

16. Hannan, Polos, and Carroll 2007.

17. McKendrick et al. 2003.

18. Pontikes 2012.

19. In this way, I am thinking along the lines of Bourdieu and Johnson's (1993) distinc-

tion between types of capital but with an emphasis on the commercialized aspect of cultural production.

20. Watts's (2011) rendition of the history behind the *Mona Lisa* is based on Sassoon 2001.

21. Pontikes 2012.

22. Elizabeth Pontikes's framework uses the concept of lenient market spaces to denote a specific kind of ambiguity in the software industry. Pontikes and Barnett (2012) show that the market for software involves a very dynamic population of both high entry and high exit rates but one in which entry rates outstrip exit rates. Thus, while the market category persists, the longevity of any one particular firm is relatively short.

23. See Pontikes 2012.

24. E.g., Podolny 1993; Podolny, Stuart, and Hannan 1996; Podolny and Phillips 1996; Stuart, Hoang, and Hybels 1999; Phillips and Zuckerman 2001; Jensen 2006; Washington and Zajac 2005; Kraatz, Ventresca, and Deng 2010; Bothner, Kim, and Smith 2012; Phillips, Turco, and Zuckerman 2013.

25. See the boundary conditions in Phillips and Zuckerman (2001, 386–90) middle-status conformity.

26. See Phillips, Turco, and Zuckerman 2013 on high-status conformity.

27. This is a question of more general interest as similar questions have partially motivated a recent set of books by major scholars in organizational theory (Hannan, Polos, and Carroll 2007; Fligstein and McAdam 2012; Padgett and Powell 2012.

28. Aldrich and Fiol 1994; McKendrick and Carroll 2001; McKendrick et al. 2003; Hsu and Hannan 2005; Wry, Lounsbury, and Glynn 2011.

29. Per conversation with Mr. Jung, the interview for *Jazz Weekly* was from February 2000. Fans of rap music around the time of this book's publishing may know of Olu Dara as the father of the rapper Nas.

30. This quote is from Granqvist, Grodal, and Woolley's interview notes and in a paper from 2011 but was edited out of their "Hedging Your Bets."

31. Consider, for example, Lena 2012 and Hebdige 1979.

32. See Terry Anderson's (1996) analysis of movements and social activism in the 1960s.

33. See Mandel 2007.

34. In other work I identify an exception to this trend where a subset of the tunes from the period of early jazz received renewed interest as re-recordings after 1990 (see Phillips 2012).

35. See Lewis 2009, 103.

36. Faulkner and Becker 2009.

37. Shermer 2003. The Penn and Teller segment can be found on http://www.youtube.com/watch?v=XfPAjUvvnIc (accessed May 2, 2012).

References

Abbott, A. 1995. "Sequence Analysis: New Methods for Old Ideas." *Annual Review of Sociology* 21: 93–113.

Adorno, T. 1941. "On Popular Music." *Studies in Philosophy and Social Science* 9, 1: 17–48.

———. 2002. *Essays on Music.* Ed. R. Leppert. Berkeley: University of California Press.

Akerlof, G. A., and P. M. Romer. 1993. "Looting: The Economic Underworld of Bankruptcy for Profit." *Brookings Papers on Economic Activity* 2: 1–73.

Albert, S., and D. Whetten. 1985. "Organizational Identity." *Research in Organizational Behavior* 7: 263–95.

Aldrich, H. E., and C. M. Fiol. 1994. "Fools Rush in? The Institutional Context of Industry Creation." *Academy of Management Review* 19, 4: 645–70.

Aldridge, B. L. 1983. *The Victor Talking Machine Company.* Westport, CT: Greenwood Press.

Alexander, V. 2003. *Sociology of the Arts: Exploring Fine and Popular Forms.* New York: Wiley-Blackwell.

Allen, I. L. 1984. "Male Sex Roles and Epithets for Ethnic Women in American Slang." *Sex Roles* 11, 1/2: 43–50.

"America's Most Admired Companies." 2007. *Fortune Magazine,* March 19.

Anderson, J. M., dir. 1930. *King of Jazz.* Universal Pictures Corp.

Anderson, T. 1996. *The Movement and the Sixties: Protest in America from Greensboro to Wounded Knee.* New York: Oxford University Press.

Arrow K. 1983. "Innovation in Large and Small Firms." In *Entrepreneurship,* ed. J. Ronen. Lexington, MA: Lexington Books.

Austin, C. 1925. "Jazz." *Music & Letters* 6, 3: 256–68.

Babon, K. M. 2006. "Composition, Coherence, and Attachment: The Critical Role of Context in Reception." *Poetics* 34, 3: 151–79.

Baraka, A. 1995. "Jazzmen: Diz & Sun Ra." *African American Review* 29, 2: 249–55.

Barnett, W. P. 1995. "Telephone Companies." In *Organizations in Industry: Strategy, Structure, and Selection,* ed. G. R. Carroll and M. T. Hannan, 277–89. New York: Oxford University Press.

Baumann, S. 2007. "A General Theory of Artistic Legitimation: How Art Worlds Are Like Social Movements." *Poetics* 35: 47-65.

Becker, H. 1951. "The Professional Dance Musician and His Audience." *American Journal of Sociology* 57, 2: 136–44.

———. 1982. *Art Worlds*. Berkeley: University of California Press.

———. 1997. *Outsiders*. New York: The Free Press.

Berger, J., and C. Heath. 2008. "Who Drives Divergence? Identity Signaling, Outgroup Dissimilarity, and the Abandonment of Cultural Tastes." *Journal of Personality and Social Psychology* 95: 593–607.

Berger, M. 1947. "Jazz." *Journal of Negro History* 32: 461–94.

Bergmeier, H., and R. E. Lotz. 1986. *The Alex Hyde Bio/Discography*. Menden: Jazzfreund Publikation.

Berliner, P. F. 1994. *Thinking in Jazz: The Infinite Art of Improvisation*. Chicago: University of Chicago Press.

Berrett, J. 2005. *Louis Armstrong and Paul Whiteman: Two Kings of Jazz*. New Haven, CT: Yale University Press.

Birchard, C. C. 1925. "What About the Saxophone?" *Music Supervisors' Journal* 1, 1: 56–57.

Block, S. 1997. "'Bemsha Swing': The Transformation of a Bebop Classic to Free Jazz." *Music Theory Spectrum* 19, 2: 206–31.

Bothner, M. S., Y. K. Kim, and E. B. Smith. 2012. "How Does Status Affect Performance? Status as an Asset vs. Status as a Liability in the PGA and NASCAR." *Organization Science* 23: 416–33.

Bourdieu, P. (1984) 2000. *Distinction: A Social Critique of the Judgement of Taste*. Cambridge, MA: Harvard University Press.

———. 1996. *The Rules of Art: Genesis and Structure of the Literary Field*. Cambridge: Polity Press.

Bourdieu, P., and R. Johnson. 1993. *The Field of Cultural Production*. New York: Columbia University Press.

Bridges, S., K. L. Keller, and S. Sood. 2000. "Communication Strategies for Brand Extensions: Enhancing Perceived Fit by Establishing Explanatory Links." *Journal of Advertising* 29, 4: 1–11.

Briscoe, F., and S. Safford. 2008. "The Nixon-in-China Effect: Activism, Imitation and the Institutionalization of Contentious Practices." *Administrative Science Quarterly* 53: 460–91.

Brooks, L. R. 1978. "Nonanalytic Concept Formation and Memory for Instances." In *Cognition and Categorization*, ed. E. Rosch and B. Lloyd. Hillsdale, NJ: Erlbaum Associates.

Brown, L. B. 2004. "Marsalis and Baraka: An Essay in Comparative Cultural Discourse." *Popular Music* 23, 3: 241–55.

Brunn, H. O. 1960. *The Story of the Original Dixieland Jazz Band*. Baton Rouge: Louisiana State University Press.

Bryson, B. 1996. "'Anything But Heavy Metal': Symbolic Exclusion and Musical Dislikes." *American Sociological Review* 61, 5: 884–99.

Burt, R. S. 1982. *Toward a Structural Theory of Action: Network Models of Social Structure, Perception, and Action.* New York: Academic Press.

———. 1992. *Structural Holes: The Social Structure of Competition.* Cambridge, MA: Harvard University Press.

———. 2005. *Brokerage and Closure.* New York: Oxford University Press.

Burt, W. 1991. "Australian Experimental Music, 1963–1990." *Leonardo Music Journal* 1, 1: 5–10.

"Bush PR Team Covers China Stamp with 'Made in U.S.A.' " 2003. *New York Times,* January 22.

Bushell, G. 1998. *Jazz from the Beginning.* New York: De Capo Press.

Campanella, C. 2007. *Images of America: Lake Pontchartrain.* Charleston, SC: Arcadia Publishing.

Cancian, F. 1967. "Stratification and Risk-Taking: A Theory Tested on Agricultural Innovation." *American Sociological Review* 32, 6: 912–27.

Carroll, G. R., and M. T. Hannan. 2004. *The Demography of Corporations and Industries.* Princeton: Princeton University Press.

Carroll, G. R., O. M. Khessina, and D. G. McKendrick. 2010. "The Social Lives of Products: Analyzing Product Demography for Management Theory and Practice." *Academy of Management Annals* 4, 1: 157–203.

Carroll, G. R., and A. Swaminathan. 2000. "Why the Microbrewery Movement? Organizational Dynamics of Resource Partitioning in the U.S. Brewing Industry." *American Journal of Sociology* 106, 3: 715–62.

Carroll, G. R., and D. R. Wheaton. 2009. "The Organizational Construction of Authenticity: An Examination of Contemporary Food and Dining in the U.S." *Research in Organizational Behavior* 29: 255–82.

Cheyne, A., and A. Binder. 2010. "Cosmopolitan Preferences: The Constitutive Role of Place in American Elite Taste for Hip Hop Music, 1991–2005." *Poetics* 38, 3: 336–64.

Christensen, C. M. 1997. *The Innovator's Dilemma.* New York: HarperCollins.

Coleman, J. S. 1988. "Social Capital in the Creation of Human Capital." *American Journal of Sociology* 94: S95–120.

Coleman, J., E. Katz, and H. Menzel. 1966. *Medical Innovation: A Diffusion Study.* New York: Bobbs-Merrill.

Connell, J., and C. Gibson. 2003. *Sound Tracks: Popular Music, Identity and Place.* London: Routledge.

Cook, S. 1989. "Jazz as Deliverance: The Reception and Institution of American Jazz during the Weimar Republic." *American Music* 7, 1: 30–46.

Crawford, R., and J. Magee. 1992. *Jazz Standards on Record, 1900–1942: A Core Repertory.* CBMR Monographs. New York: Center for Black Music Research, Columbia College.

Crosland, A., dir. 1927. *The Jazz Singer.* Warner Bros. Pictures.

Danzi, M. 1986. *American Musician in Berlin: Memoirs of the Jazz, Entertainment, and Movie World of Berlin during the Weimar Republic and the Nazi Era, and in the United States.* Schmitten, Germany: N. Ruecker.

Davidson, A. E. 1925. "Jazz Music." *The Musical Times* 66: 158.

DeVeaux, S. 1991. "Constructing the Jazz Tradition: Jazz Historiography." *Black American Literature Forum* 25, 3: 525–60.

———. 1997. *The Birth of Bebop: A Social and Musical History*. Berkeley: University of California Press.

Dickos, A. 2002. *Street with No Name: A History of the Classic Film Noir*. Lexington: University of Kentucky Press.

DiMaggio, P. 1982. "Cultural Entrepreneurship in 19th-Century Boston, Part I: The Creation of an Organizational Base for High Culture in America." *Media, Culture and Society* 4, 1: 33–50.

———. 1987. "Classification in Art." *American Sociological Review* 52, 4: 440–55.

———. 1988. "Interest and Agency in Institutional Theory." In *Institutional Patterns and Organizations: Culture and Environment*, ed. L. G. Zucker. Cambridge, MA: Ballinger.

———. 1992. "Cultural Boundaries and Structural Change." In *Cultivating Differences*, ed. M. Lamont and M. Fournier, 21–57. Chicago: University of Chicago Press.

Dowd, T. J. 2003. "Structural Power and the Construction of Markets: The Case of Rhythm and Blues." *Comparative Social Research* 21: 147–201.

Dowling, G. R. 1994. *Corporate Reputation: Strategies for Developing the Corporate Brand*. London: Kogan Page.

Driggs, F., and C. Haddix. 2005. *Kansas City Jazz: From Ragtime to Bebop—A History*. New York: Oxford University Press.

Driggs, F., and H. Lewine. 1996. *Black Beauty, White Heat*. New York: Da Capo Press.

Durkheim, É. (1912) 2001. *The Elementary Forms of Religious Life*. New York: Oxford University Press.

Elsbach, K. D., and R. M. Kramer. 1996. "Members' Responses to Organizational Identity Threats: Encountering and Countering the Business Week Rankings." *Administrative Science Quarterly* 41, 3: 442–76.

Elsbach, K. D., and R. I. Sutton. 1992. "Acquiring Organizational Legitimacy through Illegitimate Actions: A Marriage of Institutional and Impression Management Theory." *Academy of Management Journal* 35, 4: 699–738.

Elsbach, K. D., R. I. Sutton, and K. Principe. 1998. "Anticipatory Impression Management by Organizations: Tactics for Averting Expected Controversies." *Organization Science* 9, 1: 68–86.

"Eye Jazz." 1928. *British Medical Journal* 2: 1050.

Farrell, J., and G. Saloner. 1986. "Installed Base and Compatibility: Innovation, Product Preannouncements, and Predation." *American Economic Review* 76, 5: 940–55.

Faulkner R. R., and H. S. Becker. 2009. *Do You Know—? The Jazz Repertoire in Action*. Chicago: University of Chicago Press.

Feather, L. 1993. *The Encyclopedia Yearbooks of Jazz*. New York: Da Capo Press.

Fellezs, K. 2011. *Birds of Fire: Jazz, Rock, Funk, and the Creation of Fusion*. Durham: Duke University Press.

Ferm, M. 2008. "Revealing Representations of Jazz in the Weimar Republic." *Social Science Journal* 45, 2: 240–57.

Fernandez, R. M., and R. V. Gould. 1994. "A Dilemma of State Power: Brokerage and Influence in the National Health Policy Domain." *American Journal of Sociology* 99, 6: 1455–91.

Fine, G. A. 2003. "Crafting Authenticity: The Validation of Identity in Self-Taught Art." *Theory and Society* 32: 153–80.

———. 2004. *Everyday Genius: Self-Taught Art and the Culture of Authenticity.* Chicago: University of Chicago Press.

Fiske, S. T., and S. E. Taylor. 1991. *Social Cognition.* New York: McGraw-Hill.

Fitzgerald, F. S. (1922) 2003. *Tales of the Jazz Age.* Philadelphia: Pine Street Books.

Fleischmann, H. R. 1928. "The First Jazz Opera and Operetta: The Chesterian." In Koenig, *Jazz in Print*, 532.

Fleming, L., S. Mingo, and D. Chen. 2007. "Collaborative Brokerage, Generative Creativity, and Creative Success." *Administrative Science Quarterly* 52: 443–75.

Fleming, L., T. S. Simcoe, and D. Waguespack. 2008. "What's in a Name? Status, Discrimination, and the Matthew Effect." Working paper. University of Toronto.

Fleming, L., and D. Waguespack. 2007. "Brokerage, Boundary Spanning, and Leadership in Open Innovation Communities." *Organization Science* 18, 2: 165–80.

Fligstein, N. 1987. "The Intraorganizational Power Struggle: Rise of Finance Personnel to Top Leadership in Large Corporations, 1919–1979." *American Sociological Review* 52, 1: 44–58.

———. 1996. "Markets as Politics: A Political-Cultural Approach to Market Institutions." *American Sociological Review* 61, 4: 656–73.

———. 2008. "Theory and Methods for the Study of Strategic Action Fields." Working paper. University of California, Berkeley.

Fligstein, N., and D. McAdam. 2012. *A Theory of Fields.* New York: Oxford University Press.

Frankenstein, Alfred V. 1929. "Review of Reviewing." In Koenig, *Jazz in Print*, 555.

Galbraith, J. K. 2004. *The Economics of Innocent Fraud: Truth for Our Time.* Boston: Houghton Mifflin.

Gamard, E. B. 2004. "Bauhaus." In *Encyclopedia of 20th Century Architecture*, ed. S. Sennott, 118–21. New York: Taylor & Francis.

Gara, L. 2002. *The Baby Dodds Story.* Alma, MI: Rebeats Publications.

Gardner, D. M. 1975. "Deception in Advertising: A Conceptual Approach." *Journal of Marketing* 39, 1: 40–46.

Giddens, G., and S. DeVeaux. 2009. *Jazz.* New York: W. W. Norton.

Gilbert, R., and D. Newberry. 1982. "Preemptive Patenting and the Persistence of Monopoly." *American Economics Review* 72: 514–26.

Gioia, D. A., M. Schultz, and K. G. Corley. 2000. "Organizational Identity, Image and Adaptive Instability." *Academy of Management Review* 25, 1: 63–81.

Gioia, T. 1997. *The History of Jazz.* Oxford: Oxford University Press.

Gold, R. S. 1957. "The Vernacular of the Jazz World." *American Speech* 32, 4: 271–82.

Gombrich, E. H. 2000. *Art and Illusion.* Princeton: Princeton University Press.

Gracyk, T. 2000. *Popular American Recording Pioneers.* New York: Haworth Press.

Granqvist, N., S. Grodal, and J. Woolley. 2012. "Hedging Your Bets: Explaining Executives' Market Labeling Strategies in Nanotechnology." *Organization Science*.

Grazian, D. 2003. *Blue Chicago: The Search for Authenticity in Urban Blues Clubs*. Chicago: University of Chicago Press.

Green Chemistry Institute. 2011. "Green Technology Challenges and Opportunities." American Chemical Society White Paper.

Green, M. S. 1984. "Ravel and Krenek: Cosmic Music Makers." *College Music Symposium* 24, 2: 96–104.

Griswold, W. 1987. "The Fabrication of Meaning: Literary Interpretation in the United States, Great Britain, and the West Indies." *American Journal of Sociology* 92, 5: 1077–1117.

Gronow, P., and I. Saunio. 1998. *An International History of the Recording Industry*. London: Cassell.

Gusfield, J. R. 1955. "Social Structure and Moral Reform: A Study of the Woman's Christian Temperance Union." *American Journal of Sociology* 61, 3: 221–32.

———. 1963. *Symbolic Crusade: Status Politics and the American Temperance Movement*. Urbana: University of Illinois Press.

Hannan, M. T., J. N. Baron, G. Hsu, and O. Kocak. 2006. "Organizational Identities and the Hazard of Change." *Industrial and Corporate Change* 15, 5: 755–84.

Hannan, M. T., and J. Freeman. 1984. "Structural Inertia and Organizational Change." *American Sociological Review* 49: 149–64.

———. 1989. *Organizational Ecology*. Cambridge, MA: Harvard University Press.

Hannan, M., L. Polos, and G. Carroll. 2007. *Logics of Organization Theory: Audiences, Codes, and Ecologies*. Princeton: Princeton University Press.

Hebdige, D. 1979. *Subculture: The Meaning of Style*. London: Methuen.

Heckman, J. J. 1976. "The Common Structure of Statistical Models of Truncation, Sample Selection and Limited Dependent Variables and a Simple Estimator for Such Models." *Annals of Economic and Social Measurement* 5, 4: 475–92.

———. 1979. "Sample Selection Bias as a Specification Error." *Econometrica* 47, 1: 153–61.

Hedberg, B. 1981. "How Organizations Learn and Unlearn." In *Handbook of Organizational Design*, ed. P. C. Nystrom and W. H. Starbuck, 3–27. Oxford: Oxford University Press.

Heimoff, S., and H. W. Harlan. 2010. *New Classic Winemakers of California*. Berkeley: University of California Press.

Henderson, R. 1993. "Underinvestment and Incompetence as Responses to Radical Innovation: Evidence from the Photolithographic Alignment Equipment Industry." *RAND Journal of Economics* 24, 2: 248–70.

Henderson, R. M., and K. B. Clark. 1990. "Architectural Innovation: The Reconfiguration of Existing Product Technologies and the Failure of Established Firms." *Administrative Science Quarterly* 35: 9–30.

Henig, R. 1997. *The Origins of the Second World War*. Lancaster: University of Lancaster.

Heuchemer, D. 2002. "American Popular Music in Weill's Royal Palace and Krenek's *Jonny*

Spielt Auf: Influences and Usage." In *Jazz and the Germans: Essays on the Influence of "Hot" American Idioms on 20th Century German Music*, ed. M. J. Budds, 99–117. Hillsdale, NY: Pendragon Press.

Hill, E. B. 1927. "Copland's Jazz Concerto in Boston: Modern Music." In Koenig, *Jazz in Print*, 515–16.

Hirsch, P. M. 1972. "Processing Fads and Fashions: An Organization-Set Analysis of Cultural Industry Systems." *American Journal of Sociology* 77, 4: 639–59.

Holt, F. 2007. *Genre in Popular Music*. Chicago: University of Chicago Press.

Homans, G. C. 1961. *Social Behavior: Its Elementary Forms*. New York: Harcourt, Brace.

Hsu, G. 2006. "Jacks of All Trades and Masters of None: Audiences' Reactions to Spanning Genres in Feature Film Production." *Administrative Science Quarterly* 51: 420–50.

Hsu, G., and M. T. Hannan. 2005. "Identities, Genres, and Organizational Forms." *Organization Science* 16, 5: 474–90.

Hsu, G., M. T. Hannan, and O. Kocak. 2009. "Multiple Category Memberships in Markets: An Integrative Theory and Two Empirical Tests." *American Sociological Review* 74: 150–69.

Hurston, Z. N. 1942. "Story in Harlem Slang." *American Mercury* 55 (July): 89, 96.

Jackson, J. H. 2003. *Making Jazz French: Music and Modern Life in Interwar Paris*. Durham: Duke University Press.

"Jazz." 1928. In Koenig, *Jazz in Print*, 538–40.

"Jazz Bitterly Opposed in Germany." 1928. *New York Times*, March 11.

"Jazz Has Got Copyright Law and That Ain't Good." 2005. *Harvard Law Review* 18, 6: 1941–61.

Jensen, M. 2006. "Should We Stay or Should We Go? Accountability, Status Anxiety, and Client Defections." *Administrative Science Quarterly* 51, 1: 97–128.

Johnson, C., T. J. Dowd, and C. L. Ridgeway. 2006. "Legitimacy as a Social Process." *Annual Review of Sociology* 32, 53–78.

Johnston, J., and S. Baumann. 2007. "Democracy versus Distinction: A Study of Omnivorousness in Gourmet Food Writing." *American Journal of Sociology* 113: 165–204.

Jordan, M. F. 2010. *Le Jazz: Jazz and French Cultural Identity*. Urbana: University of Illinois Press.

Jost, E. 1994. *Free Jazz*. New York: Da Capo Press.

Jung, F. 2000. "A Fireside Chat with Olu Dara." *Jazz Weekly* (February).

Kahl, S. J. 2007. "Considering the Customer: Determinants and Impact of Using Technology on Industry Evolution." Ph.D. diss., Massachusetts Institute of Technology.

Kahl, S., Y. K. Kim, and D. J. Phillips. 2010. "Identity Sequences and the Early Adoption Pattern of a Jazz Canon, 1920–1929." *Research in the Sociology of Organizations* 31: 81–113.

Kanter, R. M., and R. Khurana. 2009. "Position and Emotion: The Significance of Georg Simmel's Structural Theories for Leadership and Organizational Behavior." In *Oxford Handbook of Sociology and Organization Studies*, ed. P. S. Adler. Oxford: Oxford University Press.

Karn, B. 2006. "Can Nanotechnology Be Green?" Paper presented at the Second International Dialogue on Responsible Research and Development of Nanotechnology, National Institute for Material Science, Japan.

Kater, M. 1989. "Forbidden Fruit? Jazz in the Third Reich." *American Historical Review* 94, 1: 11–43.

———. 2003. *Different Drummers: Jazz in the Culture of Nazi Germany*. New York: Oxford University Press.

Kelley, R. 2009. *Thelonious Monk: The Life and Times of an American Original*. New York: The Free Press.

Kennedy, R. 1994. *Jelly Roll, Bix, and Hoagy: Gennett Studios and the Birth of Recorded Jazz*. Bloomington: Indiana University Press.

Kenney, W. H. 1993. *Chicago Jazz: A Cultural History, 1904–1930*. New York: Oxford University Press.

———. 1999. *Recorded Music in American Life: The Phonograph and Popular Memory, 1890–1945*. New York: Oxford University Press.

Kernfeld, B., and H. Rye. 1994. "Comprehensive Discographies of Jazz, Blues, and Gospel (Part I)." *Notes*, 2nd ser., 51, 2: 501–47.

———. 1995. "Comprehensive Discographies of Jazz, Blues, and Gospel (Part II)." *Notes*, 2nd ser., 51, 3: 865–91.

Koenig, K. 2002. *Jazz in Print (1856–1929): An Anthology of Selected Early Readings in Jazz History*. Hillsdale, NY: Pendragon Press.

Koenker, R., and K. Hallock. 2001. "Quantile Regression." *Journal of Economic Perspectives* 15, 4: 143–56.

Kofsky, F. 1971. "The Jazz Tradition: Black Music and Its White Critics." *Journal of Black Studies* 1, 4: 403–33.

———. 1998. *Black Music, White Business: Illuminating the History and Political Economy of Jazz*. New York: Pathfinder Press.

Kraatz, M., M. Ventresca, and L. Deng. 2010. "Precarious Values and Mundane Innovations: Enrollment Management in American Liberal Arts Colleges." *Academy of Management Journal* 53: 1521–45.

Kraus, H. M., and H. Harap. 1931. "The Musical Vocabulary of Newspapers and Magazines." *Journal of Educational Research* 24, 4: 299–303.

Kremp, P. A. 2010. "Innovation and Selection: Symphony Orchestras and the Construction of the Musical Canon in the United States (1879–1959)." *Social Forces* 88, 3: 1051–82.

Lamont, M., and V. Molnar. 2002. "The Study of Boundaries in the Social Sciences." *Annual Review of Sociology* 28: 167–95.

Landes, D. S. 2000. *Revolution in Time*. Cambridge, MA: Belknap Press of Harvard University Press.

Lang, G. E., and K. Lang. 1988. "Recognition and Renown: The Survival of Artistic Reputation." *American Journal of Sociology* 94, 1: 79–109.

———. 1996. "Banishing the Past: The German Avant-Garde and Nazi Art." *Qualitative Sociology* 19, 3: 323–43.

Laubenstein, P. F. 1929. "Jazz: Debit and Credit." *Musical Quarterly* 15, 4: 606–24.

Lena, J. C. 2003. "Meaning and Membership: Samples in Rap Music, 1979–1995." *Poetics* 32: 297–310.

———. 2012. *Banding Together: How Communities Create Genres in Popular Music*. Princeton: Princeton University Press.

Lena, J. C., and R. A. Peterson. 2008. "Types and Trajectories of Music Genres." *American Sociological Review* 73, 5: 697–718.

Leonard, N. 1962. *Jazz and the White Americans: The Acceptance of a New Art Form*. Chicago: University of Chicago Press.

Leonhard, J.-F., and L. Stoffels. 1997. "Rundfunk und die Kultur der Gegenwart." In *Programmgeschischte Des Horfunks in Der Weimarer Republik*, ed. J. Leonhard et al., 948–95. Munich: Deutscher Taschenbuch Verlag.

Levine, L. W. 1988. *Highbrow Lowbrow: The Emergence of Cultural Hierarchy in America*. Cambridge, MA: Harvard University Press.

———. 1989. "Jazz and American Culture." *Journal of American Folklore* 102, 403: 6–22.

Lewis, G. E. 2009. *A Power Stronger than Itself: The AACM and American Experimental Music*. Chicago: University of Chicago Press.

Light, I. 1977. "The Ethnic Vice Industry, 1880–1944." *American Sociological Review* 42, 3: 464–79.

Lopes, P. D. 2002. *The Rise of a Jazz Art World*. Cambridge: Cambridge University Press.

Lord, T. 2005, 2010. *The Jazz Discography by Tom Lord*. CD-ROM (http://www.lordisco.com).

Lounsbury, M., and H. Rao. 2004. "Sources of Durability and Change in Market Classifications: A Study of the Reconstitution of Product Categories in the American Mutual Fund Industry, 1944–1985." *Social Forces* 82, 3: 969–99.

Magee, J. 2000. "Irving Berlin's 'Blue Skies': Ethnic Affiliations and Musical Transformations." *Musical Quarterly* 84: 537–80.

———. 2006. "'Everybody Step': Irving Berlin, Jazz, and Broadway in the 1920s." *Journal of the American Musicological Society* 59, 3: 697–732.

Mandel, H. 2007. *Miles, Ornette, Cecil: Jazz Beyond Jazz*. New York: Routledge.

Martin, P. J. 1995. *Sounds and Society: Themes in the Sociology of Music*. Manchester: Manchester University Press.

Maurer, D. W. 1976. "Language and the Sex Revolution: World War I through World War II." *American Speech* 51, 1/2: 5–24.

McCrum, R., R. MacNeil, and W. Cran. 1992. *The Story of English*. London: Faber & Faber.

McKendrick, D. G., and G. R. Carroll. 2001. "On the Genesis of Organizational Forms: Evidence from the Market for Disk Drive Arrays." *Organization Science* 12: 661–83.

McKendrick, D. G., J. Jaffee, G. R. Carroll, and O. M. Khessina. 2003. "In the Bud? Disk Array Producers as a (Possibly) Emergent Organizational Form." *Administrative Science Quarterly* 48: 60–93.

McWhinney, J. E. 2009. "A Brief History of the Hedge Fund." http://www.investopedia.com/articles/mutualfund/05/HedgeFundHist.asp#ixzz1pEPwlqri (accessed April 22, 2012).

Medin, D., and M. Schaffer. 1978. "Context Theory of Classification Learning." *Psychological Review* 85: 207–38.

Melosi, M. V. 1990. *Thomas Edison and the Modernization of America*. Reading, MA: Addison, Wesley Longman.

Mencken, H. L. 2003. *American Mercury Magazine: May to August 1926*. Whitefish, MT: Kessinger Publishing.

Menon, T., and J. Pfeffer. 2003. "Valuing Internal vs. External Knowledge: Explaining the Preference for Outsiders." *Management Science* 49, 4: 497–513.

Merton, R. K. (1957) 1968. *Social Theory and Social Structure*. New York: The Free Press.

———. 1968. "The Matthew Effect in Science." *Science* 158, 3810: 56–63.

Miller, D., and M.-J. Chen. 1994. "Sources and Consequences of Competitive Inertia." *Administrative Science Quarterly* 39: 1–17.

Miller, M. 2005. *Some Hustlin This!* Toronto: Mercury Press.

Mooney, H. F. 1972. "Popular Music since the 1920s: The Significance of Shifting Taste." In *The Popular Arts in America: A Reader*, ed. W. M. Hammel. New York: Harcourt Brace Jovanovich.

Moretti, F. 2005. *Graphs, Maps, Trees*. London: Verso.

Motherwell, H. 1929. "Hitching Jazz to a Jazz." In Koenig, *Jazz in Print*, 552–54.

Murray, J. M. 1996. "Saxophone Instruction in American Music Schools before 1940." *Bulletin of Historical Research in Music Education* 18, 1: 1–12.

Nakienė, A. 2003. "On Instrumental Origins of Lithuanian Polymodal *Saturnites*." *Studia Musicologica Academiae Scientiarum Hungaricae* 44, 1–2: 153–62.

Negus, K. 1999. *Music Genres and Corporate Cultures*. London: Routledge.

Nelson, L. J. 2003. *Rumors of Indiscretion: The University of Missouri "Sex Questionnaire" Scandal in the Jazz Age*. Columbia: University of Missouri Press.

Niles, A. 1928. "Ballads, Songs, and Snatches." In Koenig, *Jazz in Print*, 535–36.

Nowakowski, K. 2009. "'30 Negroes Ladies and Gentlemen': The Syncopated Orchestra in Vienna." *Black Music Research Journal* 29, 2: 229–82.

Ogren, K. J. 1989. *The Jazz Revolution: Twenties America and the Meaning of Jazz*. New York: Oxford University Press.

Osgood, H. O. 1926. "Jazz." *American Speech* 1: 513–18.

Overacker, L. 1933. "Campaign Funds in a Depression Year." *American Political Science Review* 27, 5: 269–83.

Padgett, J. F., and C. K. Ansell. 1993. "Robust Action and the Rise of the Medici, 1400–1434." *American Journal of Sociology* 98, 6: 1259–1319.

Padgett, J. F., and W. Powell. 2012. *The Emergence of Organizations and Markets*. Princeton: Princeton University Press.

Parsonage, C. 2003. "A Critical Reassessment of the Reception of Early Jazz in Britain." *Popular Music* 22, 3: 315–36.

Peretti, B. 1992. *The Creation of Jazz: Music, Race, and Culture in Urban America*. Urbana: University of Illinois Press.

———. 1998. *Jazz in American Culture*. Chicago: Ivan R. Dee.

Perle, G. 1993. "Krenek." *Musical Quarterly* 77, 1: 145–53.

Perrow, C. 1985. "Overboard with Myth and Symbols." *American Journal of Sociology* 91, 1: 151–55.

Peterson, R. A. 1997. *Creating Country Music: Fabricating Authenticity.* Chicago: University of Chicago Press.

———. 2005. "In Search of Authenticity." *Journal of Management Studies* 42: 1083–98.

Peterson, R. A., and D. G. Berger. 1975. "Cycles in Symbol Production: The Case of Popular Music." *American Sociological Review* 40, 2: 158–73.

Peterson, R. A., and R. M. Kern. 1996. "Changing Highbrow Taste: From Snob to Omnivore." *American Sociological Review* 61, 5: 900–907.

Pfeffer, J. 1981. "Management as Symbolic Action: The Creation and Maintenance of Organizational Paradigms." *Research in Organizational Behavior* 3: 1–52.

Phillips, D. J. 2011. "Jazz and the Disconnected: City Structural Disconnectedness and the Emergence of a Jazz Canon, 1897–1933." *American Journal of Sociology* 117, 2: 420–83.

———. 2012. "Orphaned Jazz: Short-Lived Startups and the Long-Run Success of Depression-Era Cultural Products." *Advances in Strategic Management: History and Strategy* 29: 315–50.

Phillips, D. J., and Y-K. Kim. 2009. "Why Pseudonyms? Deception as Identity Preservation among Jazz Record Companies, 1920–1929." *Organization Science* 20, 3: 481–99.

Phillips, D. J., and D. A. Owens. 2004. "Incumbents, Innovation, and Competence: The Emergence of Recorded Jazz, 1920 to 1929." *Poetics* 32: 281–95.

Phillips, D. J., C. J. Turco, and E. W. Zuckerman. 2013. "Betrayal as Market Barrier: Identity-Based Limits to Diversification among High-Status Corporate Law Firms." *American Journal of Sociology.*

Phillips, D. J., and E. W. Zuckerman. 2001. "Middle-Status Conformity: Theoretical Restatement and Empirical Demonstration in Two Markets." *American Journal of Sociology* 107, 2: 379–429.

Phillips, K. W. 2003. "The Effects of Categorically Based Expectations on Minority Influence: The Importance of Congruence." *Personality and Social Psychology Bulletin* 29: 3–13.

Podolny, J. M. 1993. "A Status-Based Model of Market Competition." *American Journal of Sociology* 89, 4: 829–72.

Podolny, J. M., and D. J. Phillips. 1996. "The Dynamics of Organizational Status." *Industrial and Corporate Change* 5, 2: 453–71.

Podolny, J. M., T. E. Stuart, and M. T. Hannan. 1996. "Networks, Knowledge, and Niches: Competition in the Worldwide Semiconductor Industry, 1984–1991." *American Journal of Sociology* 102: 659–89.

Poley, J. 2005. *Decolonization in Germany: Weimar Narratives of Colonial Loss and Foreign Occupation.* Studies in Modern German Literature, vol. 99. Oxford: Oxford University Press.

Pond, S. F. 2003. "Jamming the Reception: Ken Burns, 'Jazz,' and the Problem of 'America's Music.' " *Notes,* 2nd ser., 60, 1: 11–45.

Pontikes, E. G. 2012. "Two Sides of the Same Coin: How Ambiguous Classification Affects Multiple Audiences' Evaluations." *Administrative Science Quarterly* 57, 1: 81–118.

Pontikes, E. G., and W. P. Barnett. 2012. "The Persistence of Lenient Market Spaces." Working paper. University of Chicago.

Pope, K. R., and B. Ong. 2007. "The CPA as the Modern Forensic Accountant: Strategies for Forming an Effective Forensic Accounting Team." *CPA Journal* 77, 4: 64–67.

Powell, W. W. 2008. "Organizational and Institutional Genesis and Change: The Emergence and Transformation of the Commercial Life Sciences." Working paper. Stanford University.

Price, S. 1989. *Primitive Art in Civilized Places*. Chicago: University of Chicago Press.

Rao, H. 1994. "The Social Construction of Reputation: Certification Contests, Legitimation, and the Survival of Organizations in the American Automobile Industry: 1895–1912." *Strategic Management Journal* special issue: Competitive Organizational Behavior, 15: 29–44.

———. 2008. *Market Rebels: How Activists Make or Break Radical Innovation*. Princeton: Princeton University Press.

Rao, H., P. Monin, and R. Durand. 2003. "Institutional Change in Toque Ville: Nouvelle Cuisine as an Identity Movement in French Gastronomy." *American Journal of Sociology* 108, 4: 795–843.

Rayno, D. 2003. *Paul Whiteman: Pioneer in American Music*, vol. 1, *1890–1930*. Studies in Jazz, no. 43. Lanham, MD: Scarecrow Press.

Reinganum, J. F. 1983. "Uncertain Innovation and the Persistence of Monopoly." *American Economic Review* 73: 741–48.

———. 1985. "Innovation and Industrial Evolution." *Quarterly Journal of Economics* 100, 1: 81–99.

Rich, M. F. 1976. *Who's Who in Opera: An International Biographical Directory of Singers, Conductors, Directors, Designers, and Administrators, Also Including Profiles of 101 Opera Companies*. New York: Arno Press.

Roberts, P., and M. Khaire. 2009. "Getting Known by the Company You Keep: Publicizing the Qualifications and Former Associations of Skilled Employees." *Industrial and Corporate Change* 18, 1: 77–106.

Robinson, J. B. 1994. "Jazz Reception in Weimar Germany: In Search of a Shimmy Figure." In *Music and Performance during the Weimar Republic*, ed. B. R. Gilliam, 107–34. Cambridge: Cambridge University Press.

Rosch, E., and B. Lloyd, eds. 1978. *Cognition and Categorization*. Hillsdale, NJ: Lawrence Erlbaum Associates.

Rosenbloom, R. S., and C. M. Christensen. 1994. "Technological Discontinuities, Organizational Capabilities, and Strategic Commitments." *Industrial and Corporate Change* 3, 3: 655–85.

Roy, W. G. 2004. "'Race Records' and 'Hillbilly Music': Institutional Origins of Racial Categories in the American Commercial Recording Industry." *Poetics* 32, 3–4: 265–79.

Roy, W. G., and T. Dowd. 2010. "What Is Sociological about Music?" *Annual Review of Sociology* 36: 183–203.

Ruef, M. 2000. "The Emergence of Organizational Firms: A Community Ecology Approach." *American Journal of Sociology* 106, 3: 658–714.

Rust, B. 1969. *Jazz Records, 1897–1942*. Vols. 1 and 2. Essex: Storyville Publications.

Rye, H. 2009. "The Southern Syncopated Orchestra." *Black Music Research Journal* 29, 2: 153–76.

———. 2010a. "The Jazz Kings and Other Spin-Off Groups." *Black Music Research Journal* 30, 1: 85–92.

———. 2010b. "Southern Syncopated Orchestra: The Roster." *Black Music Research Journal* 30, 2: 385–87.

Sampson, E. E. 1963. "Status Congruence and Cognitive Consistency." *Sociometry* 26, 2: 146–62.

Sassoon, D. 2001. *Becoming Mona Lisa: The Making of a Global Icon*. New York: Harcourt.

Satterfield, J. 1956. "The Defining of Jazz." *Music Educators Journal* 42, 5: 84–88.

Saunders, T. J. 2004. "How American Was It? Popular Culture from Weimar to Hitler." In *German Pop Culture: How "American" Is It?*, ed. A. Mueller. Ann Arbor: University of Michigan Press.

Scherer, F. M., and D. Ross. 1990. *Industrial Market Structure and Economic Performance*. Boston: Houghton Mifflin.

Schmidt, K. F. 2007. *Green Nanotechnology: It's Easier than You Think*. Washington, DC: Woodrow Wilson International Center for Scholars.

Schuller, G. 1986. *Early Jazz: Its Roots and Musical Development*. New York: Oxford University Press.

Schumpeter, J. A. 1942. *Capitalism, Socialism and Democracy*. New York: Harper.

Schwartz, E. I. 2002. *The Last Lone Inventor: A Tale of Genius, Deceit, and the Birth of Television*. New York: HarperCollins.

Schwarz, A. E. 2008. "What Makes Green Technology So Smart?" Paper presented at the NanoCap Working Conference, Darmstadt, Germany, September 11.

Segell, M. 2005. *The Devil's Horn: The Story of the Saxophone, from Noisy Novelty to King of Cool*. New York: Farrar, Straus and Giroux.

Seldes, G. 1924. "Jazz Music Not Such an Enfant 'Terrible' After All." In Koenig, *Jazz in Print*, 324–25.

"Shady Dance Steps Barred by Police." 1922. In Koenig, *Jazz in Print*, 214–15.

Shaw St., J. H. 1924. "The Potentialities of Jazz Music." *Musical Times* 65: 1117.

Shenoy, S. S., and R. Eeratta. 2011. "Green Software Development Model: An Approach Towards Sustainable Software Development." Paper presented at the Annual IEEE India Conference (INDIACON).

Shermer, M. 2003. "Is Bottled Water Tapped Out?" *Scientific American* 289: 33.

Simmel, G. (1908) 1950. *The Sociology of Georg Simmel*. New York: The Free Press.

———. 1957. "Fashion." *American Journal of Sociology* 62: 541–44.

Simon, G. G. 1992. *The Book of Hungarian Jazz*. Budapest: Hotelinfo, Ltd.

Sine, W. D., and B. H. Lee. 2009. "Tilting at Windmills? The Environmental Movement and the Emergence of the U.S. Wind Energy Sector." *Administrative Science Quarterly* 54, 1: 123–55.

Slotkin, J. S. 1943. "Jazz and Its Forerunners as an Example of Acculturation." *American Sociological Review* 8, 5: 570–75.

Smith, E. L. 2003. *African American Theater Buildings*. Jefferson, NC: McFarland and Company.

Smith, J., and L. Guttridge. (1960) 1988. *Jack Teagarden: The Story of a Jazz Maverick*. Cambridge, MA: Da Capo Press.

Stanfield, P. 2002. "An Excursion into the Lower Depths: Hollywood, Urban Primitivism, and 'St. Louis Blues,' 1929–1937." *Cinema Journal* 41, 2: 84–108.

Stark, D. 1996. "Recombinant Property in East European Capitalism." *American Journal of Sociology* 101, 4: 993–1027.

Steinmetz, G. 2007. *The Devil's Handwriting*. Chicago: University of Chicago Press.

Stinchcombe, A. L. 1965. "Social Structure and Organizations." In *Handbook of Organizations*, ed. J. G. March, 142–93. Chicago: Rand McNally.

Strang, D., and N. Tuma. 1993. "Spatial and Temporal Heterogeneity in Diffusion." *American Journal of Sociology* 99: 614–39.

Stringham, E. J. 1926. "'Jazz': An Educational Problem." *Musical Quarterly* 12, 2: 190–95.

Stuart, T. E., H. Hoang, and R. Hybels. 1999. "Interorganizational Endorsements and the Performance of Entrepreneurial Ventures." *Administrative Science Quarterly* 44, 2: 315–50.

Sudhalter, R. M. 1999. *Lost Chords: White Musicians and Their Contribution to Jazz, 1915–1945*. New York: Oxford University Press.

Sutton, A. 1993. *A Guide to Pseudonyms on American Records, 1892–1942*. Westport, CT: Greenwood Press.

———. 1994. *Directory of American Disc Record Brands and Manufacturers: 1891–1943*. Westport, CT: Greenwood Press.

Sutton, A., and K. Nauck. 2000. *American Record Labels and Companies: 1891–1943*. Denver: Mainspring Press.

Sutton, R. I., and A. L. Callahan. 1987. "The Stigma of Bankruptcy: Spoiled Organizational Image and Its Management." *Academy of Management Journal* 30, 3: 405–36.

Swidler, A. 1986. "Culture in Action: Symbols and Strategies." *American Sociological Review* 51, 2: 273–86.

Thomas, G. V. 2002. "The Canonization of Jazz and Afro-American Literature." *Callaloo* 25: 288–38.

Titon, J. T. 1995. *Early Downhome Blues: A Musical and Cultural Analysis*. Chapel Hill: University of North Carolina Press.

Tschmuck, P. 2006. *Creativity and Innovation in the Music Industry*. Dordrecht, The Netherlands: Springer.

Tushman, M. L., and P. Anderson. 1986. "Technological Discontinuities and Organizational Environments." *Administrative Science Quarterly* 31, 3: 439–65.

van der Tuuk, A. 2003. *Paramount's Rise and Fall: A History of the Wisconsin Chair Company and Its Recording Activities*. Denver: Mainspring Press.

Veblen, T. 1899. *The Theory of the Leisure Class: An Economic Study of Institutions.* New York: MacMillan.

"Von Dr. Hoch's Konservatorium: Erstes Konzert der Jazz-Klasse." 1929. *Sudwestdeutsche Rundfunkzeitung* 5, 9: 9.

Walser, R. 1999. *Keeping Time: Readings in Jazz History.* New York: Oxford University Press.

Walsh, J. 1942. "Favorite Pioneer Recording Artists: Arthur Collins, I." *Hobbies* (November): 11–12.

Ward, G. C., and K. Burns. 2000. *A History of America's Music.* New York: Alfred A. Knopf.

Washburne, C. 2004. "Does Kenny G Play Bad Jazz? A Case Study." In *Bad Music: The Music You Love to Hate,* ed. C. Washburne and M. Derno, 123–47. New York: Routledge.

Washington, M., and E. J. Zajac. 2005. "By Invitation Only: The Institutional Evolution of Status and Privilege." *Academy of Management Journal* 48, 2: 281–96.

Watts, D. J. 1999. *Small Worlds: The Dynamics of Networks between Order and Randomness.* Princeton: Princeton University Press.

———. 2011. *Everything Is Obvious, Once You Know the Answer: How Common Sense Fails.* London: Atlantic Books.

Welburn, R. 1986. "Duke Ellington's Music: The Catalyst for a True Jazz Criticism." *International Review of the Aesthetics and Sociology of Music* 17, 1: 111–22.

Welch, W. L., and L. Burt. 1994. *From Tinfoil to Stereo.* Gainesville: University Press of Florida.

Wertheim, A. F. 2006. *Vaudeville Wars: How the Keith-Albee and Orpheum Circuits Controlled the Big-Time and Its Performers.* New York: Palgrave Macmillan.

Westphal, J. D., and E. J. Zajac. 1994. "Substance and Symbolism in CEOs' Long-Term Incentive Plans." *Administrative Science Quarterly* 39, 3: 367–90.

———. 2001. "Decoupling Policy from Practice: The Case of Stock Repurchase Programs." *Administrative Science Quarterly* 46, 2: 202–28.

"What's the Matter with Jazz?" 1924. In Koenig, *Jazz in Print,* 214–15.

White, H. 1981. "Where Do Markets Come From?" *American Journal of Sociology* 87, 3: 517–47.

Whiteman, P., and M. M. McBride Whiteman. 1926. *Jazz.* New York: J. H. Sears and Co.

Whiteoak, J. 1994. "'Jazzing' and Australia's First Jazz Band." *Popular Music* 13, 3: 279–95.

Who Was Who in America: 1897–1942. 1962. Chicago: A. N. Marquis.

Witmer, R. 1994. "Standard." In *New Grove Dictionary of Jazz,* ed. B. Kernfeld, 1155. New York: St. Martin's Press.

Wolfe, T. 1929. *Look Homeward, Angel: A Story of the Buried Life.* New York: Charles Scribner's Sons.

Wry, T., M. Lounsbury, and M. A. Glynn. 2011. "Legitimating New Categories of Organizations: Stories as Distributed Cultural Entrepreneurship." *Organization Science* 22: 339–463.

Zeitz, J. 2006. *Flapper: A Madcap Story of Sex, Style, Celebrity, and the Women Who Made America Modern*. New York: Crown Publishers.

Zerubavel, E. 2003. *Time Maps: Collective Memory and the Social Shape of the Past*. Chicago: University of Chicago Press.

Zuckerman, E. W. 1999. "The Categorical Imperative: Securities Analysts and the Illegitimacy Discount." *American Journal of Sociology* 104, 5: 1398–1438.

Zukin, S., and J. S. Maguire. 2004. "Consumers and Consumption." *Annual Review of Sociology* 30: 173–97.

Index